Beyond Lost Dreams

Beyond Lost Dreams

Janusz Nel Siedlecki

The Moving Finger writes; and, having writ,
Moves on: nor all thy Piety nor Wit
Shall lure it back to cancel half a Line,
Nor all thy Tears wash out a Word of it.

*The Rubaiyat of Omar Khayyam,
rendered by Edward Fitzgerald.*

The Pentland Press Limited
Edinburgh • Cambridge • Durham

© Janusz Nel Siedlecki 1994

First published in 1994 by
The Pentland Press Ltd.
1 Hutton Close
South Church
Bishop Auckland
Durham

All rights reserved.
Unauthorised duplication
contravenes existing laws.

ISBN 1 85821 140 9

Typeset by CBS, Felixstowe, Suffolk.
Printed and Bound by Lintons Printers, Crook, County Durham.

To my wife, without whose insatiable curiosity, great patience and still greater help, this book would never have been written.

J.N.S.

CONTENTS

Preface	ix
PART 1 : CHILD AND YOUTH	
Chapter 1 Prelude	3
2 Home in the Twenties	5
3 Early Teens	10
4 Widening Horizons	17
5 Wasted Time?	27
6 The Fourth Dimension	39
7 A Glimpse of England	48
PART 2 : WARRIOR AND SLAVE	
Chapter 8 The Incredible Defeat	53
9 Turbulent Interlude	76
10 Pilgrim's Progress	84
11 It is Better to Travel Hopefully . . .	101
12 Love and Folly	116
13 Prison Bars	132
14 The Bottom of the Abyss	147
15 Wheel Of Fortune	160
16 The Gypsy Camp	178
17 The Old Numbers	201
18 Travel in the Third Reich	208
PART 3 : WANDERER AND CITIZEN	
Chapter 19 Displaced Persons	223
20 God Helps Those . . .	236
21 The Friends in Need	248
22 Back to School	255
23 Apprentice	263
24 People without Future	270
25 Reincarnation	279
Map of Poland 1939	284
Map of Europe 1939	285

PREFACE

This is the tale of my life, a life shattered into three parts enjoyed, suffered and endured in different languages, different lands and different epochs. There was a happy Polish childhood, the gruesome experiences of the Second World War and the new home in England.

All my life I have believed that one can attain any reasonable aim providing that its pursuit is exclusive and relentless. Whilst this belief seemed justified by my early life, it also spurred me to actions which often resulted in adventure and trouble. Even with hind-sight I do not know whether these adventures were written into my fate or if I created them unwittingly while chasing chimerical dreams. But in the twilight of my life, I suspect that the dreams, as well as the actions, were more a logical consequence of my environment and background than a result of personal whims.

When I had no country and no family the people of Britain accepted me into their midst. I learnt their language and customs, and with their help built my new life in England. Now I write this to show them the mysteries of survival against long odds in other lands, amongst other people. Reading this story you might spare one thought, one tear, for the thousands who travelled as I did but fell by the wayside. This thought, this tear, will become the only memorial to the men, women and children who vanished without a trace, without a name.

J.N.S.
Ilkley, 1982/1989

PART 1

CHILD AND YOUTH

CHAPTER 1

PRELUDE

The fertile plains of Poland stretch from the Baltic Sea to the Carpathian Mountains. The people of Poland, sandwiched between Germany and Russia, belong to Western Europe as do their culture and Catholic religion. For ten centuries the nation resisted the aggression of Turks, Tartars, Danes and Swedes, but first and foremost of the Russians and the Germans. At the end of the eighteenth century the enemies triumphed and Polish lands were partitioned amongst Russia, Prussia and Austria though the Poles never ceased their armed resistance. In the south-east of the Russian zone of Poland lay the walled town of Kamieniec, 'bastion of Christianity'. In the eighteenth and nineteenth centuries there prospered the long line of physicians from which came Anna Farenholc. Around the town spread the estates of the Siedlecki family impoverished by their patriotic activities. Eustachy Siedlecki, the eldest of the four brothers, married Anna when they studied medicine in Warsaw. Police penetration of their resistance group forced them to flee and continue their studies in Petersburg where, in 1916, I was born to them. The first years of my life I spent in Kamieniec under the care of my grandmother whilst my father fought for the freedom of Poland and my mother ran a hospital for infectious diseases which were rife in the war-ravaged district. In 1920 the Bolsheviks reached Kamieniec and, abandoning their possessions, the entire family fled to Warsaw.

Kamieniec I know only from old photographs, literature and my mother's stories. My own recollections in the form of dreamlike pictures reach back to our journey north: skeletal horses plodding across sandy fields, people pushing heavily-laden carts, an enormous lorry rumbling and jolting on its solid tyres. I remember disused marshalling yards with rusty rails and endless strings of stranded goods-wagons full of nomadic humanity. I remember my nest of soft blankets amongst the black trunks. Sometimes our train stopped in hot, silent forests smelling of resin. But whenever we walked, shuffling in sand and dry pine needles, I was terrified of being left behind. Still, as the wagons jerked and bumped somebody always managed to scoop me up from the tracks and pass me into the safe hands of my mother. Thus we reached Warsaw and succeeded in renting a one-room flat where we spent the next ten years.

CHAPTER 2

HOME IN THE TWENTIES

Mother spent more and more time in the hospital. She stopped coming home at night and appeared only for short meals at odd times. She was always tired and preoccupied except when sometimes a wounded soldier brought us a letter from Father. Of course she never called him 'Father' as his family pet name was Stalek and we all called him Stalek. The long days I spent with Granny who read to me stories of Lech and his Royal Bird seen against the setting sun – the White Eagle of Poland on its scarlet field. She read of the Princess Wanda and her supreme sacrifice for Poland.

Granny also took me for long walks and that particular August day we were going for our 'allocation' – the sugar and flour which we collected every week because Stalek was still fighting the Bolsheviks. Yet I would much rather do without and have him at home. Anyway, it was deadly dull to stand for hours in a mile-long queue where thin, pale women gossiped and argued. But that day was different. The streets were quite empty and we waited only a few minutes. Also the constant rumble of the guns sounded louder and we could hear it not only near the Vistula, but all along our way. At home, Granny would not read to me and I went to bed very early. It was dark when I woke up and there was mother laughing and cuddling me. I did not know why she wept, because she was very happy and told me that we had finally beaten the Bolsheviks and Stalek would be coming home.

It was the day when the women and children of Warsaw held, against all odds, the single line of trenches whilst Pilsudski's Legions, counter-attacking with every last man, routed General Budienny and all that Soviet Russia could throw at us in 1921.

Days were getting shorter and frost etched fantastic white feathers on the windows, so that you couldn't see the small quadrangle of the yard. But life was good and full of surprises. First Stalek came home and the three of us were together. Of course, Granny also lived with us, but she was more like a piece of furniture, quiet and agreeable, always there. Then, with book-shelves and a hanging curtain of Persian carpet, the large single room was divided into halves. The first part, nearer the kitchen, held the dining table in front and, far back, Granny's bed, whilst I got a whole bed for myself. It was a folding one and it always tried to nip my fingers, when I was opening it up at night. The second half of the room was very beautiful – near the window was Stalek's roll-top desk and against the wall stood a magnificent sofa. When you grabbed it by its little ears it turned upside down and there was the bed and blankets and all.

Soon after I got my bed Edmund came home. He was my mother's younger brother, noisy, boisterous and great fun as he often played with me. Outdoors he looked ordinary, but indoors his six-foot frame and extremely wide shoulders made everything around him shrink to toy-like proportions. Edmund came back from fighting the Germans who had tried to take from us the whole of industrial Silesia. But I never managed to get out of him the story of how he won there the highest military decoration of Virtuti Militari. He had nowhere to live and I was very proud to give him my new bed which he used to put up in the kitchen. I slept in a corner on a few blankets spread over a Moldavian rug.

Then the time came for me to begin school and all too soon we started reading and writing, which entailed pages and pages of homework. This reading business had another serious drawback. Before I could read, Stalek would answer fully any of my questions. But this changed gradually and he would just glance round the book-shelves and casually remark:

'I am not sure, but you will find it, I think, in this encyclopaedia under ...'

Later he would suggest a dictionary or a text book with which he would help a little. Much later, skipping through some 'Who done it', I landed myself with three volumes of forensic medicine which took me half a year to get through.

There was also fun. There were presents – magnificent presents – some that I will never forget. One Christmas, Stalek fixed two hooks and hung on them a trapeze. But after swinging for an hour, I became thoroughly bored. Then he showed me how to turn forward and backward somersaults, how to climb and hang by the knees or toes. I never again tired of it, inventing newer and better holds and tricks. Not all were quite successful and once a most ingenious leg grip proved useless. My head thumped heavily on the floor and I sprawled there in a heap when Stalek looked round:

'You should be more careful, you could damage the floor!'

Another time when swinging upside down I began to wonder if one could eat in this position and enquired whether it was possible to swallow upwards. Stalek explained about the ring-like muscles contracting in sequence to push the contents of the gullet towards the stomach, regardless of the body position. It sounded convincing, but in my mind I saw an inverted well – try pouring up it a glass of water! Stalek must have seen my doubts and added:

'Try it for yourself.'

Instead of a glass of water I decided to use a sweet which I had saved for a special occasion. To swallow the sweet instead of slowly savouring its flavour would be calamitous, but its huge size seemed to offer additional insurance even if Stalek was right. I caught the trapeze, swung up and over and, hanging by my toes, I swallowed and the whole lump disappeared upwards into my stomach. It was a sad loss which confirmed further the utter infallibility of Stalek.

After the main meal of the day, about three or four o'clock, Mother often helped me with my homework. Then she would take me for a long walk to the University. They both worked there but Stalek often stayed late unless we fetched him home.

In the evening, as we walked through the empty streets, Mother taught me to sing: not the nursery rhymes but the songs of the Napoleonic Wars and those of Pilsudski's Legions. But I liked best the martial rhythm of the 'Oath':

> To the last droplet of our blood
> For Fatherland we shall fight
> Till the oppressor's heavy flood
> Ebbs and broken be his might.

The University building was deserted, mysterious; our steps rang loudly on the stone staircase and reverberated in the dark corridors until we reached Stalek's office in the Pathology Department. Usually they both had more work to do and in the long summer twilight I could wander through the adjoining laboratories, their shelves and tables full of fascinating instruments and machines. Sometimes Mother finished before Stalek and then she showed me their purpose and operation.

We also used to visit the Museum which had thousands of glass jars containing odd specimens, but I never could recognise more than the most characteristic ones like brain or heart. Easier to follow and understand were the fully-assembled skeletons on which I learned the names and the shapes of the bones so well that, when asked, I could pick up the right one from the loose piles in big drawers.

Frequently Stalek and Mother had so much work that she would not take me with her. If Granny was away I double-locked the door and, armed with the sharpest kitchen knife, checked that nobody had sneaked in. I looked under the beds, thoroughly inspected the wardrobe and the kitchen cupboards and felt behind the overcoats hanging near the door. Then, satisfied and at ease, I would begin homework or play. I was never worried about being alone, but the possibility, however remote, of concealed brigands or even Bolsheviks terrified me.

The holidays were always marvellous: for Christmas and Easter two uninterrupted weeks of play. I had lead soldiers who marched in endless parades under Stalek's desk and a box of magnificent wooden bricks suitable for long walls or even a castle. The castles were difficult to build because there were never enough bricks and even using old cigarette boxes I still had to place the fortress against the sofa, but these unscalable heights just added to the mystery of the castle. The two days of the real Christmas were still more special, because Stalek and Mother were all the time at home. Stalek's brothers, Chris and George, came as well as Edmund, who by then lived away from us. We had a marvellous dinner and afterwards all the figs and nuts that we could eat. Then they would talk long and seriously with Stalek and Edmund would often give me a present. Once he brought a fret-saw and taught me how to use it. Soon I could make things better than he did, and without breaking blades which he snapped by the dozen. But it was Stalek who showed me how to plan on paper the more complicated shapes and things so that they would properly fit together.

In the summer holidays Granny took me to some dull country places acceptable only because of limitless supplies of fruit which I devoured wholesale. Then we went to the north-east border of Poland where Edmund had a restaurant. There was no garden, no fruit, and we could walk only to the village but not to the woods – this was too dangerous because of the Bolsheviks. We did not see much of Edmund as he was always working until locking-up time. This began with closing all the shutters and barring them with great iron bars. Then the heavy round table was dragged to the front door and Edmund mounted on it the machine gun which lived in daytime in an old oak cupboard. Finally Granny would go with me upstairs while Edmund settled down on a mattress just behind the gun. 'They' did not come when Granny and I were there, but the cross-border raids continued unabated. For years robber bands came from Soviet Russia, leaving along our frontier trails of corpses and smoking ruins.

Later came the best holidays of all. Stalek and Mother and I went to the seaside. We lived in a tiny room in a fisherman's cottage with nothing to eat but fishes all full of bones. Then came the surprise of the sea itself: the incredible expanse of water with gigantic waves. Stalek said that all of it was salty but seeing the vastness of it I could not quite believe him – nobody could have salted all this water. So he told me to try it. Familiar with quiet lakes and streams I walked to the edge and bent to have a sip. But, like a vicious beast, the sea rose up, smacked my face and rolled me to and fro in the wet sand. It was not only salty, but nastily bitter and my nose and mouth were full of sand and·this fantastic water. I soon got used to the sea, Mother taught me to deal with the fish, and best of all were the long walks when Stalek used to tell Mother and me endless, fascinating tales of Tarzan, of Ivanhoe, of the Count of Monte Cristo; the tales that I remember for ever in all the smallest details.

CHAPTER 3

EARLY TEENS

The primary school days ended and after passing a competitive entry exam I was accepted into the King Batory's High School. This National School Number One, a quadrangle of cream-coloured building, stood in its sumptuous grounds with playing fields, tennis courts and botanical gardens.

Unfortunately, a prolonged illness delayed my schooling for a full year which I spent in the country at the house of my paternal grandfather. It was not a completely wasted time as he had three university degrees in divergent subjects and a fair amount of time to spend with me. In a most informal way he taught me some botany, zoology and the beginnings of astronomy. Then, fully recovered, I began the real school.

Out of our flat in the centre of Warsaw I walked along the gardens surrounding the Parliament Building, and turned at the ornamental park to descend the high scarp which centuries earlier had formed the left bank of the Vistula. There, on the low-lying land, was the school, just over half an hour from home. Of the first days I remember only the enormous scale of it all. There must have been millions of boys, all so much bigger than we of the first form. Some, wearing long trousers, looked really grown up.

The building was equally bewildering in its white spaciousness, in the blinding gloss of the parquet floors, and the royal width of staircases falling down in cascades of golden oak. We learned the layout of the cloakrooms in the basement, and memorised the numbers of our hooks, where the overcoats and shoes were left as we changed into slippers. Our own classroom, as well as that allotted to the boys of the parallel stream, was situated off a spacious corridor on the high ground floor. We, or rather our parents, were asked to choose one of two foreign languages:

French or English. Stalek and Mother considered English more useful whilst I already had a strong preference for the people who had never lost a war, who made BSA bicycles and Purdy's guns. In the class we – 'the English' – were a minority which gave us better cohesion in the endless wars with 'the French'. So, at the end, though nobody really won, we (the filthy slavers, oppressors of India and murderers of the Boers) emerged triumphant over the disorganised bands of the frog-eaters and slayers of their own Kings.

Hour after hour there were lessons on different subjects each with its own master: a mosaic of history and physics, religion and physical training, languages and handwork. The tall, soft-spoken maths teacher was followed by a fire-spitting dragon of literature, and the enormous priest with a thundering voice was succeeded by a red-faced and grim English 'Sir'.

Of the boys some were noisy, some quiet and frightened, others pushing and aggressive. Many were already making friends, or enemies, chattering and laughing. I observed and learned, but tried not to get involved in this crowd. Like everybody I had to be in school, but there seemed to be no point in becoming one of the herd. I did not jeer with the mass when two big boys ran away afraid to face a cocky little devil. I stood aside when a bully started walloping a clumsy fatso. But then, the little fighter approached me and offered to show me something 'fantastic'. We interlaced fingers and suddenly, without any warning, he pressed down with both hands. My loosely held fingers bent backwards, and before I knew what was happening, I was kneeling, whilst he crowed, 'Grovel to your master, now!' and pressed harder. My fingers were almost breaking, but I would not grovel, and I began to realise that I had started resisting, pressing back, whilst his hands shook and vibrated with a last effort. Then, pouring all I had, all concentrated will and thought into my fingers, I felt the balance tip. Slowly, further and further, till I was standing again and he was writhing on the floor. Only then, I saw all around us the open-mouthed, breathless crowd. Disgusted, I let him go: 'Try again and I'll break your arms.' They all wanted to be my friends but I shrugged my shoulders and walked away.

But the school was really about lessons and learning. Learning I deplored, whilst for the lessons I soon developed my own classification. I found gymnastics an exhilarating challenge with the unending surprises of new equipment and more daring exercises. Equally fascinating and exciting was the introduction to physics, where I tried to go further than our course by reading the encyclopaedia and other books found at home. Handwork started slowly with technical drawing, but soon provided a necessary basis for real craftsmanship which I much coveted. My second group of subjects comprised those which I found dull but easy to cope with, like Polish language, painting and chemistry. Last came the lessons which I disliked, such as music.

Thus slowly passed my first year of 'real' school and summer brought the longed-for holidays which I spent again in Grandfather's house. But though only a year had passed since my last stay there, the place had changed: the stairs were not so high, the attics had shrunk and were now more dusty than mysterious. But the biggest changes were outside. Each day I ventured further and further past the smoothly grazed meadows, past the weed-choked ponds, to the meandering stream known to the locals as 'the Sticky'. This twisting and looping creek cut deep into the peaty soil, undermining the banks, setting innumerable traps for the unwary explorer. In a few places the farmers had dug a length of straight trench to reclaim boggy islands encircled by the Sticky. In these narrows the water, confined by straight-cut banks, ran smooth but slow, and after careful exploration I found that I could stand with my head above the water all along the canal: this was the place to learn swimming. I plunged forward, just as I had seen Stalek and Mother do in the sea, but the result was not the same. My legs shot up in the air, whilst my head seemed to go down and down, right to Australia. Somehow, I scrambled up, coughing and spitting gallons of water which had poured into me through the nose, ears and eyes. I reconsidered the matter, and decided to go at it slowly. I simply bent my knees till the water came level with my mouth, and started paddling with my arms like a dog. I drifted with the current, my feet dragging or partly lifting. It really worked, and I practised for hours till I could swim through the cut with, or even against, the current. Two days later, after cycling to the next village, I pinched my nose firmly and jumped confidently into the bottomless millpond – I had learnt to swim.

I cycled a lot, going to outlying villages or to the great forest which reached to the lake district some hundred miles away. The heather-covered glades were light, fairy-tale places, where one had to sit quietly or lie concealed on the edge of the shadowy forest, waiting patiently for the elves to resume their dancing play. But they were so shy, so difficult to spot, that only seldom one caught a tantalising glimpse of them behind a shimmering swarm of dragonflies. I stretched and smiled, smiled at summer, at the happy forest-elves, and I laughed, remembering the silly city boys who thought that all the Little People were only 'kid's stuff' for babies.

Later that summer Chris came over for a few days, bringing from Warsaw Edmund and my parents who were to stay a fortnight. Now, every day, Stalek would take Mother and me deep into the forest, or swimming in the mill-ponds, or on foot, past the Sticky, into the Sandy Mountains. There were also other wonders. Christopher was now in the Police Force and came in his new six-cylinder Buick, a sleek torpedo with fluted bonnet and a chauffeur who once had been an Italian racing driver! He showed me the engine, and the controls, and how to clean the carburettor, but sent me home before I got completely covered with oil and dust. Then Edmund produced a long parcel: a present for me! I should have known it was something very special by the way everybody gathered round when I began to untie the strong cord. Inside the outer brown paper were layers of white tissue with golden stains of oil. From this soft cocoon emerged a slim, slightly tapered, blue-black barrel and a smooth walnut stock. The two superbly-fitted parts seemed to click together of their own accord and there, in my hands, was a rifle, the lightest, the most beautiful rifle in the whole world. When everybody had examined this princely gift, Edmund casually dipped into his pocket and, producing a full box of shells, winked and called me to come hunting.

We skirted the potato clamp and the high coppice of the ice-house and walked along the elm alley towards the meadows when Edmund pointed:

'See that chicken there? I'll bet you can't hit it from here!' – the big black hen was some forty yards away, and I, used to the old 'musket' firing a BB shot for about half this distance, just laughed:

'Nobody can hit it at this range. But I might frighten it away.'

'This rifle will hit it all right if you aim straight.' He dived again into his pocket, and produced another box of shells.

'You are a chicken yourself! I'll give you this box if you hit it!'

I knew it was no good trying such a long shot, but asked him whether to aim one or two feet above the hen. He laughed so loudly that the hen turned round to look at us.

'Don't make any allowances, just aim straight at it! Oh you've lost it – it's now behind this big stone.'

Cross with him for laughing at me, I brought the rifle to my shoulder, aimed just a fraction above the rock and whistled. The hen popped its head above the stone and I squeezed the trigger. The noise was not as loud as I had expected and the empty shell sailed slowly sideways to fall by my feet. The hen jumped straight up and lay flat by the side of the big stone. Edmund was rolling with laughter, extending to me the promised box:

'That's good shooting, Nel! I'll soon take you with me to have a go at ducks and water-hens.'

But I stood still trying to sort out so many things: the incredible range and accuracy of the rifle, the hen which I did not really mean to kill, the coming row about the silly bird and the nagging doubt that I should not have aimed at it anyway – yes, I knew that Stalek would think so, even though he might not say it because of Edmund's involvement.

The days grew shorter, the emerald of the leaves changed into dark jade, whilst the fields ripened into gold. Then the receding summer left the fields bare, and the leaves began to lighten and bleach into all shades of yellow, from a touch of ochre and chrome to splashes of sienna and umber browns. More and more swallows swirled like falling leaves, formed endless rosaries on the telegraph wires, and suddenly vanished like a puff of smoke from the steam-engine which sweated in the yard driving the ever-hungry thresher. It was time to leave, time to go back and start the next school year.

The everlasting school was the same as it had been the previous year. Only when we looked at the new first form we realised our own growth and progress by one infinitesimal step from the very bottom. Inside the class the extreme groupings of Goodies and Baddies shrank, leaving in the middle a motley crowd of mediocrities. The crudity of the left repelled me as much as the snobbery of the right whilst the bland inferiority of the centre left me still uncommitted. Nevertheless I began to make friends of my own.

Eric and I walked to school along the same route and gradually found more and more common interests. He knew more than I did about cars, and this brought back my memories of Edmund's Fiat and Christopher's Buick. Soon we held competitions in spotting and recognising various makes, of which there was then a fantastic variety. Slowly and painstakingly, from overheard remarks, from odd catalogues and leaflets, we began to learn the anatomy and physiology of a horseless carriage. We also found fascination in wiring simple battery-powered circuits. Beginning with a bell, we moved to the telegraph which progressed from a simple buzzer to a complex machine which sometimes printed Morse signals on carnival streamers.

My friendship with Kitty began in the most unlikely circumstances. In spite of his small size and delicate build, he was one of the most aggressive nuisances of the class. If not nudging, shoving or tripping somebody, he would use his sharp tongue on the biggest boys, till, in desperation, they turned on him with clenched fists and murder in their eyes. But by then he would be miles away or winking from behind the shoulder of some temporary ally. In extremity, the small but wiry Kitty scratched and bit like a polecat. In the class, he sat behind me, and during a geometry lesson began to test his new set of compasses by pricking my back. The first stab was the most effective as I squealed like a stuck pig, and was promptly chastened by the teacher. Kitty was delighted with the effect, and, undeterred by my threats, continued to jab me. There was nearly a quarter of an hour to the bell, but it seemed the longest lesson of all my school career. At last, the bell rang and, as it was the final lesson of the day, we all knelt and rattled off the customary prayer. Kitty had taken off over the desks well before the 'Amen', but expecting this, I managed to grab one of his legs. He crashed to the floor, and I sat on his head till the teacher left the classroom.

'Now get up! It's no use whining, I told you to stop. I said you'll regret it and you shall!'

The whole class stopped and watched, first delighted, then frightened, as I beat him up. It was not all one-sided, as he scratched me considerably, but I did not stop till, with a bloody nose and two black eyes, he begged for mercy. He missed the next two days, and then was brought by his father straight to the Headmaster's study. They had a long session there, but finally Kitty came back to the class. It was a very colourful Kitty, with a face like a rainbow, who, smiling sheepishly, told the teacher that he 'just fell' – and that was the beginning of a friendship which lasted many long years.

But somehow, though with few and not too close friends, I was popular with the whole class and was often asked to arbitrate in disputes, quarrels or even fights arising from some 'affairs of honour'. My free time, of which there was never enough, was filled with cycling, model-making and wireless.

Though affiliated to the International Movement of Baden-Powell, Polish Scouting was more nationalistic and competitive than the English organisation. It also encompassed older boys as we joined at the age of fourteen. Anyway, the whole class went mad filling in application forms, and talking only of the Troop they were about to join. I was not enamoured with this new enterprise because of my aversion to crowds and group activities. They all joined the Scouts and were formed into patrols led by older boys loaded with badges of merit, distinction and rank. I looked at the small fleur-de-lys displayed on school uniforms and was having second thoughts on my decision, when I was approached by one of the patrol leaders asking me to join! – a thing unknown in the annals of the school and the troop. Apparently, the boys talked so much about me that, after consultation at 'higher level', the patrol leader invited me to a couple of meetings, 'without obligation', and a month later I joined the Scouts.

Our first year of scouting was crowned by the 1931 Jamboree in Prague. There, too young to appreciate fully the international brotherhood, we still enjoyed sight-seeing. However, for most of us the exchange of badges with boys of other nationalities became not only a hobby but almost the sole reason for existence. Obsessed by this mania they approached not only other scouts but also policemen, soldiers and firemen, sometimes carrying off vital, if not lethal, bits of their equipment.

Our own summer camp, in the Carpathian Mountains, followed the Jamboree. The leader of our patrol could not come and, by common demand, I took over in spite of my age and inexperience. With the help of all the boys our patrol finished the camp as the best of the juniors.

CHAPTER 4

WIDENING HORIZONS

At the November meeting of our troop came the announcement about the winter skiing camp. As it was our first winter venture there was only a score of applicants with very few of the juniors among them, and I would never have dreamed of going if it were not for Stalek's remark that skiing is an interesting sport and worth consideration. I pressed for more positive advice, but was told to make up my own mind. I was still tempted to stay at home, but could not miss the camp knowing what Stalek thought about it. I was appointed quartermaster and was very busy seeking information on balanced diets, intake of proteins, fats and sugars, even measuring our own household consumption of various foodstuffs, as well as finding the cheapest sources of supply. I also had to buy skis and other equipment of which I knew nothing, but learned a lot by visiting, one after another, almost all the sports shops in Warsaw.

We marched a few miles from the tiny railway station to 'our own' pair of cottages in a snow-bound hamlet. They were deserted and buried so completely, that it took us half an hour of snow-clearing to open the front door. Only then, we dug further into the yard and began chopping big blocks of wood into smaller chunks which were fed into the rusty, cast-iron stoves. Ages passed before these began to dissipate any heat into the empty, frozen rooms. Gradually we got used to the primitive existence, to rising in the darkness and breaking layers of ice on the water-buckets before attempting a wash. Then we melted more ice for coffee, and fried the breakfast bacon. At dawn, after greasing our skis, we dispersed: the seniors heading for distant mountains, whilst we explored the nearby nursery slopes. Our classmate, nicknamed Poppy, showed us how to grease the skis, adjust and fasten the bindings, and how to move on snow. We had more spills than thrills, suffered tired and painful muscles, cold and even hunger, but at the end of our ten days, we had gained a surprising amount of experience and had learned to climb in sharp zig-zag, or in the 'fir-tree' pattern, 'shus' or plough down hill, walk, run, turn and even make little jumps of a few yards length. We enjoyed it, and were immensely proud of our achievement.

But I really learned to ski during the next winter's training camp. It was a well-planned though spartan affair, organised by the Warsaw Scout Headquarters. We were billeted in local schools, and fed with plentiful, if not palatable, army rations. On the first day, one by one, we followed a gruelling trail covering a stiff climb and vicious descent with unexpected obstacles. From a hillock the experts observed our performance and graded us accordingly. Then the instructors, graduates of the Institute for Physical Training, picked their own groups, each taking a dozen boys of the same level of skill. Poppy, Bob and I, friends from the nursery slopes of the last year, were classed as advanced and taken by an American, one of many foreign students at the Warsaw Institute. 'Our Yank' spoke little Polish, and that with a Texan drawl. With a curt 'Follow me!' he lit straight into the mountains at a racing speed. In the first three days he reduced our group to just five as the others had dropped out with exhaustion or minor injuries. A great believer in modern method, he taught us the low, squatting posture with one ski forward, which we soon learned to appreciate as faster and more stable than the old straight and heroic-looking Austrian School stance. He was just as adamant about old-fashioned turns like the telemark, and insisted on various forms of christianias from the slow, almost plough-like, side drift, to the sharp and vicious jump. Still, after the first week, no group could keep up with us, whilst we acquired technical skill, with a staunch team spirit and a deep affection for our Yank.

In summer, after swimming and life-saving tests I was accepted for a 'water-camp' – sailing for seniors and canoeing for us. There I teamed with another adventurous spirit and we soon rigged our kayak with side dagger-boards, a tall mast and a sail similar to those carried by Thames barges. She was most unstable and unwieldy but before the wind she flew like a bird.

Amongst my increasing scouting activities I attended a short Civil Defence course and became so interested in the subject that in the following two years I obtained a third and a second class Instructor's grades. These studies extended from chemistry and decontamination to shelter construction and care of casualties (the last of which, so much later, helped me to survive).

I was too single-minded and busy to look further than my immediate environment, and so the family affairs, as well as national matters, were passing me by. Already, more than a decade had passed since Poland had regained independence. A decade of hard and enthusiastic effort resulted in unprecedented progress. From a divided, agricultural country, we were growing into a cohesive and prosperous nation. With stable currency and full employment, with growing industries and commerce, Poland was racing forward, and Warsaw grew faster than the provinces. With the building programme in full swing we moved to a brand new flat in the Warsaw suburb of Zolibor. Stalek left the University and took charge of the Pathology Department at St. Lazarus Hospital. Mother soon obtained an identical position at the Holy Ghost Hospital, but at home they both continued work on cancer research. Edmund after many false starts settled into a career in the Police Force while Chris changed to politics and was already in the Cabinet.

At about this time I experienced – no, I was hit by – two traumatic events. These changed my trusting, childish outlook into one of suspicious caution. The first incident concerned my class master's suspicion that I had forged Mother's signature on the monthly school report. The signature was conspicuous because all the other ones had been my father's and also the round, large lettering of my Mother was very similar to my own best efforts. The idea of forgery or even lying was so alien to me that at first I did not understand what he was driving at. Then my spluttering, almost incoherent, denials did not improve the situation. At home, completely unruffled, Stalek remarked that, however suspicious the circumstances, the teacher should not have made any such remarks in front of the class and now would have to apologise also in class. Next day I delivered my father's letter to the master who turned crimson and babbled something about a misunderstanding. By then I was so embarrassed for him that I let it go without a formal apology. But now all my admiration and respect for this excellent teacher and writer was completely and irretrievably lost. I also realised that truth and honesty were not natural and self evident.

The second misadventure was even worse as it happened in scouting which was so dear to me. A boy was caught cheating but as he made restitution and appeared truly sorry I dealt with the offence rather lightly instead of referring the matter to my superiors. However, the boy ran to his father and, denying any transgression, complained of being victimised. With his besotted father he stormed to the headmaster's study calling for the scoutmaster and vengeance. Because of the father's position and in spite of the indisputable evidence I was told to hush up the matter. Young and uncompromising, I refused and offered my resignation. The affair came into the open and a number of boys resigned in sympathy with me. Pressured even by my best friends I saw the insignificant original problem threatening the existence of the whole troop but still I would not compromise. The case resolved itself with the collapse and public confession of the offender. But I had already seen that being honest mattered only to myself whilst in this tarnished world loud shouts carried more weight than the truth.

The process of growing up was further advanced by a new friendship with a B stream boy whom I knew from the English class where both streams were studying together. For weeks, squeezed in some far corners, we travelled on the same tram, each reading his book but never acknowledging the other's presence until, one day, I noticed that he was engrossed in the English number of *Flight*. We started talking and I soon found out that he was fanatically dedicated to this one and only interest. Technology formed the immediate basis of our association. At school after woodwork and sheet-metal work, we graduated to machining at which he excelled. When building his superb models of current aircraft he was glad to share with me his skill and knowledge. But there was another and different aspect of this friendship. He had no father and his over-worked mother could not control him. It made me realise my own good fortune in having Stalek whom I always took for granted. It also brought home to me the difference between the 'haves' and the 'have-nots'. Though we were not wealthy, maybe not even well-to-do, I never felt poor or deprived and other boys' electric trains, or their replica model cars, left me unmoved. But now I observed how he lived with his mother and sister. They never went hungry, but the amount of jam or cheese tended to be sparingly rationed. Also, whilst I had my bike and some tools, he had to pinch and scrape and earn money for the smallest luxuries. When helping him with some maps which he was doing for a pittance, I learned that he was supposed to hand over to his mother half of his earnings. With stunned disbelief, I heard him lie to her about the sum he had been paid. But then I asked myself whether I could be sure of my own actions especially if my newest and best model plane needed the last coat of high-gloss paint. For the first time in my life a lie ceased to be an unforgivable sin.

But however important these incidents appeared at the time, the world did not stop, lessons continued and new activities overshadowed the recent past. Fired by the aviation madness of my new friend I became interested in gliding which was then in its infancy. I joined the Scout Gliding Club and attended the evening theoretical course as a prerequisite to the real flying. There I was staggered by the amount of knowledge and the speed with which it was ladled into us but at last I passed with honours in all the subjects: meteorology, aerodynamics, instrumentation and structures. The end of the school year brought with it the final catastrophe - my annual certificate showed two marks below the pass level and this meant no progress to the next form but an ignominious stay for another year in the same class. I faced losing a whole year, leaving my circle of friends and joining another, younger group of boys. At home Stalek raised his eyebrows and asked whether I intended to finish school, as otherwise I was taking the place of somebody who would really benefit from it. But there were no recriminations and later Stalek himself told me not to look at it as the end of the world but to take advantage of the experience. I was so dejected and contrite that I intended to resign my place in the flying school when Stalek pointed out that it would be a further waste of knowledge already acquired. So in summer I went to Polichno Flying School, vowing to improve my scholastic achievements - and indeed, three years later I obtained my matric with excellent marks in all subjects.

We were sprawling on the rocky slope in the scanty shade under the wings of the gliders. We were sunburnt, hot and bored with the ridiculous weather. All summer, it was either stiflingly hot with not a breath of wind or, without warning, heavy clouds would flood the horizon and lash us with streams of water blown by merciless, gusty squalls. Either way, we could not fly: with catapult launching we had to have a steady wind, and in Polichno we had neither cars nor planes to tow us. Of course, it only seemed that we never had a chance to fly, whilst in reality, we did manage quite a lot of training. It began on the gentle slopes with only six men at the rubber rope hooked to the glider which was held by a quick release shackle. For the first little 'jumps' of some hundred feet, we used the almost prehistoric CWJ gliders with wings stiffened by dozens of wires which whistled and sang in the lightest breeze. Then we graduated to the much lighter Crows with their aerodynamic struts supporting the square wings. The pilot, perching on a flimsy, open seat below and in front of the wing, would shout the commands of the time-hallowed ritual: 'Ropes ready?' – 'Tail ready?' – 'Pull!' – and the men would walk away with the ropes, 'Run!' – and the men ran down straining at the stretching rope till the 'Let go!' released the tail and the glider shot forward. This was the critical moment, when the pilot's body was pressed back against the frame, when one felt like a human cannon ball. The fierce acceleration lasted only a few seconds but if you jerked back the joy-stick, you could cripple the men by the snap of the suddenly released rope and the rearing glider losing the lift would plummet to the ground. But if you held still, the machine would overtake the slackening rope, releasing it gently. Then you were on your own, absolutely free, soaring silently. It was a marvellous, exhilarating feeling to be up there with the blue sky around and the chequerboard of fields spread below, whilst the hands and feet on the controls made the glider an extension of your body, an integral part of yourself. But it did not always work out like that. Sometimes a flying glider looked like a wounded bird with a wing hanging down whilst the red-faced instructor bawled after it, at the top of his voice, new orders and admonitions. Sometimes an inept learner, scared of losing speed, pushed the stick forward and the whistling machine would land too fast, scattering fountains of earth and gravel, even splintering its skids. But the opposite was even worse when, climbing too steeply, the glider would stall and plunge down like a falling stone. Because of these potential dangers we were not allowed to fly in shirtsleeves but had to wear a jacket which provided some protection against minor abrasions and light splinters from the wooden structure. On the other hand, between the flights, in the sunshine, we lolled about, almost naked, awaiting our next turn. There, one day on the rocky mountain ridge, I found under my windcheater a large grass-snake. There was a good three feet of a beautifully patterned, sinuous, green body, perfectly smooth except for the middle point of its back which seemed sharply bent, swollen and scratched. As it did not move, I left it there till after my flight which, with the lengthening shadows, was the last one of the day. I talked to the beastie which watched me closely with its black, unblinking eyes, and slowly wrapped itself, or rather its upper half, round my arm. I lifted it gently and lowered it into the voluminous folds of my windcheater, which had a strong, elastic hip-band. In the little cottage where six of us lived together the snake was delighted with a raw egg and a saucer of milk. It lived and flew with me snug in the windcheater or, in the hot weather, loosely wrapped round my neck, like a precious jade necklace. It must have been seriously hurt, but was recovering fast and when left on its own tried to follow me. At first, the slithering movements were slow and laboured, with the tail-end dragging inertly. But in a few days, the tail began to move, and soon it could flow gracefully at a good pace. When I found it I had already acquired the 'A' grade, and, whether due to my fast reactions and sense of balance, or to the green mascot, I obtained the 'B' pilot-licence in record time. The snake seemed to know that it was time to go home, and, during the next morning walk, slithered away. It stopped at the hedge, lifted its head above the high, dense grass and looked back at me for a long moment before disappearing into the surrounding meadows.

The school year, my second in the sixth form, began more easily than I had expected. Nobody cared about my personal catastrophe, and the new class accepted me as a matter of fact. But what really cheered me was the attitude of all the boys of my old class who continued to treat me as one of themselves to such a degree that when, after their own matric, they formed a close-knit association, I was the only outsider who was proposed, and unanimously elected, a member. Meanwhile I settled down and, finding the work easy, continued my scouting activities and read voraciously. Long past Sherlock Holmes and Stalky, I plodded through Dickens, loved Lady Rowena of *Ivanhoe*, and Rosamund of *Sea Hawk*. I wallowed in Jack London from the *Greenhorn* to the *Sea-Wolf*. But also, however unlikely the mixture, I put a lot of time into forensic medicine and into *Das Kapital* which I bottomed and dismissed as unacceptable.

In addition to this literature, I enjoyed motoring when Chris took me to a few local rallies. He soon changed his Mercedes to a BMW and twice completed the Monte Carlo. As cars were so expensive I began to think of a motorcycle. My finances were based solely on my pocket money – the equivalent of about fifteen shillings a month. Half of it went on tram fares and the other half had to pay for pencils, rubbers, copybooks and school charities before tools or other toys could be considered.

At that time in Warsaw, there were no easy ways for a boy to earn money. There were no paper-rounds, except by the licensed news vendors, the idea of baby-sitting did not exist, because of cheap and plentiful labour in the domestic market, whilst nobody would even consider paying a teenage student for odd tasks or evening labour. However, with great difficulty, I found some tracing work which, though of a high standard, paid little. Better, though scarce, were posters required from time to time, by small cafés or dance-halls. But I really solved the problem by the invention of a partnership and, after a long thought, offered it to Poppy, who accepted with alacrity. From then on, my life became more difficult as I saved like mad. The authorities did not allow cycling to school because of traffic hazards, but cycling most of the way, leaving the bike with friends and walking, I saved daily a third of a zloty – a whole threepence. I also had a lot of trouble with my new partner who, with unbounded enthusiasm, would go hungry to save twenty groshes, but the next day would lash out ten times as much on an irrelevant fancy. There is no doubt that my single-mindedness caused him a lot of hardship and difficulties; it also imposed a great strain on our friendship. Yet in spring, with over a hundred zloties saved, I began to study advertisements of garages, wreckers yards and even those of scrap-metal dealers. Unfortunately, with the money at my disposal (about four pounds sterling) I was either laughed at, or shown heaps of incomplete and rusty parts. Thus, finding a machine with two wheels and an engine, I proceeded to beat down the vendor's price which had been twice the sum I commanded.

After two hours of hard bargaining, I bought the thing for ninety-seven zloties and fifty groshes with half a gallon of petrol thrown in.

It took hours of cleaning and polishing, before I could see details of the thin spidery wheels, the moss-green square tank with the last traces of gold lines, and the brass, hand-operated, oil-pump. Below, there was the heavy-looking cylinder sitting proudly on a narrow crank-case, the oil bath with chain to gearbox, and the final drive by a pitifully shaggy belt: my very own 500 cc. 1918 Sunbeam. Without a clue as to what it was all about, I started on the engine by unscrewing all the bolts and taking it slowly apart. Not only did I have to find out what held what, but I also had to figure out the why and wherefore before I could do something to make it work. A fortnight later, the engine coughed, spat and burbled into life, and I was away. It was an unbelievable feeling to relax in a wide and supple hide saddle, and be pulled along at a dizzying speed, without pedalling, without any effort. It was easy to pass the driving test, but it took weeks to modify the ever-slipping belt to a chain-drive, and change the block-brake for a modern drum which I designed and made in the school workshop. In summer I really learned to ride, though I also developed extra muscles pushing the 'old dame' many weary miles. I learned to improvise field repairs of pipes, tyres, springs and clutch, using miles of wire, pounds of solder and, of course, string. During my heroic tours, Poppy was happy riding horses and sailing his dinghy on the family estates. I even felt guilty about his half-share in the bike until I reached his place where he managed in half an hour to wreck the machine by smashing at speed into the cedar timbers of the old country mansion. This completed my first summer of motorcycling and almost finished the old Sunbeam.

My last two years of school passed slowly and uneventfully. In spite of the ever-increasing load of homework, I managed to obtain good marks and still continued scouting, motorcycling and skiing at Christmas and Easter recesses. Both my parents caught some of my motorcycling enthusiasm and helped me to buy my next machine which was a 600 cc. Douglas twin belonging to my gym-master. He had just broken his leg and smashed up the bike, so that I got it really cheap and managed most of the repairs on my own. The same winter I completed a course which qualified me as a skiing instructor so that teaching covered the cost of my winter holidays. More important for me were the International Ski Trials in Zwardon, where I represented the Warsaw Scouts. Taking part in two events I finished in the first half, but not in the medals. There, in the fierce downhill run, I saw skiers technically worse than myself passing me fast, losing control and smashing into the trees. Similarly, I was overtaken in a gruelling climb by weaker boys some of whom not only failed to finish, but had to be carried down. Whether it was cowardice or lack of competitive spirit, I realised that I valued my own skin far above ribbons and medals, and decided never to compete again and to leave the honour to the brainless fanatics.

In the late spring the final exams came, and we sat them with all pomp and circumstance, each at a separate table in the spacious gym. They were followed by the orals, when I got the whole board of examiners in stitches having forgotten the name of dandelion and given instead the Polish folk name 'Man's Virtue' which, according to the village maidens, disappeared in a single puff of wind, as easily as the ripe seed-head of the plant. But I passed well, and after the formal distribution of certificates, I proceeded to demonstrate my maturity and independence. In the very centre of the school quadrangle stood the bust of King Batory. At night I squeezed between the sharp top spikes of the gates, climbed the solid granite base and, to the immense satisfaction of my colleagues, sat myself down on the bronze head of the King.

CHAPTER 5

WASTED TIME?

The matric, so distant and unattainable for years, once won changed from the glittering golden fleece into the first little step to further education and profession. The new climb began from a highly competitive University entrance exam and, for most of us, a year's National Service which we preferred to complete at once to avoid later disruptions of the studies. However, the summer was upon us and instead of swotting I accepted an offer of joining a group representing Polish youth at the Berlin Olympiad 1936. The games were truly magnificent but I failed the University entrance exam which seemed less important viewed from the Signals Training Centre in Zegrze where I began my Army Service.

The first weeks were the worst. We all felt naked and alien in the strange and unknown surroundings. The strident, continuous shouts of the NCOs; the remote, god-like figures of the commissioned officers; the utilitarian barracks which had to be kept spotless twenty-four hours a day ... Our shorn heads, tight uniforms buttoned to the chins, and of course, rifles. These should have been mentioned first, as they were the most important: handled like holy relics, unceasingly polished and inspected. But soon, in spite of the seemingly impossible demands on our wits and muscles, even the most unmilitary-minded of us learned various combinations of stars, stripes and chevrons and instead of whispering: 'If you please, Mister ...' roared: 'Yes, Sir!' When we were just getting used to running, jumping, square-bashing and saluting from six in the morning to ten at night, they threw in lectures and equipment instructions. Electricity and magnetism started innocuously enough, but in a couple of hours we already were deep in superheterodyne circuits! Those without technical background were bewildered in the first week, and began swotting at night.

It seemed unbelievable that in the early weeks of run, spit and polish, nobody was injured, nobody collapsed or died. But still more amazing was the fact that, in this breathless and bewildered crowd, there was already a certain pride and competitive spirit. The individuals, only yesterday's schoolboys, engineers and lawyers, panted and sweated, shining their boots more brightly than anybody else, springing to attention straighter and more quickly. Each troop licked the floor cleaner, and waxed old telephone cables smoother, whilst our 'A' company was obviously better than the 'B', and smarter than the first year of the 'professionals'. We learned the rules and regulations, the terrible punishments which might befall us, but I do not remember a single instance of any penalty being imposed. On one side the shame of doing things wrong, and on the other, the potential reward of a weekend pass home, was more than enough to keep everyone on his toes.

My own original conviction that the army, though necessary, was in peace time just 'bull and showing off', changed completely in view of the volume of knowledge and skills required by the service. The most obvious of these was physical fitness which appeared, at first, considerably impaired by our clumsy cavalry boots. But soon, even shinning up a telegraph pole, the boots became as inseparable a part of us as the rifle. We began to associate wave-length and frequency with changing capacitance and the big black knob on the front of the receiver. And when stringing new lines at night, we understood the seemingly mindless insistence of our instructors on always placing each tool and each spare part in the appropriate order and place. Even the repetitive and endless building of telephone field lines, as well as cleaning and rewinding of cables, became bearable when we began to out-perform other teams of the garrison. We fired Very pistols, read light signals, built permanent telephone lines and listened to Morse code speeding up to a hundred letters a minute.

Between the lectures, instructions and field exercises, there were less common activities. Some, like demolition, were exhilarating with their taste of danger; others, such as horse riding, did not appeal to me. We groomed and saddled awkward beasts which kicked, bit and took every opportunity to obstruct the soldiers in their duty - any one of us would have been shot for half of their tricks! Yet in spite of all the opposition, we trotted and galloped round the exercise yard, out into the open fields and then cross-country through hedges and over ditches. But that, however painful, was just the beginning, and soon, side aprons of thick leather were buckled on to the brutes whilst we started training with drums of cable, each weighing about ten pounds. It was child's play to ride at a walk unrolling the cable from the drum clutched desperately in the left hand as the right one controlled the reins. Trotting soon found us wanting, especially when the horse stopped and the fast-spinning drum continued to revolve like a great flywheel spilling yards of cable which always enmeshed the horse and rider in a tangle of Gordian knots.

'You big bazooka of a professor! Yes, you! You there in the saddle! You think that the thumb is only for sucking? God gave you the left thumb to press the drum brake! And if you haven't got a left thumb hold the cable in your teeth!'

The gallop produced other snags – invariably in the cable on the drum! However carefully we rewound the drums (like the early pilots packing their own 'chutes) it was always at full speed that the cable would tangle and, with its two hundred pounds breaking load, the result was inevitable; the enormous mass of the horse continued unchecked whilst the rider, halted by his own wire, would stop dead in mid-air and, as an afterthought, plummet down, still clutching the jammed drum. Once, landing in this fashion, I burrowed deep into a muddy stream, and when I emerged half-drowned, I was met by a real barrage from the quartermaster-sergeant:

'I and the government don't give you a uniform to go swimming in! You can fall off at the Grand National, that's what the fences are for, but in the army you go with the horse, you little Cossack!'

And I remained the 'Little Cossack' for the duration of my service – the Polish diminutive of Cossack held many implied meanings, the foremost being a reckless gambler rather too quick on the trigger.

After the unpredictability of horses, the reliability of hand-guns was a great relief. I was quite familiar with revolvers and automatics, but it was more the ineptitude of my colleagues than my own marksmanship which made me the best revolver shot in the company.

Yet, with childish delight in good bangs and fireworks, I enjoyed even more the grenade practice. Throwing from a shallow trench, I repeatedly scored direct hits on the target which erupted in a fountain of earth and smoke. It was difficult to understand why so many of us were apprehensive of this exercise, though some were scared out of their wits and, from a deep communication trench, I witnessed an episode which could be described as roaringly funny. The next grenadier, though a brilliant Ph.D., was an extremely timid and clumsy soldier. Given a real, live grenade, in spite of all the instruction and training, he grabbed it in his left hand instead of the right one, and pulled the safety pin. Then, with the pin clutched tightly in his right he casually opened the left hand letting the sizzling bomb drop to his feet. As all of us, he was supervised by the Company Commander who, bending low, scooped the grenade out of the trench and, continuing the smooth turn, tripped the bewildered Ph.D., falling on top of him, whilst from a few yards away came the roar of an explosion and the hail of splinters over their heads.

With the training programme as full as it was, we were rarely on guard duty. It was quite an experience for us and an event dreaded by the whole garrison. All rules and regulations which we knew by heart could be summarised simply: one challenge, one warning and shoot to kill! Also, in our situation of being constantly observed and assessed, we all stuck like leeches to the smallest letter of the law. After polishing all our equipment brighter than ever, after washing and shaving till our faces shone, we were issued with live ammunition and marched to the guardhouse and the simple ceremony of changing the guard. In the standard, often ill-fitting, khaki uniforms seen against the background of dismal barrack blocks, we were infinitely remote from the spectacle of Buckingham Palace Guard in all but the precision of drill. From then on gloom and oppression reigned in the garrison. Within an hour, at every gate there were queues of officers' wives as well as various civilian craftsmen. Well known to everybody but us, they rarely carried the official passes or other documents and were reduced to calling their friends or husbands by shouting over the heads of unrelenting sentries. Even the appearance of always furious and sometimes high-ranking relatives did not help: we were fearless and firm, sending the newcomers to the CO of the guard. The night produced other problems and more nerve-racking experiences. There were two especially 'dangerous' and vulnerable posts: the arsenal and the quartermaster's safe. The first held little lethal equipment but nevertheless was fortified like Fort Knox, whilst the cash content of the second would hardly fill a wallet. But the magic names gave them enough importance and status to be guarded and defended to the death.

The sentries there were at the treble disadvantage of poor lighting, confined space and vague gossip of instructors creeping up to wrench the rifle from an unlucky soldier. In these circumstances, when I drew the duty at the famous safe I made up my mind that they were not going to get me. Every quarter of an hour before entering the wide, pitch-black corridor, I lunged a bayonet thrust to the right followed by a vicious sweep to the left and, feeling no resistance, crept along, with rifle well back as in instructions for 'close quarters combat', then at the blank end of the passage I pressed the push-button to illuminate the safe in the next room which I inspected through a barred window.

Another disquieting night task was that of inspecting disreputable pubs which were 'out of bounds' to military personnel. Leading a three-man patrol I approached the first of the listed dens of iniquity on the bank of the river. From a distance we heard the rowdy songs and snatches of gramophone music from the large building and through the screen of trees saw the flicker of brightly lit windows. It required some courage to follow the instructions and leave the comfort of my three musketeers outside, and enter the place alone. I climbed the four rickety steps and pushed through the squeaking door. Almost blinded by the strong light within, I stopped on the threshold and inspected the room slowly. A crowd of people talking and drinking, small tables and large bar at the back, and a silence spreading from my point of entry like circles from a stone dropped into a pool. And, as the Red Sea opened for Moses so the hushed crowd receded leaving a wide passage to the two back rooms which I duly inspected. Then I was back in the dark alley, leading my patrol further whilst I began to realise how silly and groundless were my misgivings: the armed forces, never employed to quell civil disorders, were regarded as friends and defenders of the people. They were 'our troops' composed of 'us', and, with the compulsory military service, everybody knew and understood what they were about, just as well as they knew the thin red binding on our sleeves denoting the budding ensigns with their 'holier than thou' attitude of new converts. The people of Poland not only knew and understood, they also were proud of us and anxious to help. The uniform lifted the wearer from his own class putting him firmly into the poor but noble warrior caste.

There were forced marches and field exercises, nights of service on busy exchanges and hours of coding and decoding. There was rifle and machine-gun practice as well as continuous, never-ending work at laying miles and miles of telephone cable, rain or shine, day or night... But also there was more and more stress on leadership and command. From two-men patrols we progressed to sections, platoons and a full company. We began with our own mates who strained to help interpreting rightly any incorrect order. But the instructors would always pull us up so that when the time came to command a strange company we not only managed, but, feeling sure and confident, took charge of professional NCOs and soldiers so much older than ourselves.

There were also more individual challenges, of which the line of faults was the most dreaded. This was a two-mile loop of single telephone cable, beginning and ending at the small exchange in our barracks. Every night a patrol of three men was called to check and repair the line, which during the day had been 'doctored' in a most fiendish way by our equipment NCO. The theory was simple enough: one man was left on the exchange whilst the remaining pair, equipped with a field telephone and a tool-bag, walked along the wire mending breaks and other faults till the man on the exchange could 'ring himself' getting a strong signal through the repaired loop. It was a dark and cold night when the dubious honour of commanding the line patrol was conferred upon me. There was a whole night before us which meant not only loss of much-needed sleep, but also the longer we took, the lower were the marks so much coveted in this furiously competitive environment. Even so, we knew that at least a quarter of all the patrols failed to complete the task. I was set on succeeding, and succeeding fast, but knew better than to cut corners. A check of the exchange before leaving the building showed some internal faults which we soon repaired.

However, even then we could not contact the exchange from outside until we discovered a faulty earth-wire. After reconnecting the damaged cable, we plunged into the night on the double, checking the line every couple of hundred yards. The cable snaked most ingeniously under the densest and most prickly bushes, or was slung high over the tallest and smoothest trees. It was cut in the middle of an enormous hawthorn bush with both ends tied to the branches so that we could not pull them out, and we had not only to repair the damned thing, but also to report all faults in detail. There was no end to the ingenuity of our sergeant, but the trick that took the most time to sort out employed a number of invisible thin needles with which the cable was pinned to the high trees. One needle does not cause much leakage, but a series of them earths the cable and short-circuits the whole line. But at last, about one o'clock in the morning, we were back with a list of twenty-three faults and the line working perfectly.

There were intervals of fun and camaraderie between the unshed tears of exhaustion and frustration, but above all, there was the unceasing sweat of maximum effort sustained by pride and competitiveness. I kept myself to myself acquiring the needed skill and knowledge; but I loathed the system of blind obedience, of being shouted at and ordered about by anybody with half a stripe more than me. I saw clearly the necessity for obedience and discipline, for the saluting and 'Yes Sir'-ing, yet this did not make it any easier to bear. I was friendly to all, but friend to no one. Some of them were miserable, just enduring and struggling to stay the course. Many saw themselves as heroic defenders of Poland, and gloried in their blue-black colours of the Signal Corps, in the ring of their spurs and the admiring glances of the girls. I dreamed of finishing this useless interval of my life. But I had to finish well.

By Christmas I got my first stripe and, at Easter, I was a full corporal. It was also at Easter that we were herded by the sergeant-major to confession. In the quiet church I took my place in the queue and in due time reached the army chaplain in the confessional.

'Excuse me, Father, I do not feel any need for confession, and I am not sure that I believe in any of it, but I do not wish to lie or to offend you and the Church.'

'Then why did you come to me, son?'

'Well, Father, the sergeant-major is watching from the choir and making notes in his black notebook.'

'Oh ... I see. Well, my son, thank you for being honest and for telling me. Please keep kneeling whilst you count to fifty, then go and sit down ... and remember to beat your breast, it's fashionable amongst the believers and sergeant-majors!' He absolved three or four men following me and only then did he shoot out of his confessional and roar loud enough to shame any NCO:

'Sergeant! You there, in the choir! It's no use ducking, stand up and leave my church on the double! Report to me when I have finished here

– understand?' It was typical of the army at its worst and of religion at its best.

The relentless training continued to the very last day before graduation. Of our company four men did not complete the course whilst the best three finished with full sergeant's chevrons which I missed by a whisker, being fourth in the honours list. Still, I was one of the next three who boasted platoon sergeant's stripes. Also, like all of us, I was an ensign which meant a commission in three years. But in the meantime, the remaining months of my service passed uneventfully at Skierniewice, my permanent posting to the 26th Infantry Division.

When I left the army I was expert at building and servicing telephone systems and firing small arms. I could blow up a bridge and had learnt to box and ride. Admirable achievements, no doubt, though of little use in my intended career. At the time I completely overlooked the less tangible results of the training, like the ability to lead, the habit of command and the self-assurance backed by the certainty that I could stand on my own two feet alone and unaided.

After a year in the army there was no point in taking again the failed entrance exam and, to avoid wasting a whole year, I decided to try the Danzig University. There the condition of entry was a year's apprenticeship in the Shipbuilding and Engineering Company of the same city. I already had some experience of factory work, but the rigid regimentation and vicious anti-Polish atmosphere coupled with the German language drove me out of Danzig before Christmas. Back at home I really concentrated on physics, chemistry and maths which was always my weakest subject. The studies progressed so well that I decided to take an Easter break skiing in the Tatra Mountains. But I had to seek younger companions as my close friends were too busy: Bob filled every second of his life with engineering studies and Poppy used every moment in a headlong pursuit of the fair sex. So I approached two boys to whom, long ago, I had taught skiing. Both accepted eagerly and joined me with the wholehearted approval of their parents. The first one, nicknamed 'Long', seemed even higher than his six and a quarter feet, and his close friend, by contrast called 'Little', was almost a head taller than I. They were strong, excellent skiers and trusted my leadership whilst I knew that I could fully rely on them.

The small, sleepy station of Zakopane, the very centre of Polish winter sports, came to life with the arrival of the overnight express from Warsaw. The train, leaking small jets of steam from the engine and the snow-streaked carriages, spilled its load of passengers. In a few seconds the empty platform was filled with a milling, multicoloured crowd. Young men in navy blue and girls in colourful sweaters were in the majority; but there were also family groups and some older men accompanied by young ladies in furs. Near the station some distraught adults tried hard, but ineffectively, to collect their own group of an excursion or skiing school. Everywhere the local highlanders in their white, heavily embroidered trousers and flowing short capes wove through the crowd, calling the names of hotels, or touting for passengers for their little one-horse sledges. We piled out with the rest but, carrying only rucksacks and skis, we were away within a couple of minutes. We attracted a fair amount of attention and quite a few ribald comments on account of our dress. In spite of Long's parents' wealth and the comfortable financial position of Little's family, all three of us were doing things our own way 'on the cheap', and as each of us had a winter scout uniform, we used the very loose, baggy 'plus fours' of khaki colour almost offensive in this snowy landscape. We also wore white gaiters and waterproof windcheaters, well worn and faded but still showing various shades of lovat. All this greenish clothing was enhanced by a kerchief and headband in the colour of our scout troop which was the most vivid orange!

We skied past the large tourist establishments, and climbed higher to places where local people ran small rest-houses. I was already familiar with them and we soon became known in the locality as 'those wanting discounts for scouts, and lower rates for a group, and ...' We often chopped wood for a pot of boiling water and sent Little to charm a dozen eggs out of the 'kitchen ladies'. But it was all good fun and we were liked and accepted by the highlanders as friends – not tourists. Once we took part in a night rescue operation and on another occasion were lucky enough to find and bring down a group of tourists lost in a blizzard. By then we knew the terrain and local conditions but nevertheless we ran into trouble. It started with the decision to cross one of the higher passes to the next valley. Deep snow, slowly melting in the noonday sun, was heavy and ripe to break off and fall in avalanches. From a distance we saw a small one, an unstoppable torrent of boulders, ice and snow rolling downhill, leaving behind a track of destruction. We only heard of the deadly dust avalanches and of the plate type where the complete covering of a hill would move like a gigantic escalator in one enormous solid plate which, reaching the end of the slope, would shatter in a violent explosion – but that seemed too fancy to be true. We left the forest and climbed traversing a steep slope above which, on our left, were several large lips of menacing snowy overhangs. This was the danger point and, after a short discussion, we agreed to proceed silently, without speaking but watching the threatening edge. If anything moved there, we had a good chance to escape the consequences by a straight downhill run into the old forest. Over the steep virgin slope I led diagonally, getting cross-eyed from watching the edge on our left as well as the pass marked by a solitary tree in front of us. This tree, at last no more than a hundred yards away, suddenly started moving upwards – it was just going uphill! Disbelieving my own eyes, I glanced round: everything further away was moving uphill. Then the penny dropped – the whole slope, the complete field of snow with us in the centre, was flowing downhill faster and faster – the plate avalanche.

'Follow me down! Now!' – I yelled and jumped in a straight downhill race. After gathering speed, I turned to escape sideways into the gently rising edge of the main field. My speed over the snow was too high for comfort and the snow moved also at a fair lick. With these two combined velocities I crossed the cracking, smoking edge of the plate, lost control and crashed into the thickly tangled bushes of dwarf pine. A few yards above me, Little was similarly wedged into another thicket, and just below Long ploughed into a plantation of young saplings, breaking several of them and coming to a stop bruised but unhurt. Behind us the solid mass of the flowing snow and ice thundered into the wood below, shaving a wide clearing.

It took us hours to reach the pass climbing the steep ridge instead of taking another chance on the again silent snowy field with the overhangs still poised above. Finally, resting in the shallow saddle of the pass, we spread out the remaining bread, the last of the butter, sugar and the lemons for a sumptuous meal. I was sucking the very last lemon when Little with his cherubic smile remarked:

'Johnny, I don't want to worry you, but did you look at the beauty of nature lately?' They all called me John or Johnny since my Texan instructor rechristened me that way. I raised my eyes from the delicious lemon – but there was nothing to see: from the valleys around us a white, solid veil of fog was rising fast. Even as I looked, like a spreading milky flood it reached the plateau of the saddle and moved towards us blotting out everything. Within five minutes the three of us squatted in the snow, each seeing only the ghostly outlines of the other two. We all knew the mountains too well to move though it grew unbearably cold under this white, wet blanket. Each of us carried about ten yards of light, strong line and knotting together the three pieces we had enough to undertake a bit of exploration.

'Long! Tie the end to your belt. Take one of your ski sticks and try the snow well before you step on it. This rope won't hold your weight if you drop into a precipice. I want you to circle round us – till you find those nice bushes which were on our right when we settled down here. When you are there, shout and we will join you with all the clobber!'

Within an hour we set up camp under the dense bushes. We had made for ourselves sleeping bags of airtight balloon fabric and the boys squeezed into them after dressing up in all the clothing that they possessed. They settled down on a thick layer of pine branches leaving me a place in the centre, whilst I covered all with more branches and, with my dixie, shovelled as much snow as I could manage over the whole heap. Exhausted and half-frozen, I pushed in and soon found it really warm and snug. We slept through the evening and the whole night and, ravenously hungry, woke up to a glorious morning. A careful search revealed a couple of mouldy slices of bread, half a bar of chocolate and the bacon. This two-pound fatty piece had come with us from Warsaw, but unfortunately it had seemed slightly off and a week ago we decided to give it to some hungry dogs. Now Long, completely unabashed, explained triumphantly:

'Well, they just wouldn't touch it and it was a shame to throw it, so I kept it. It's a Godsend now!'

We did manage to consume everything and the same afternoon returned to civilisation none the worse for our experience.

It was an unforgettable holiday full of the sheer physical effort of climbing ever higher, through the enchanted valleys to the deep forests. There each fir was dressed like a Christmas tree with a light sprinkling of snow or the long delicate needles of hoar-frost, with ice stalactites glittering like diamonds in the sun or, in shadows, showing only opalescent milky hues. Farther were endless vistas of mysterious paths and in the background the ever-changing views of the rocky crests. The upper reaches, where we spent most of our time, were almost deserted. The mountains of the snowy fairy-tale belonged only to us as did the triumphs and exhilarations of headlong flight downhill. The boys, though impressed and overjoyed with their first time in the high mountains, tended to take it all for granted: winter and snow, ski and speed. But for me it was a heady mixture of unparalleled, almost abstract beauty, and physical delight verging on some still unknown, but only guessed-at, feelings of infinite love and repose, of power and victory.

At home I continued my studies though I felt quite confident about the exams. In spring it was time to consider my bike which was growing rather unreliable. As in the past Mother enjoyed riding pillion and as I had taught Stalek to ride the bike I was not surprised when they both hinted at the possibility of a 'decent' bike with a sidecar. And behold – in no time at all – we had our own, almost new, Norton combination.

CHAPTER 6

THE FOURTH DIMENSION

One warm spring night I got into a most involved discussion with Poppy when his sister knocked on the door: 'Johnny – be an angel and take my friend home – it's too late for trams or buses!' Over her shoulder I had a glimpse of a slim, ash-blonde girl – I think they introduced us, but I only remember her long, shapely legs when she perched side-saddle on the pillion. I just had enough sense left to tell her to sit astride as she was bound to fall off on the potholed suburban streets. With a doubtful grin and a casual 'Don't look' she hitched the tight skirt over her hips. Those were the pre-war days of almost Victorian propriety in a country much more formal than England: the time and place where it took months for 'Miss Smith' to become 'Miss Judith' and still longer for her to be just 'Judy'. My achievements in sports, in the army, the hard-won matric – all seemed useless and irrelevant by the side of this glamorous girl. I was tongue-tied, afraid of even a casual physical contact – but I was not letting her go and vanish from my life.

Three days later we met again and looking into her blue eyes I said:

'I just can't call you 'Miss' – it's so silly, so remote ...' And from then on she was just Veesa. Veesa loved motorcycling and the next Sunday we went far into the country. Coming back at night we had a puncture – a frequent occurrence because of the wicked nails shed by heavy horse traffic. She held the torch as I struggled with tyre-levers and the little vulcanising kit. A good hour passed before, streaming with sweat, I straightened my creaking back and leaned against a tree at the side of the dark, deserted road, whilst Veesa, shivering in the cold night air, huddled against me. My arms went round her slim waist as she nestled closer and somehow, incredibly, our lips met in a first kiss. The budding romance was shattered by the blinding glare of headlights from a lorry rumbling round the corner, lighting up the edge of the road and holding us in the spotlight as if in a farce. Red and furious I could have slaughtered the driver who let out a triumphant series of honks; but Veesa, still holding me tight with one arm, waved happy greetings to the offending vehicle which trundled away into the night. This was the beginning of a glorious spring and a carefree summer, of sailing on the Vistula, lazing in the sun and motorcycling through the country, my Veesa and I in a happy, intimate friendship verging on real love.

In the absolute scale of time these were only a few months of my life but they unleashed a whirlwind of feelings and emotions which I never before could have imagined. Trivial actions and episodes acquired a new meaning and importance. Sun on the beach shone brighter when she smiled, the road unwound faster when, sitting behind, she gripped me tighter. There was happiness and rapture in her uninhibited embraces. There was also an overwhelming sense of responsibility for her, and the need to protect her from any real or imaginary danger. There was laughter and fun, or quiet, idyllic repose but never a misunderstanding or a cross word. This was Veesa, in shortest shorts whenever possible, a slim beautiful blonde of blue eyes and soft ready lips.

During this summer I was called out for six weeks of the army 'refresher'. I trained recruits, built miles of permanent telephone line and finished with two weeks of manoeuvres involving several infantry divisions and an armoured brigade. It was an extremely tiring long slog in which I was gratified, but apprehensive, at being in sole charge of the headquarters signals platoon. The 'Blues' and the 'Reds' advanced, retreated and skirmished whilst we ran faster and faster, stringing miles of field lines, missing meals and sleep, but maintaining the necessary communications till the main 'battle'. Just before it I was pulled out, given another platoon and ordered to maintain the 'White' liaison of the safety net serving the observers and referees. It was a devil of a job but we just managed the last connection as the 'battle' commenced. I was standing behind the headquarters of the 'White' observers on top of a hill dominating the surrounding country. Only a few yards away was my exchange with lines to the headquarters of both 'armies', their artillery, and other subsidiary units. The lines were tested every few minutes and all were 'bunched', that is, cross-connected at the exchange so that everybody on the network would hear simultaneously any orders coming from us. An hour later the 'Blue' infantry advanced behind the rolling barrage of their own artillery firing live ammunition. I was watching them through my binoculars when suddenly everything went haywire; the 'Blue' infantry took another fifty yards jump whilst their own barrage, instead of rolling the same distance forward, shortened the range. I saw the first eight shells bursting right amongst the soldiers and, God knows from where, four extra ones exploding just behind them. I roared to my exchange:

'Corporal! All artillery stop fire! All artillery stop fire!'

I was grossly exceeding my responsibility but it seemed the only thing to do. I heard my 'talker' repeating on the safety net my order, which should stop anybody pulling the trigger whatever the load or state of the gun. I stood with the binoculars glued to my eyes but not a single shell followed the twelve which had been fired into the ranks of the infantry. It was only then that I started sweating - after all, I had just casually with this order usurped the responsibility of the General commanding the whole show! It was another quarter of an hour before I was called into the presence:

'Ensign! Who gave the order to stop fire?'

'I did, Sir.'

'Well done, my boy, well done!'

And luckily the abused infantry got off as lightly as I did - without any serious casualties.

I passed the exams more easily than I had expected and, a week later, our crowd poured into the old, imposing building of the Polytechnic - Warsaw Technical University. On this first day we had little to do but locate various lecture theatres and laboratories where we expected to work for the next five years - the duration of the mechanical or electrical course. During the first year both these departments had an almost identical curriculum and their students attended many of the same lectures. There were some acquaintances and friends: mostly boys a year or two younger than I but catching up by postponing their army service till later. At noon we all met at the canteen crowded with hundreds of male students and, at the far table, a dozen girls taking the same course. We ogled with interest this small but highly valued minority. There was a spectacular swarthy beauty with sparkling eyes, assessing openly the surrounding admirers. She was flanked by two mousy blondes, one well rounded, the other thin and gaunt, both providing a perfect setting for the central jewel. Slightly further, was another trio, an almost white blonde with kittenish face, and a small girl whose long, black plaits made her look no more than fourteen. Between them was a golden-haired, statuesque young lady with a regal expression on her serene face. Across the crowd our eyes met by some odd chance and we both looked for long, long seconds – or was it hours? Somebody slapped me on the back: 'They are the two Irkas. The brunette lives next door to me and she is my own little Irka, the gold one – big Irka – is her best friend. Want to meet them?' – and, not waiting for my answer, he yelled over the noise and hubbub of the place, calling them over to our group. They pushed through the crowd carrying their half-finished meal. The small dark one flowed daintily, weaving between the densely-packed students so that no one felt her passage. The golden blonde just walked, and the crowd opened before her leaving a wide passage. Somebody squashed in the throng called 'Princess!' but nobody laughed and the path lined with hundreds of admiring eyes widened still more. We were introduced and got lost in the general conversation. The crowd thinned as there was no more to do and I walked her home. She had refused dozens of other offers with a meaningless, polite half-smile and a shake of the head which set the bell of her hair dancing in a shower of golden lights. We strolled slowly, hardly speaking, just being together.

Later, I did not catch a tram, but walked along the Vistula, up hill through the Old Town, round the Citadel to Zolibor. I thought of her, trying to understand what had really happened. I had just met a girl, a good-looking girl but not a classical beauty. A quiet girl in a coat the colour of a red squirrel, a dark green woollen dress and flat-heeled, brown shoes. The golden hair and large grey eyes. And I did not know her at all, I still called her 'Miss Irene', not daring the diminutive 'Irka'. She appeared cold and remote – I might never break down the barriers surrounding her, I might not speak to her again! She had not a trace of the happy, forthcoming camaraderie of Veesa, nor the slick chic of the frivolous blue dresses usually just a trifle short and tight. No, there would be no hesitation in choosing between the two if there were a choice. But for me there was no choice and, making the bravest decision of my whole life, I went to see Veesa for the last time.

We kissed, hers were always long, lingering kisses, and she asked about my first day at the Polytechnic.

'Darling, it's very difficult to say, but I met a girl there, and I feel ...' She just laughed at me:

'But you are here now! It doesn't matter. I am not the jealous, possessive type!' And it is so difficult to explain something that one does not understand oneself. Yet she understood better than I did. She did not say one word of recrimination or complaint. With tears in our eyes we kissed and parted.

'You should go now. But if you've made a mistake come back to me.'

I felt as if I had lost part of myself, an important, vital part. I could hardly imagine life without her, but at the same time I knew with absolute certainty that I had done the only possible thing. So I lost Veesa because of Irka. But in my mind's eye I had already seen the Fates weave and knot together the threads of our lives: Irka and I belonged to one another.

The academic year started slowly, but soon its pace quickened into a dizzying whirl of lectures, tutorials, drawings ... In enormous, steeply tiered auditoriums famous professors followed one another with bewildering rapidity. Each subject, each new idea, was presented clearly and logically but at such speed that a momentary lapse of concentration left one floundering and lost. After being spoon-fed in school and regimented in the army this free, almost 'happy-go-lucky' system appeared beguiling but, in reality, was hard and demanding. Still we were there and had to manage.

All the girls drifted together, but soon split into two small groups. The one with the two Irkas, elegant Black Ada and flaxen-haired Hala stuck to me and my friends from Batory's school. We sat together at the lectures and the girls concentrated and worked as hard as, or harder than, we did. Inevitably the work brought us closer as we helped one another to grasp the elusive dogmas.

In the evenings I used to take Irka home and, if the weather was not too bad, we walked a long way round through the beauty and mystery of the Lazienki Park. There we sat on benches half-hidden in the foliage and fed red squirrels who came to play around our feet and who jumped on our knees in search of a nut or a piece of chocolate. By that time we were both well known in the University: Irka for her cold, regal poise and beauty, and I as her one and only boy-friend. She was always called

Princess and to me she became my Golden Princess. All the world accepted us as a duo, twins almost, all the world except herself. She liked me well enough but rejected the idea, or even the vaguest inkling, of love. This worried me only because of the waste of time from which we could have extracted so much more happiness. But walking hand in hand was not too bad a beginning and, in the end, she could escape our common destiny no more than I could. I did not push, insist or importune, and left her as free as she wished to be, especially as I gradually discovered that her reserve and almost disdainful manner were only an armour against the unknown and feared world. Beneath this mask she was even more shy and romantic than I was.

Only a month or so later, direct as ever, she announced:

'Look, I like you, but I am falling in love with Kazik!'

It was as if a fluffy, young kitten suddenly fell in love with a tortoise. I liked Kazik and knew him well, so well that I just laughed and told her to go ahead and not to worry about me. Later Kazik came to see me and, rather embarrassed, asked whether Irka was still my girl.

'Well, she can do what she likes, and I certainly won't try to stop her or you.'

'I like her, but I haven't looked even - I thought that you and she ...'

'Kazik, she *is* my girl but she doesn't know it yet, so that you both can do anything you want, it will only make her come back to me more quickly.'

'I mean ... I would like ... if you ...'

'I don't mind. Go walking, talking, courting, and I won't interfere whatsoever. I'll wait till she knows and comes to me of her own free will.'

If there were anything wrong with Kazik I would not have let it go so far, but he was a good man and a good friend. I thought that with his background of a small farm, his keen but entirely practical mind, little imagination and no sense of humour, he would not get far with Irka. At a guess I gave this new friendship a month but I was wrong. In a fortnight they both came to see me, Kazik rather sheepishly, she with her devastating honesty and courage. We shook hands and I walked with her to the Lazienki Park.

In spite of the autumnal mists and cold weather we explored on the bike the country around Warsaw. Once I picked her up at home in the early morning of a dull Sunday and, in search of sun, we rode south.

Through empty streets, along muddy deserted roads, we splashed and skidded almost aimlessly till we saw the Czersk signpost. We passed the sleepy village when the clouds parted and there, in front of us, stood the proud walls of the ruined castle. In the sudden spotlight of the unexpected sun the ageless brick towers shone like red torches. We walked along the ramparts and climbed to the top of the keep. Below the castle hill spread the plain of Central Poland and the grey waters of the Vistula rolled amongst the golden sand dunes. It was the time and the place, and she came into my arms slowly, hesitantly, but with the full lips slightly parted for our first kiss.

Irka was bewildered by crystallography whilst I was sinking in the morass of differential equations. Nevertheless we still found time for a long walk or for an escape into poetry. She loved Tuwim, one of the few Polish poets whom I read with real pleasure. But whilst I enjoyed Tuwim's frivolous romantic nonsense and took in my stride his many serious and tragic thoughts, she skated lightly over the surface of his potent love dreams and dwelt in the sadness of spent passions. This tendency to expect the worst, to believe in a malicious fate, was an attitude which I deplored and hoped to change as otherwise she would exist in misery instead of enjoying the wonders of life.

As a frequent visitor I knew her mother, a daunting though small lady, separated from her husband who ran an electrical workshop. Irka had a sixteen-year-old sister Maryna who, having absolutely no use for men, remained polite but distant. The mother was a disciplinarian, outspoken and tactless with the girls. Irka told me straight that she wanted me to 'make a good impression' at home and luckily my quiet, shy manner proved entirely acceptable. Then came the day when I really scored a hit. Her mother, active in many feminine organisations, lectured from time to time and on one occasion had overlooked an engagement some ten miles out of town. This came to light some twenty minutes before the event and I promptly offered the services of myself and my combination which was outside the door. As the local train had just gone she was glad to accept, stipulating that we must be there 'as quickly as possible'. Like most young men, I tended to drive fast and on this occasion surpassed myself, delivering her with a minute to spare. She got out rather pale and shaken but really grateful. The next day Irka told me of her mother's comment on the drive: 'You must thank this half-devil of yours from me. I won't ever go with him again ... but he can drive and I asked for it.'

As the spring days grew longer I exploited my advantage to the full. Irka loved the Holy Cross Mountains and wanted to take me there, but it remained a theoretical wish as the trip would take more than a day, and she believed that her mother would never allow her to go with me for a longer period. So, without mentioning that matter to Irka, who was anything but a diplomat, I tackled the mother alone, mentioning vaguely the beauty of the mountains and their long distance from Warsaw. She was a botanist and as one thing led to another soon suggested that Irka and I could go there provided we stayed with her relatives, as otherwise the girl's reputation would suffer. Irka could not believe it when I told her. She remarked that if I could get round her mother I must be more than a 'half-devil of hers'. Soon, even Maryna accepted me and we became good friends.

The passage of time was bringing Irka closer and closer to me. We enjoyed the cinema, delighted in the forgotten forests and streams, loved books ... though our tastes differed radically. Nevertheless we both became obsessed with the current best seller *The Lover of the Great Bear* and, for her birthday, I made a silver brooch with the seven magic stars. It was admired by everybody and loved by Irka who never parted with it.

Whenever I approached Stalek or Mother about Irka they remained totally non-committal, remarking that it was my life and the choice was mine alone. They had seen Irka casually when she came to work with me at home, but with the approaching summer Stalek suggested that it might be the right time for a more formal meeting and, after Mother's 'official' invitation, she arrived with her own mother one Sunday afternoon. This was the only occasion that I remember seeing Irka rattled, if not obviously frightened. I was also apprehensive about this visit as we never entertained and the infrequent visitors were doctors completely immersed in research. To make it worse I had never heard my parents indulge in small talk or show any interest in sociology so dear to her mother. But I should have known better as, with the introductions over, I was the only one left in the cold. Both ladies were at once immersed in some intimate discussion whilst Stalek, always so sparing and cold with words, was talking animatedly to Irka who responded with a happy smile. I listened to both conversations but caught only meaningless, jumbled phrases, and soon Mother signalled me to bring the tea and sandwiches. The conversation became more general and rather jerky with the pouring of tea. Stalek, who liked neither sandwiches nor odd meals, was toying with his glass of lemon tea whilst Irka with the appetite and enthusiasm of youth tucked into the ornate open sandwiches. There was a momentary silence in which, clear as a bell, rang the voice of her mother:

'Irka! You are guzzling these sandwiches! They will think I never feed you at home!' - and everybody was suddenly talking together except Irka who, red as a beetroot, left the half-bitten piece of bread on her plate. Luckily the meal was practically over and I got up to clear the tea things and masses of left-over sandwiches. But Stalek anticipated me saying:

'You *stay* and entertain the ladies. Irka will help me to clear up.'

I nearly dropped a cup as Stalek never entered the kitchen unless somebody was ill or a similar calamity required his help. Still, there was such a stress on the word 'stay' that I sat down whilst he disappeared with Irka into the nether regions. A good quarter of an hour later Mother suggested that I should find out what had happened to them. I discovered them in the kitchen where they sat flanking a pile of empty plates. I just overheard Stalek's last sentence: 'That's better, I hate these posh parties when you can't really eat!' And I thought that nobody but he would have gone to this trouble to make her feel really at home simply because she was my girl.

CHAPTER 7

A GLIMPSE OF ENGLAND

Whilst Irka and I lived our dreams, planned the next meeting and worried about maths and geometry, our whole world was balanced precariously on the edge of a precipice. But the warning tremors were hardly felt and people around us went quietly about their own affairs, confident of themselves, sure of Poland which they had rebuilt from the ashes and ruins left by the First World War.

In this summer of '39 Bob and I seized the opportunity of a vacation apprenticeship at Metro-Vick though I grudged the time which I had planned to spend with Princess.

A long train journey and a Channel ferry brought us to England. I was not sure whether it really was so different from other countries or if it was just our own anticipation and excitement that gave us such an impression. After the noisy, arrogant Germans, after the excitable, gesticulating Frenchmen, the people of Dover seemed quiet, slow ... phlegmatic like the English of all the popular jokes. Even the train with its luxurious but quaintly Victorian wood-built coaches belonged more to Sherlock Holmes than to twentieth-century Europe. London was overpowering with its sheer size and bustling masses of people. After the whirling kaleidoscope of views and faces it was a relief to close the door of our hotel room and relax in the confines of four walls. But we had no time to rest as our plans squeezed the whole English history and heritage into a few days of sight-seeing, to which the language was another obstacle. My school English allowed only a laborious construction of rather primitive sentences which surprisingly were quite often understood. The trouble came with the quickly gobbled answers which certainly did not sound like the same language. The endings of most words disappeared completely, the middles were garbled with the lost 'H's and barely sounded 'R's (unless we met a Scot). So I was glad to leave the communications in the capable hands of Bob who had visited England before this trip. Then, as planned, we went to buy a car for which transaction I was responsible. We looked for the smallest contraption on four wheels but soon found out that, because of some quirk of English taxation, the big foreign cars were by far the cheapest. So we chose a Big-Six Citroen and, after a long haggle, bought her for twenty pounds to my entire satisfaction and the great relief of the whole staff of the garage.

Driving home was not so easy. The density of rush hour traffic was intimidating, the left hand rule of the road daunting and the 'wrong' position of the steering wheel made driving a real nightmare. On the first busy crossing I stalled the engine repeatedly, creating a solid traffic jam and becoming completely flustered in the process. The enormous shadow of an English policeman loomed over me, speaking slowly but still utterly incomprehensibly whilst I just gave up and sat there looking at him. Ponderously he leaned into the car and stretching his arm across me tapped the lever of the hand-brake:

"If you release the 'and brake, Sir, you might move from 'ere.'

I tried to thank him but he just waved me on:

'Please go, just move from 'ere, Sir!'

Visiting Windsor, Oxford and other famous places we began to discover England. Our own country of lakes, mountains and fertile plains was beautiful but here everything was so different. There was the parkland landscape of which we had read but neither fully comprehended nor believed. There were cities with sprawling suburbs where millions of people lived in their miniature dolls' houses. The houses, and their postage stamp gardens, stretched for miles, joining the towns into an enormous urban maze. After our compact cities connected by miles of straight roads, the labyrinth of English streets and lanes was incredible. But we were even more astounded by the weekends and the national pilgrimage to the seaside. The little houses spewed their families, and the nose-to-tail string of Baby Austins and Rover Eights loaded to the gunwales with prams, kids and beach-chairs, rolled along the narrow roads, waited patiently at innumerable traffic lights and crept round the strange obstacles called 'roundabouts'.

To us everything was strange and either awe-inspiring in its scale like the London Underground, or quaint and confusing like the monetary system. It was spelt L - S - D, pronounced pounds, shillings and pence and contained farthings, florins, half-crowns (though no crowns) and guineas (a concept but no coin). Still, it was a marvellous country with God-awful weather and with calm, soft-spoken people who minded their own business but when approached were invariably kind and helpful.

In the industrial Midlands, we spent a day at the BSA factory and another one at Herbert's Machine Tools, before reaching Manchester's Trafford Park and Metro-Vick. We were welcomed by the Training Officer who supplied us with a local map and a list of suitable lodgings. In no time we settled down with the Sinclairs – a tall, thin couple and their pretty daughter Joyce – all of whom were to become our staunch friends. The next day we were taken on a detailed tour of the whole factory and finished in the small-turbine assembly shop where we both were to work. The shop was clean, the people friendly and eager to teach us all they knew. But the most amazing was the attitude of the men to their own work: they were highly trained craftsmen proud of their skills and the resulting product. Their pride was fully justified by the perfect fitting of all the components, slow hand-scraping of bronze flanges and gradual tightening of all bolts so that, on the test bed, not a single wisp of steam escaped from the finished machine. They were unhurried but not slow, and as I worked I remembered Papa and his Purdy's guns ... Stalek and the BSA bikes ... The English seemed to lack our enthusiasm, drive and panache just as they lacked cavalry, but the unrelenting, purposeful effort might count for more in the long run ... and they had built the Empire.

Our own work was simple enough and, in addition to manual skills, taught us to pay attention to details, to take time over a given task and complete it to perfection. Sometimes, however, our own outlandish ideas were accepted and even applauded. One morning our group finished the assembly of two turbo-generators and the work came to a halt. We enquired about this unexpected stoppage and were told that nothing could be done before more rotors were delivered from balancing which was carried out at the far end of the long shed. Unfortunately, the travelling crane had broken down and we just had to wait, though it affected adversely the production bonus of the men. As the rotors weighed not much over a hundredweight we thought that they could be easily fetched without the use of the ten-ton overhead monster but apparently that was unthinkable.

'Don't be silly, you can't lift and carry a rotor!'

Bob and I looked at each other, got up and sauntered to the balancing bay where, after a word with the operator, each of us picked a finished rotor, heaved it on to his shoulder and marched back. The whole shop had gone rather quiet till it suddenly erupted in a loud round of handclapping and shouts of 'Hurrah for the Poles!'

At weekends we went on sight-seeing trips or visited our friends. In London we had already met our fellow scout Alec who was a continental correspondent of *The Times*. But in the north we looked up Malcolm, Bob's old friend from the Hungarian Jamboree. We also took Mrs Sinclair and Joyce to Blackpool and revelled in the fun of the 'Golden Mile'.

The Metro-Vick works closed for a week of the annual summer holidays and we set out on a tour of the east coast and Scotland. We crossed the Pennines and rolled to a stop at the home of John's and Jane's parents at Ilkley. The brother and sister, just a year or two older than ourselves, had toured Europe a year previously and had spent a few days in Warsaw where we took them around. The long tarmac drive winding through the magnificent garden staggered us, but the warmth of the welcome by Mr and Mrs Ford put us at ease. After an epicurean lunch, Jane took us for a walk on Ilkley Moor so that we could do justice to a sumptuous tea. Soon it was time to say goodbye and depart for Scarborough. Our engine coughed and spluttered as I let the car roll down the drive. It descended through the gardens and some hundred yards down the road where, a couple of hours later, Jane found us amongst the parts of a dismantled engine neatly laid out along the grass verge. The family not only offered us hospitality but insisted on us staying with them whilst the car was being repaired. Jane took us around the Yorkshire Dales. We saw Bolton Abbey and Barden Towers, the Strid and Kilnsey Crag. We visited some scout camps and cub colonies as Jane was a Cub Mistress. Somewhere I was given a narrow paddle and a charming young lady instructed me in swiping away a small ball aimed at three sticks standing behind me but, though I managed quite well, the principle of this pastime eluded me completely. After a couple of days we continued our interrupted journey.

I sent Irka a postcard from Gretna Green and thought that she was romantic enough to elope there with me if it were nearer home. We visited Edinburgh and Stirling, slept rough on the Scottish moors, looked for the Loch Ness monster and enjoyed every second of the holiday in this magical country. All too soon we had to turn back to Manchester where the time passed just as quickly, bringing the end of summer. In the second half of August I set out for home and Princess. Bob, extracting the absolute maximum from our apprenticeship, decided to stay on and flew home via Sweden on 2 September 1939.

PART 2

WARRIOR AND SLAVE

CHAPTER 8

THE INCREDIBLE DEFEAT

The hot, dry summer baked the streets of Warsaw till the little dust devils danced on the softened tarmac. But through the open balcony door a gentle draught wafted into the flat a scent of roses from the park and the cooler breeze from the banks of the Vistula. At the door the postman handed me his receipt book and the long, buff envelope addressed with my military title: 'PLATOON SERGEANT, ENSIGN (RESERVE)'. Folded inside was an official form. At the top, fat black letters screamed MOBILISATION and, further down, two stamps indicated when and where to report: 29 August 1939 and Auxiliary Signals Centre, Baranowicze. So I had another two days at home but instead of joining my own 26th Infantry Division I was ordered to some odd outfit on the north-east border of Poland. Still, it wasn't too bad: in spite of the general unease in Europe, we knew that there was not going to be any war and, with luck, I would be back in a month to begin my second year in the University. And, putting first things first, Princess was coming back to Warsaw from her holidays.

The call up papers were delivered in the morning and the afternoon passed in a visit to the hospital where I was due for a dressing. Only two days previously my Mother had taken me to her former pupil, now a young surgeon, who had operated on my big toe for a deep abscess. The surgeon removed the drain but dismissed the idea of a call-up. However I was adamant about joining up and received unexpected backing from Mother: '... he heals like a puppy and should be all right in a couple of days.' So the next day I brushed up my uniform though I still could not squeeze my aching foot into the long cavalry boot. Irka returned on my last day and we talked on the phone. I discarded the heavily padded dressing and found that a short bandage with a tuft of cotton wool allowed me to put on the boots and to walk with only a slight limp. A small suitcase and heavy pistol completed my preparations. Mother, with tears in her eyes, kissed me goodbye. But it was the firm clasp of Father's handshake which made me think that the whole affair might be serious. And, of course, Irka came with me to the station. It was only a quarter of an hour from Warsaw Central to the East Junction and she got in with me for the last few minutes together. She was not in her usual form. No longer casual and off-hand, she appeared anxious, almost frightened. We sat side by side in the empty compartment not speaking, not seeing, just holding hands. The click of the wheels was like the tick of a clock, like time itself. She turned, looking straight at me with tears in her large, grey eyes: 'Will you come back to me?' And I knew that come hell or high water I would return to her.

A hollow echo followed my footsteps along the endless corridors of the empty barracks in Baranowicze. The division had long since departed leaving only a skeleton staff of a few aged NCOs who had never heard of a Signals Centre. But, at last, I found the communications room, where a duty sergeant handed me a teletype message addressed to the Senior Signals Officer. I was very much a junior, but as the only signals officer there, though beset by doubts, I tore open the envelope:

'YOU WILL FORM THE SECOND AUXILIARY SIGNALS CENTRE. REMAIN BARANOWICZE UNTIL 31 AUGUST. ENTRAIN ALL SIGNALS PERSONNEL AND EQUIPMENT. PROCEED TO BRZESC AND REPORT TO THE FORTRESS C.O.' It was signed by somebody for the GHQ Chief of Staff. I stood there reading and re-reading the incomprehensible order until my peripheral vision registered the gawping faces of the communications crew. The military training reasserted itself and I barked an order at one of the men to get me the quartermaster. With the same impetus and bluff I prevailed upon the latter to open the padlocks on the stores. Imagining already my defence at a Court Martial I broke the seals and found mountains of signals equipment ... either bust or obsolete. But I was cheered by the information that 'masses' of reserve signalmen were reporting for duty. There were two hectic days of turmoil, of foraging for bread and coffee, of imposing some military order on the civilian rabble. At last two hundred elderly men were fed and, as order is order, the piles of useless signals gear were crated and loaded. On 31 August we marched to the station. Except myself and a few senior NCOs the whole crowd was still in 'civvies' and their uneven ranks shuffled with bundles and parcels bumping against their legs. Slowly we boarded the train which puffed, groaned and began to move. Along the platform raced the sergeant from the communications room and I just managed to pluck from his outstretched hand an envelope addressed to me in Irka's bold script. Inside was a single sheet and above her signature the words of the old song:

'Who stole my heart away? Who makes me dream all day? ... No one but you.'

So at last she saw the light – suddenly the cares and troubles of my strange command dropped away – nothing mattered but Princess and her acknowledgement of our love.

The Brzesc garrison looked like a disturbed ants' nest and after parking my men on the barrack square I sought the CO. Pleading, threatening and cajoling I finally reached his Aide, but didn't get further than a smart salute – he simply exploded: 'What the hell do you want? Report to the office! Out!'

Clicking my heels again I thrust at him the telegram as there are few people who can resist taking something pushed into their hands. While he read I noticed his unshaved beard and black shadows under his eyes – he must have been days on his feet.

'Well, where is your Commanding Officer?'

'I am, Sir.'

After a lot of explanation I saw the Fortress CO and received new orders to go by train to Lublin where the Centre would be formed and properly equipped. That night we dozed in the square, whilst around us milled crowds of called-up men, half-formed units marched hither and thither and messengers on foot and bikes cut through the bedlam.

In the first light of dawn I organised black coffee and bread for all of us. There was neither time nor facility for washing, but I managed to change the bandage on my toe. Before six I formed up the men, finding about twenty more than I had brought in. Probably my brass lungs attracted to us the lost or unattached Signals men. I led them along the straight, tree-lined avenue back to the station. With the crowded barracks behind, blue skies above, and brilliant sunshine in front, we cheered up. My reservists, in spite of their uncomfortable night, lost their hang-dog expressions and marched like a military detachment.

Then, from behind, from the direction of the barracks came a sudden thunder. Not the protracted, grumbling peal of a summer storm. Just one, two and a whole series of solid crumps, each like the slamming of an enormous door. And there, in the dense greenery of the trees, shot up white flashes crowned immediately by black geysers reaching into the sky. Time stopped. We stopped. Only the flashes and the thundering explosions were coming nearer. Somewhere in the distance the sirens took up a mournful wail and we woke up from our trance to the new, changed world. We heard shouts, cries and screams from the stricken barracks, saw black smoke and red flames defying the serene sky and the indifferent sun. It was early morning, 1 September 1939.

The journey to Lublin lasted almost two days instead of a mere few hours. There were crowded stations with milling masses of people, jolting trains with civilians and soldiers on the buffers, on the running-boards, on the roofs. There were endless stops, detours, changes of engines and trains. But, at last, dirty, thirsty and hungry, we reached Lublin. Of the original complement I had lost nearly a half, but gathered twice as many other reservists unable to reach their proper destination.

In the barracks I found senior officers and more chaos. The major in charge of the Centre had disappeared and his second in command was obsessed with one idea only: find the boss - we almost beat the bushes for him. The men sprawled higgledy-piggledy everywhere, most of them dozing uneasily in the scanty shade of dusty trees. But common sense and two young lieutenants prevailed. We organised three companies, quartered them and began kitting out. But there was neither any signals equipment nor a single round of ammunition for the standard issue of Mauser rifles.

In the Quartermaster's stores, I sleepily watched the 'clerks' slinging bits of uniform over the counter. The men of my own third company were being slowly and unsatisfactorily kitted out. Unsatisfactorily, because of totally inadequate stocks. In this situation I was not surprised when a quarrel flared up in some dark corner of the hall. I pushed through and saw a half-dressed soldier kneeling on and, with both fists, laying into a feebly struggling body. As my roared order produced no results, I grabbed the soldier by his hair and yanked him off the victim, whom I recognised as one of the storemen. Though somewhat messed up he jumped to his feet, picking from the floor an entrenching tool.

'Stop!'
In the sudden silence my yell froze them all and I continued quietly: 'There is a war on. War, you understand? Just stop it or I'll have you both shot!' – and whether I could or not, I meant it.

'Now I want to know what it's all about. You first!' – pointing at the storeman – 'Drop this bloody shovel and stand to attention.' He had been viciously attacked without the slightest provocation ... On the other hand, my soldier, a lance-corporal, claimed that he was given a dixie with a big hole and while complaining was hit with the shovel. The dixie was produced in evidence and the crowd supported him with murmurs of 'Yes, Sir ... That's right ... Go on Blondie ...' The other storemen kept their mouths shut and seemed frightened of their own man who now wanted a court-martial.

'There won't be a court-martial. There won't be even a report. You will forget it and behave yourselves or I will make something of it – and you will be bloody sorry. If you don't like it – report tonight to your own CO.'

Kitting up continued with whatever remnants were left in the stores. I kept yawning, but also had my eye on Blondie. Tall, very thin, he had vivid, almost lemon-coloured, hair and an unusually pale complexion. With a fixed sneer on his face he moved quietly, slowly, cat-like.

In the evening one of the newly-arrived officers was appointed to take over the Third Company while I became a general dogsbody with the resounding title of the Centre's Aide-de-Camp. Later there was a knock at my door and, dressed in the most elegant uniform, which certainly was not a standard issue, in came Blondie bearing gifts – like the Greeks? There were no water bottles in the stores, but he produced a brand new one with a wide neck, baize cover and fittings. Thanking him, I refused, and mentioned casually that I was no longer his company commander.

'Oh! We will see about this!' and he sounded like a hissing snake. I suspected that this lance-corporal could create a hell of a lot of problems and trouble, but somehow I liked him.

'We will NOT see about this and there will NOT be any trouble ,Blondie!' He stared straight into my eyes, it seemed for hours, and suddenly he smiled. His whole face was transformed, the vicious sneer permanently frozen on his lips vanished and the whole face lit up like that of a happy child.

'Yes, Sir, I mean No, Sir! But, Sir, do take it – it's the best French brandy, Sir.' I was still green enough not to accept the gift, but we parted friends. Though we were to meet several times, I never knew his name, where he came from, or even what happened to him in the end.

Next morning I sneaked to town and, paying double, got my rather thin boots re-soled. I also wanted some ammunition for my automatic, but though I tried everywhere, I could not get a single 9mm. round, and was left with the one clip which I had brought from Warsaw. The same night Blondie brought me a full box of shells but that was much later.

Returning from town I looked for the Army hospital to scrounge some bandages for my toe. In the corner of the military complex, this four-storey building fronted a vast square of parched grass criss-crossed by dusty tracks of countless footpaths. I was in the middle of this urban desert when the lazy stillness of the hot September day was shattered by the wail of the sirens. Then, against the persistent moaning, came the menacing beat of innumerable aircraft engines and soon, a clear whistling sound. This became louder and higher, rising to a terrifying scream. I was flat on my face pressing as hard as I could into the sun-baked earth and the earth kicked me in the stomach, and thundered, and rained all about me. Now I could not hear a sound but saw everything like a silent slow-motion film. I could have counted the bricks erupting high, hesitating and falling slowly to thump before me, behind me, beside me. A large gap opened up in the building and separated the left wing from the main block. A half-folded tin sheet, like an enormous vulture, flapped to land in front of me: on its torn surface the broken arm of a red cross. Then the front wall leaned out, the whole wall with its open windows. It leaned further, accelerated and hit the ground, crumbling into small pieces. There, inside the open doll's house, were all the floors still full of beds, equipment and people. The left wall folded and the exposed corners of all floors began to sag slowly. The white dust of crumbling ceilings, some joists bending, falling out and the whole sandwich collapsed spilling out beds, bedding and doll-like figures in striped pyjamas, in white coats. They turned and tumbled to disappear in the clouds of dust and smoke rising from the rubble.

We marched in long columns leaving behind the smouldering ruins. Farther away, above the sun-splashed roofs of the town, church spires pointed at the sky. But, in the centre of this idyllic vignette dark pillars of smoke were still rising, spreading, polluting the vivid blue with an ever-increasing brown stain.

Later, resting and waiting, we were bombed and strafed by the dive-bombers. With a banshee scream down they came, aimed at every one of us. The screams ended in the thunder of explosions, and fountains of fertile black earth. Little spurts of dust stitched straight lines between us, across us. We huddled in the ravines of dried-up streams, in the thick clumps of bushes, under the spreading trees. They came again and again in never-ending waves. And with them came fear, the panic fear of the ancients, the blinding mindless fear of trapped wild animals. Somebody ran away and fell silent forever. Somebody emptied a puny little automatic shouting abuse at the planes, but the noise of the shots was lost in the shattering din of planes and bombs. More men ran away and were killed or wounded. I would run too if there were no responsibility for the men:

'Keep down! Down! Don't move!' They quiver and shake on the ground but, they stay, and I stay, and after a century there are no more planes.

At night we marched north-east, plodding slowly to nowhere along the minor roads and winding tracks. Minutes, hours, whole days were the same. Cloudless skies, hot sun, scattered farms, an odd village. Peasants working in the fields, peasants standing in the fields and waiting, as bewildered as we were. We crossed bigger roads, all choked with traffic. Civilians fleeing on foot, in peasant carts, in cars. Military convoys, industrial convoys, overheated lorries, cars out of petrol and abandoned, or dragged by a failing horse, pushed by children, by women. Summer dresses, fur coats, broken high heels and tattered silk stockings, or just dirty, bloody bare feet. People with sweaty, dusty faces, preoccupied, silent people trudging, pushing, panting. Crowds of people, but each one separate and alone with his or her own fear in staring, unseeing eyes.

Every day, every mile there was more wreckage. Not just broken-down cars, but whole transport columns abandoned, pitted with machine-gun bullets, blackened by fire. Even side-roads bore more and more scars. Burnt buildings, unburied corpses, scattered luggage. There, by the little brook, stood an enormous white Mercedes, and on a tartan rug were spread open suitcases with leather and silver fittings, a pile of transparent undies on top of a gentleman's dress-suit, and not a trace of the owners.

Once we passed a field full of horses, dead horses. They were long dead, because those not ripped to pieces were swollen horribly, like brown balloons blown up to bursting point, thin legs sticking straight up. And the stench, the horrible cloying stench pursuing us for miles. We crossed the borders of the Lublin ordnance maps and tried to navigate by a road atlas taken from a wrecked car, but more often than not we slogged through the large white areas between the marked main roads. The nights were cold and we quickly learned to find accommodation in barns and other buildings. I almost managed a night in a magnificent four-poster in a deserted manor house. It was the first time for days that I pulled off my cavalry boots and felt the soft carpet with my toes sticking out of the torn socks. The filthy bandage was in shreds, but the incision appeared healed. A commotion broke out when I was vaguely considering the choice between a much-needed wash and the temptation of the luxurious bed by my side. I was spared this decision by the sergeant's report that one of our outer guards had heard the Germans! It was not only ridiculous, here, so far east of Warsaw, it was impossible. Weary, cross and disgusted, I almost told him to get stuffed. But already the CO was telling me to take out a patrol, whispering to go easy, to avoid risks. To be on the safe side I borrowed a rifle for myself. The glint of fixed bayonets reassured us more than the weight of the empty guns for which we still had no ammunition. A mile from our manor house was a solid clump of trees with vague shapes of buildings. We saw flashes of light and heard distant voices. I left the men lying low in the roadside ditches and, with three volunteers, circled through a cornfield. We stopped against a half-open gate in a stone wall. The farm lay in darkness, the edges of the yard velvety black. But in the centre, in the dim moonlight, moved silhouettes with the square heads of men in German helmets. I heard the guttural sounds of German and a whisper in my ear ... 'We take them now!'

Crouching shadows around me, white gleams of bayonets. We jumped, ran into the frozen group, collided. Somebody yelled, somebody flailed with a rifle held by the barrel, and there was only a heap of bodies at our feet. Shouts on the road, more running feet, a shot.

'After them!' and a roared hurrah. We chased the fleeing men. A burst of automatic fire cut short by a piercing scream, and the growl of starting engines. Lorries, bikes and running Germans disappeared into the night. My volunteers and the rest of the section gathered on the road – all but one. And from the yard I heard Blondie's triumphant shout: 'Sir, we got ourselves some ammunition,' and we carried back cartridge pouches stripped from the dead.

My report to the CO was interrupted by a lance-corporal: 'Sir, it's the ensign who told us what to do and led us all the way!' I talked to the boys later and they all swore that they heard only me, not Blondie ... and I will never know for sure.

After the maze of meandering sandy tracks we marched along a real road which, with its blinding white limestone surface, ran straight across the endless fields of freshly cut golden wheat. Along this road our straggling column approached a sizeable town. But, in front of the town a dark line lay across the road. Coming closer we saw the haphazard pile of a barricade, a few men in front and a crowd behind. The men in front dispersed and a flickering flame appeared in the centre: the long burst of a machine-gun sounded flat in the noon-day heat. Bullets whipped up a cloud of white dust halfway between them and us. Our front rank stumbled and hesitated. When they moved on, the machine-gun chattered again, bullets crackling above our heads. The CO halted the column and we stood still – two opposing crowds. For we also were a crowd with our scruffy uniforms and the men's shattered morale. Using borrowed binoculars I saw more details: a narrow passage through the pile of overturned carts and upended furniture, a heavy Maxim in the middle and civilians with red armbands. After two more futile attempts at an advance the situation developed into a stalemate. The soldiers sprawled comfortably on the grass verges, the group of officers stood motionless, the CO kept looking through his binoculars, shifting his weight from one leg to the other. We might have stayed there forever in this silent tableau. But suddenly from the rear of our long column came the sound of the heavy tread of advancing infantry. We all turned and stared. In the centre of the road moved a dusty single file of men, Polish round helmets on their heads, cavalry Mausers slung across their backs. They marched with long, measured steps, looking straight ahead, oblivious of us, of all the world. There was about a score of them led by a young giant with the single star of a second-lieutenant. His equipment was almost the same as theirs: rolled blankets and carbine slings crossed their chests, bulging shoulder-bags alongside sheathed bayonets, their belts sagging under the load of grenades hooked into them. His belt carried also the weight of a black Vis, the best pistol of the war. Framed by the deep helmet, etched with tiny rivulets of sweat, his face resembled more the sculpture of a warrior than that of a living man. His arms swung in time with each stride and, most incongruously, at his wrist hung a rawhide whip with a loaded grip and a long, wicked tongue. When they reached the van of our halted column the CO called to him:

'Lieutenant, you can't go further – Reds!'

'Fuck the Reds' – and, seconds later, after a long glance at our captain, he added, 'Sir.' They did not stop, they never missed a step. After passing through our column their single file swung to the grass verge and kept going. We gaped while they went on and on. They reached and passed the halfway point – a few random shots rang up from the barricade but they marched on. They marched with the long measured tread, inexorably, like Nemesis herself. They reached the barricade and the terrible whip rose and fell, rose and fell. The screaming crowd resolved into running people fleeing the barricade, leaving the guns, vanishing, as vanished in the distance the single file of marching soldiers. Such was our first clash with the 'fifth column': the Ukrainian rabble of malcontents and criminals whipped up by Soviet agents to pillage and murder.

We marched further, soon reaching the almost deserted army barracks in the town. Soldiers sauntered aimlessly in and out of the unguarded gates. Nobody was in command, nobody knew anything, but everyone looked over his shoulder for some unknown danger. It seemed that we might stay there indefinitely, and so two of us decided to explore the town. We walked towards the centre along wide streets devoid of traffic, of pedestrians. Shops were shuttered, windows closed. Sometimes a vague shadow moved inside, sometimes running footsteps sounded in the distance. A ginger cat melted into a hedge. The uneasy silence was broken by shouts and two girls raced out of a side street. The first, with a bulging shopping basket and wide open panting mouth kept running. The other, with flaming red hair and heaving breasts, was completely spent. Staggering, she cowered behind us and, between two sobbing breaths screeched:

'Red Ukrainians!'

We moved the few steps to the corner. There, running towards us, was a group of shabby men with red arm-bands. Some had army rifles, the others an assortment of knives and cudgels. Confronted by the two of us they slowed, hesitated and stopped. But spotting the girl they spread across the street and advanced again. Then the uncanny silence was shattered by a rifle shot from behind and the body of the girl slammed into us. Stumbling from the blow which spun me round, I stared at the row of grey tenement houses, saw only one open window and a rifle barrel rising and foreshortening slowly. I don't remember reaching, opening the holster, or pulling the slide – just the heavy automatic bucking in my hand. The top pane shattered first, but before the shards of glass reached the pavement, the whole window disintegrated. The body behind jerked and disappeared. The rifle dipped, slid out of the window and clattered to the street below. I turned back to face the Reds, but their running figures seemed already miles away, fleeing for their lives, whilst my friend kept firing down the street with his Browning. The girl sat on the pavement, the rucksack, which she had carried, was torn and oozing a sticky red mass of strawberry jam. She was not even scratched!

After taking her home two streets away, we gave up our sight-seeing and headed back to the barracks which we could hardly recognise. At the wide open gates two sentries smartly came to attention. In front of the guard-house an NCO bawled orders at a platoon strung in perfect lines. The open square was a hive of activity, even the uniforms looked smarter, boots shone, equipment sparkled.

On the steps of the main block, dwarfed by the enormous double doors, was poised a little figure of a colonel in the stance of a sergeant-major from a comic-strip. In spite of all the bustle he spotted us immediately and roared in a voice disproportionate to his size and grizzled hair:

'You two! Report!'

The whole atmosphere of the place must have been contagious, as both of us straightened up and almost ran to click our heels the prescribed three yards before him. He listened intently and not one of his silver hairs fluttered in the breeze – it wouldn't have dared.

'Right, take a platoon from your signals unit, lieutenant, and patrol the town. You, ensign, march one section to the railway station and try their telegraph – I want information!'

My friend saluted swiftly, turned and marched off. I hesitated and saw

the colonel's eyebrows come together, his mouth opening for another roar, but I stood my ground:
'Colonel, Sir! We have no ammunition.' His face relaxed.
'Get from the arsenal what you need. Paper and pencil?'
The only piece of paper I had was the letter from Princess and I produced it reluctantly, blank side up. He turned it over, scrutinised it for a few long seconds, and not bothering to turn it back scribbled at the bottom the authorisation for the arsenal with an illegible zigzag of a signature.

I found Blondie trying to restore his boots to the Army standard. This did not interfere with the stream of his vile invective directed at the fire-eating midget of a colonel from nowhere. Blondie's fluency and vocabulary were so startling that I hated to interfere. However, he was delighted to have an alternative occupation and only remarked that no one could blame him for dying in dirty boots when attacking the Ukrainian rabble.

Most of the men seemed eager to go with him, but he was rather choosy in gathering his little group. Yet, even in our crowd, they seemed to be the scrapings of the barrel – sloppy, scrawny, shifty fellows. Blondie, noticing my lack of enthusiasm, brought his thumb and forefinger together in a gesture of approval, winked, and whispered something about them 'doing just fine'. So we went to the arsenal with his men, as I did not want to undermine his authority by taking another squad.

The heavy, wide door stood open and behind the counter skulked two old armourers. One with a sergeant's chevrons held an old St. Etienne revolver from the 1914/1918 war.

'Get out! Nobody's getting aught! Thieves! Bandits!' I argued, but even the colonel's scribbled order didn't help. Obviously, neither his authority nor his personality had yet penetrated to the arsenal.

I was eased aside so gently that I only realised it when the armourer's voice suddenly faded out and I saw at his throat the point of a flick-knife held by one of Blondie's choice soldiers. There were no more automatic rifles, but we left with a light machine-gun, a few belts of ammunition and more than enough grenades.

In the fading twilight we reached the station which suddenly, at point-blank range, erupted with fire from a hundred windows. Houses and high walls hemmed us in, and we all spilled into a goods-yard through the gap of the open gates. Machine-gun fire followed us, and we tripped and tumbled over the rails and wires of the signals. Bullets clanged on the rails, crunched the ballast and drummed on oak sleepers. Squeezed against the rails and hugging the ground we stayed flattened like rugs scattered on a floor. The cannonade stopped and from the station came a few people, a group and then a crowd. They seemed to flow towards us, disappearing in the deeper shadows, emerging against a lighter background. Some carried acetylene lamps, which, with their brilliant aureoles, only added to the darkness of the night. Two rifle shots exploded almost in my ear and two lanterns shattered whilst others were quickly doused. Some automatic rifles opened on us from the crowd. It was all so senseless, unbelievable, unreal. I was no longer paralysed, frightened to death, and Blondie's men were 'doing fine'. Ricochets whanged and screamed through the air. The menacing crowd advanced. I was in charge, with gravel up my nose and something boring holes in my stomach – the hand grenades.

'Keep down when I throw. Wait for it and scatter.' And Blondie's voice behind me: 'Run down the embankment to the meadows!' I pulled the pin, knelt and threw. But in the last moment I pulled to the side: I just could not kill the stupid bastards. The most satisfactory, deafening bang was followed by dead silence. We ran and slid down the steep slope of the embankment to finish in a heap against a barbed wire fence. Screams, curses and, in a few seconds, shots from above. Slowly, deliberately I freed my left hand, got a purchase on the slippery grass and tore my trousers off the fence. The Ukrainians kept shooting wildly, and I felt anger and blind rage. I didn't start it! I didn't slaughter them with my grenade! I was sweating with fury. Their dark silhouettes on a lighter sky were like targets on the range. Holding my pistol in both hands I aimed slowly, deliberately, and one by one they tumbled back till the hammer clicked on the empty chamber.

We scrambled through and over the fence, ran across squelchy meadows, stopped and fell down exhausted. We had lost two men, but nobody knew when, where and how. The rest were not even seriously scratched except one with two deep gashes right across his face. It was this one as well as Blondie who resisted most fiercely my decision to return to the barracks. By then I did believe that these men could take the station, but except for revenge, there was little sense in such a mad enterprise.

As we marched back I could not resist wondering about Blondie and his men. That they, or at least some of them, were criminals was obvious. But, they also were adventurers, patriots ... possibly heroes. Are there clear demarcations between these? And a ne'er-do-well, an ordinary reservist years past his training, would never hit a lantern at a hundred yards. Also, Blondie was a born leader, a well-liked and closely-followed leader who, surprisingly, took my orders without hesitation. And the colonel? ... certainly retired many years, seizing his last chance and turning it into a moment of glory. Still able to impose his will, still obeyed implicitly by a rabble like us. Does any group without a strong leader become a rabble, or is it only in war? Total war, not just the heroic charge of the Light Brigade. My scratched hand ached, my boots pinched and my eyes were closing as we entered the barracks.

Dawn was breaking whilst we stood in front of the colonel's desk from which the flickering candles cast long, slowly-fading shadows. Straight as a ramrod he came through the side-door and began a resumé of the situation. We were isolated by lack of communications. National news ceased, local transmissions were vague and contradictory. German armour had penetrated deep into our country. Our duty was to maintain law and order, guard property and lives. He followed with detailed individual orders. I was put in charge of No. 4 lorry in the motorised patrol which, under a full lieutenant, had to reach a small town thirty miles to the East.

The main square was abustle with soldiers running amongst a dozen lorries. Next to the driver of an almost new Sauer, with freshly painted number four, Blondie grinned from ear to ear. Days later I found out that the last flimsy of the typed orders 'stuck' to Blondie's hand and so my number was painted on the best lorry.

It was grand to be driven on a cool, dew-spattered morning instead of marching in the noon-day sun, and a freshly-baked loaf tasted wonderful after the sparse diet of the past week. Suddenly, without warning, machine-gun fire came from the crest of a steep ridge parallel to the road. Long bursts whipped spurts of turf, raised fountains of white dust and brought down showers of leaves and small branches, like a gigantic though invisible hedge clipper. A red and white rocket shot up from the leading lorry. Obeying the signal we stopped and dismounted then and there, on the open road in full view of the gunners. If they had found and held the range it would have been a massacre. Actually the streams of bullets ploughed the meadow and hosed the trees with only a few shots ricocheting off the road. The fearless lieutenant came fast leading his men, bravely and stupidly, in tight formation. Pointing at the ridge he roared orders to fix bayonets and charge. Somebody shouted and they all yelled and cheered and charged. Pounding boots, purple faces and bulging eyes fixed on the distant crest. Scrambling and slipping I was with them, but not of them. They ran and panted – a herd of maddened animals. I saw the slackening tempo and the long distance to the top. I heard their brave roar fading to breathless sobs, but, above all, I heard the long bursts in front and screams behind. And still we staggered upward, for no longer could it be called a run, and still less a charge. By then I was well forward and suddenly, on the crest, I saw a man rise. He hesitated, turned and ran. Almost immediately two more, three, a group, two groups vanished behind the ridge and the guns were silent.

Though my watch still ticked evenly, I could hardly believe that only half an hour had passed since the rocket had flared. Again we rolled forward, richer by two heavy Maxims, poorer by the silent dead and the moaning wounded.

We passed deserted villages, some puny barricades, isolated farms. The cab was getting too hot and I felt better outside, crouched over a light machine-gun resting its stubby feet on the roof of the cab. I took the gun because none of my crew was really happy with it. We also regrouped so that I led the convoy with the best armed vehicle, and we felt triumphantly invincible. Then the shots came from the side. The loader slumped on my shoulder with a neat hole in the centre of his helmet. The convoy screeched to a halt. I was still entangled with the loader whilst from the corner of my eye I saw the lieutenant sprint to a cottage opposite his lorry. My man was stone dead, shot straight through the head. There, on the road, the soldiers dragged out an old peasant, his woman shouting, pleading. The lieutenant came out of the cottage, a long rifle in his hands, his distorted snarling face like the muzzle of a mad dog. He didn't speak or shout – it was just a growl: 'With the same rifle ...' and he shot the old man through the head. Blood and white brains spattered everywhere. The woman was frozen still, silent as her man, as my man. Little tongues of fire flickered in the thatch of the cottage. The lieutenant pocketed his lighter and the yellow flames spread and grew into a roaring inferno.

Before us, in the shimmering heat, the dusty road stretched endlessly till we stopped at a broken bridge. Lazy dark water swirled in little eddies around the shattered timbers of both spans. Only the centre pier stood defiantly, its ice-cutter shedding the current evenly to both sides.

The heat, the hunger, the pointlessness of it all made the return journey long, depressing and at the end there was nothing. No barracks, but the empty shells of smouldering buildings. No colonel, but the demoralised remnants of the returning patrols. Fear spread, men were difficult to control. There were no clear objectives, no chain of command, no leaders. Chaos grew into anarchy as, leaving the town, we again marched to nowhere.

I remember only one bright episode when Blondie unearthed an abandoned Skoda tourer and I contributed petrol from a tanker bogged down in a soft meadow. By then our little band had grown closer together and formed the only hard core of the disorganised herd. It was an odd relationship. They still called me 'Sir', sprang to attention and carried out orders – maybe because there were so few to give. At night, almost invariably, one of them brought me a dixie full of some damned good and utterly unexpected food. It began with a pound of tinned lobster, an almost unknown luxury in Poland. The offering staggered me for a moment. 'This is looting!' I barked. From behind came Blondie accompanied by a witness, not one of his cronies, but a sergeant-major whom I had not seen before. 'No Sir! We bought it in the last village. Your share is fifty groszes.' They had about ten more witnesses and I ate the lobster. They took enough care never to be seen sneaking away or rummaging any likely premises. But, Blondie, apart from food, acquired for us a few Browning automatic rifles and we were armed to the teeth. Then we had the Skoda and the petrol, I just reported to the Captain that I would carry out a reconnaissance and we drove off.

A solitary house at the crossroads seemed deserted, but I noticed the row of porcelain insulators with a bunch of wires at the gable-end, and told Blondie to check it out. Almost immediately he called me to an abandoned post office exchange. I tried a few sockets but the lines seemed dead. We turned away just as the box woke up with the rattle of an incoming call. All flaps had been down but I saw one of the catches fluttering anxiously. The cord plugged in, the key depressed and a shriek from the earphone: 'Help! Help! They are here! They will kill us!' After hours on postal exchanges I was used to dealing with excited women and, overcoming her panic, I slowly got the facts. Besieged by the Ukrainians, three women in their manor house had one shot-gun and were almost out of shells. It was only three miles away and I drove flat out all the way. The gravelled avenue curved round the rose-beds in front of the house. Rifle shots sounded everywhere, running men flashed between ornamental shrubberies and hedges. The car, skidding and drifting, threw showers of gravel as I fought the steering wheel. In a spiralling curve we seemed to accelerate when Blondie, swaying just behind me, opened up with the Browning, and I felt an avalanche of hot empty shells falling over my head. We came to a halt in front of the stone terrace. The car leaned crazily with the front tyre shot away and the wheel buried to the axle in a rose-bed. Now the gardens seemed deserted and in the still silence one heard only the crackling of the cooling engine and the low buzzing of bees in the roses. There was not a pane left in the house windows, but the empty frame of the front door opened wide, and a tall slim woman came to us picking her way daintily through shards of shattered glass. She wore a white, low-cut gown and a string of pearls shone against the golden skin of her neck. Behind her, out of the same door jumped a teenage girl with a wild mop of chestnut hair and a young howitzer cradled in her arms – 'Daddie's elephant gun,' we learned later.

The next day, 17 September, came the end. We were strung along a road whilst across the fields rolled a long line of tanks firing just over our heads. Red stars on the turrets, open cupolas with commanders leaning out, shouting to the Polish comrades to give up, to surrender, to throw down their arms. Most of our gear was on commandeered peasant carts and, grabbing a light machine-gun, I ran for my life, away from the approaching tanks, away from the accursed Russians. In a few seconds I covered a couple of hundred yards and crashed through the bushes and seedlings to reach the old forest, solid and dense enough to halt the advancing monsters. As I stopped, on the ground at my feet thudded two boxes of ammunition, and Blondie was already opening one and shoving at me the end of a new belt. More of our people crashed through the undergrowth. I was setting up the gun, somebody was tying together a bunch of hand grenades. One of the tanks trundled slowly, ponderously, and stopped in the flattened bushes a hundred feet away, the commander still shouting from the turret. From behind me came a strangled quivering voice of somebody trying to shout in a whisper.

'Stop, you bloody madmen! I tell you, stop it! It's the end! The end of the war! Stop! We will all be killed!' There, white as a sheet stood our captain – 'Stop or I shoot!' – he mouthed, trying to cover us all with his little pistol. I saw Blondie turning slowly from the gun to face the captain. I saw his glance drift sideways, one eyelid coming down in a wink, and I remembered the arsenal, the man with a flick-knife. Through my head flashed a tumult of incoherent thoughts – Germans, Ukrainians, Russians. No armour-piercing ammunition. White brains splashed everywhere. I knew the captain would die and I shouted 'No!' The shadow of a man rising behind the captain relaxed and melted away.

As the sun set and daylight faded there were about a hundred of us in the forest. The captain thanked us and officially dissolved the Second Auxiliary Signals Centre. His voice broke and he wept. We disabled the machine-guns and buried the ammunition. Men in twos and threes began to disperse. Blondie and his band came to shake hands before heading south.

I and two lieutenants had a long argument: this could not be the end; yes – we had met the Germans in East Poland; we had just escaped the tanks of the second invader and had barely survived the Ukrainian banditry. But our fortresses, our Air Force, the Navy – they did not collapse and flee? Even our own mob had been willing! And finally, we decided to march to Warsaw, though it was some three hundred miles. We had no food, no rucksacks, and the only personal possession was my little safety razor amongst the three of us. This left room for magazines and grenades which we stuffed into our tunics and pockets till we looked like pregnant women. Then with two Brownings we set off in the north-westerly direction.

That night, hidden in a small ravine, we slept a few hours and half-eaten by mosquitoes, wet with dew, shivering in the grey light of a waking day, we marched on. We were famished, as for several days we had lived on bread, and very little of that. But to avoid Russian tanks we by-passed all dwellings and roads. On the second day of our marathon, with the choice of food or starvation, we approached a small village. With guns loaded and cocked, crouching low we ran through the fields into a small orchard. Suddenly above my head, resounded a high-pitched yell: 'Mum, Mum!' I froze against the gnarled trunk of an old tree. But the voice, a healthy strident soprano, continued: 'Mum! The Army! Our Boys!'

There in the tree, just above my head, were sun-bronzed legs, long, slim and perfectly rounded. From bare feet they stretched high into a skirt hitched up to the waist. She looked down, caught my eyes and, trying to pull down the skirt, lost her grip and fell, flattening me to the ground in a tangle of arms, plaits and flying skirt from which spilled a cascade of apples. From the cottage 'Mum' and girls and boys ran to us laughing, waving and shouting. We were 'our boys', 'our soldiers' – there was love and affection and food – it was Poland.

Further and later was another village where a young school-teacher, a mere slip of a girl, produced an atlas from which she tore a one-page map of Poland to guide us. Everywhere the people, young and old, rich and poor, were our people who warned us of German positions, of cut roads, who gave us food and help, and would have given their lives and souls for Poland. They also brought us news: besieged Warsaw was still fighting, some fortress in the West still defied the aggressor, but our decimated armies were broken by the ultimate blow from the East. The Russian commissars had joined forces with the German megalomaniac and his master race. We listened and disbelieved. We talked, argued and hesitated. But, at last, we threw the rifles and ammunition into a river, my friends went south-west to their homes, and I was left alone. The immediate need for action receded and to the fore came the anxiety about Princess, about home. But maybe the English, who had guaranteed our borders, who had already declared war with Germany, maybe the English ... the French ... I must reach Warsaw as quickly as possible. So I kept on, in full uniform with the heavy pistol and three grenades on my belt. Nearer to Warsaw I began to recognise the towns and, though the German columns were more numerous, on my own ground I moved faster, avoiding main roads, sneaking behind hedges, marching and running, marching and running, mile after mile.

The last night of this race against time I spent in a big dilapidated manor-house. A tall, silver-haired gentleman took one look at me and opened the door wide. He and an old, slightly-stooped lady led me through the dark hall into the salon and seated me in a deep armchair. A door slammed somewhere and two girls rushed into the room and stopped short. The spell broken, I scrambled out of the chair and introduced myself. But he just waved me back and, opening a walnut cabinet, produced crystal goblets and a bottle of mead. Still silent we drank slowly. Then, after refilling my glass the host introduced himself and welcomed me into their family. We sipped leisurely in the surroundings and style of the past century. Gradually the present intruded on us and I saw the threadbare Bokhara carpet, the tapestries faded to a uniform sandy grey, felt the uneven springs of the antique chair. I recognised their natural courtesy and hospitality, but also their fear and anxiety for their sons in the forces. I shared their mystic belief that, as they helped me, so someone, somewhere, would succour their own kin. The girls, disappointed in seeing a stranger instead of their beloved brothers, still remained eager to help, to please. The older one showed me to a bedroom, fetched a ewer of hot water and insisted on pulling off my cavalry boots. Over the marble washstand was an age-darkened looking-glass in a gilded frame. From it looked at me the dust-streaked face sunburnt to a deep mahogany. The high cheekbones were made more prominent by the sunken eyes. Sprouting moustache and beard didn't improve my looks. The picture was completed by crumpled, battle-stained uniform with an outsize holster and green eggs of grenades – a caricature of a Mexican bandit minus the sombrero. Horrified, I seized my razor and a piece of soap.

At dinner I heard that Warsaw had fallen on 27 September and for the first time realised that our war was lost. I also learned that officers in uniform were arrested, and anybody caught in possession of arms was shot on the spot. The girls found a sports jacket and riding breeches which fitted me well and matched my cavalry boots. I left my spurs and the black holster. The grenades went into the capacious pockets, the pistol was held firmly by my waistband and at dawn, I was on my way approaching Warsaw along the right bank of the Vistula, where Princess and I had so often sunbathed and swum together. But the sandy dunes and quiet beaches were cut by trenches and tangled concertinas of barbed wire. There was only one open pass, guarded by a German detachment. Screened by dense willows, I sat and watched the long line of civilians queueing to enter the town. I waited and looked and learnt – learnt to remember and hate. Fat, coarse faces under the square helmets, kicks and curses, fists lashing out at men and women alike. Obscene leers and guffaws of ribald laughter when they frisked girls. A young woman squealed and was stripped naked. A young boy was shot for a penknife. They took all they fancied – watches, rings, food, even brighter scarves and better boots. The pile of loot grew bigger and bigger, but the small items went straight into the pockets of the heroes of the Third Reich. I crept away and carefully hid my remaining arms after greasing them with a piece of bacon. I pushed my wristwatch into my bootleg and generously smeared my boots with muck and river mud. Only then did I join the patient queue. Stooped carefully, with a meek expression, I got through unscathed. I traversed quickly the streets of Praga, crossed the long bridge and stopped. Scarred, bullet-pitted houses stared on to the street with blind holes that once had been windows. Looking further one saw great gaps where whole buildings had collapsed. The road was blocked with piles of masonry over which led narrow, deeply trodden paths. At my feet were barricades and, right across the street, half-levelled anti-tank ditches. Along the houses many paving stones were raised and leant against the walls. They all bore roughly marked crosses and on each there was a scribbled name or two. Below each lay a Polish helmet or a workman's flat cap, sometimes a woman's hat or beret, There were also people, grim, hurrying, silent. A people conquered but not defeated. I straightened my shoulders and joined them.

Long streets, more devastation and many more pathetic graves. But, her house stood almost untouched. I ran to the third floor and she opened the door. She was in my arms, hugging, kissing, loving. A changed Princess, really truly mine. There was her Mother holding my hand. And Maryna, her younger sister – with no use for men, and 'all that' – kissing me inexpertly but hard and straight on the mouth and blushing to the roots of her hair. And my parents were all right, and our house still stood.

CHAPTER 9

TURBULENT INTERLUDE

I was left alone with Princess, but we could not talk. It was impossible to put into words the events that had overtaken us in the past month, but looking at her I said, 'Princess, I did get your letter.' She stayed silent, suddenly miles away as if my words, or her letter, had built a wall between us. We sat close, almost touching, but no longer together. Slowly she turned to face me, again there were tears in her eyes, just as in the train that had carried me away to war. But the eyes were laughing and her lips were on my lips now and forever. She disentangled herself, slipped off her wrist the chain bracelet and snapped it over my hand:

'You are my cat now and you will no longer walk by yourself. Anyway, it's high time I took you home to your mother,' she said, knowing well that my mother always called me Cat.

We walked across the town, till we reached Zolibor and our long block of flats. By the standard of Warsaw it was untouched – nobody would count the pock marks of rifle fire or a couple of jagged holes left by the artillery shells. Scanning the façade my eyes reached the middle of the block and there were our windows: the only ones miraculously sparkling with a complete set of glass panes!

There were Mother and Stalek welcoming Princess as much as they welcomed me. I could not keep my eyes off the expanse of spotless glass and they just laughed at me, and with me, and we were together again. Stalek explained the windows which before the siege they had dismantled removing to the cellars the inner leaves so that only the outer glass was lost in the fighting. Then Mother took me to the kitchen where, in the small alcove, were piled big hundred-kilo sacks full of rice, sugar and chocolate. I glanced at Stalek who hesitated a moment before replying: 'Uncle Edmund "won" them after the surrender and now I think that he was right. It is war and we should deny the Germans everything that is in our power to deny. Also, more than ever, our duty is to our families.'

For several days the town lived in a curious limbo. The German Army removed the surrendered arms and ammunition. They filled the trenches and removed barricades to open through-routes; they issued several proclamations about arms and sabotage, each ending in 'Will be shot immediately'.

The German forces did not enter the town but, maintaining a ring around it, allowed only a few people in or out and these without luggage. Thus the city of a million inhabitants was cut off from any supplies, though our own people managed to restore electricity, gas and water services to most districts. Otherwise the town as an entity was dead. There were no buses or trams, no police, all public offices and schools were shut as were the shops and factories. It was a strange situation with no work, no play and no children, who were still kept indoors. Groups of bewildered inhabitants wandered here and there in a fruitless search for food. Single people, distraught with grief, ran somewhere seeking lost families, or joined in small bands still digging desperately in the piles of rubble. A few individuals rushed purposefully on their own secret missions. But all the people, the lost and the busy, knew that this was only a momentary lull before worse calamities befell them.

The day after my return home Uncle Chris came to tell us that his wife was all right. He looked the same as always: black suit, immaculate shoes and, in his gloved hands, a bowler hat and gold-mounted cane. Smiling happily he unbuttoned the elegant overcoat and, inviting himself to dinner, produced a large live chicken! We all stood dumb like children at their first encounter with a magician. But it was Mother who recovered first: 'I will not kill it! I will not touch it! And I don't know how to prepare it!' After all, Mother's cookery was restricted to making cocoa for Sunday breakfast. Then Stalek came to the rescue as a true pathologist. 'I can dissect it and remove the gall-bladder, intestines and lungs, the rest is edible.' Chris offered to pluck it and they all looked at me, whilst I knew there was nothing with which to shoot it! But, as Stalek had said, it was war, so I took the chicken and retired to the kitchen. By then I would not mind killing a German or a Ukrainian, but the chicken presented a different problem. It was a gruesome, inhuman deed to murder a trussed, defenceless bird but I had to do it. I chopped its head off with an axe, blood spurted and the headless chicken hopped round the kitchen. To this day it remains one of the more unpleasant episodes of my life. I cleaned up the kitchen and called Chris to take over, whilst Stalek was already waiting with his rubber gloves and lancets. When they had finished I cooked the bird with rice and enjoyed it as much as the others, though Mother kept looking at me strangely for a few days.

The following week I joined forces with Little and Long, my old skiing companions. We found a suitable pair of abandoned cars and cannibalizing one we got the other working. Then, with our own transport we began scrounging in expectation of future shortages. Into our cellars went sheets of tin from blown off roofs, plywood from a ruined factory, odd tools and anything of potential value. Also in factories we looked for any food-stuffs, as shops and warehouses had been emptied long ago. All along we were helped by the people, some urged us to take more, some were glad to sell at pre-war prices, 'so that the bloody Krauts won't get it!' With petrol running out we raided a German depot and 'liberated' a two hundred-litre drum.

Soon orders and proclamations, backed by the arrival of the Gestapo and the German police, heralded the start of the real occupation. First came the re-registration of all motor vehicles, though just a few owners received the new papers. Cars of German make were shipped to the Reich, whilst tens of thousands were parked in the fields and left to rot. Uncle Chris smashed his new BMW and acquired a Citroën 'Light Fifteen' with a temporary municipal registration. I surrendered an ownerless moped with the number-plates of my Norton which had been hidden in a well-camouflaged cellar. Next came the demand to give up all radios, and everybody holding a licence had to obtain a receipt. As with cars, non-compliance carried dire penalties. Here Princess was a great help. From her father's workshop she brought a big suitcase of burnt-out valves and faulty parts which she quickly assembled into good imitations of receivers. These we gave to the Germans whilst the best sets 'went into hiding'.

Then came the shock of Vaver. In this small village a few miles from Warsaw a gendarme was knifed and killed in some drunken brawl. The same night the heroic German Army rounded up one hundred Polish men from the vicinity of the incident and hanged them all. The lists of the victims were plastered all over town.

When Princess asked for help with transport of some packing-cases which 'the Germans shouldn't see' I realised that she was the first of us in real work. I borrowed Chris's Citroën and after shifting a hundredweight of explosives, returned it with only one bullet-hole in the boot.

The Germans began issuing streams of Identity Cards, Ration Books, Certificates of Employment and Pass Cards – all in unreadable Gothic script. Stalek was the first to receive an Identity Card and a Special Pass for 'The Supervising Doctor in charge of ... '; there were about three lines of the heading and we began to learn that the longer and the more complex the title, the more important the document. Mother, as a married woman, was classed as a housewife and thus unfit for a post of responsibility. She had a whole three days at home before being reinstated in her hospital as there were too few doctors and various infectious diseases were already spreading. Then Chris, no longer a Minister of State, stepped into the shoes of a man killed during the siege, and became a director of an import-export firm. My Princess was employed by her father as a 'Domestic and Industrial Electrical Heating Technician', whilst I with my two friends established ourselves as the 'Super Glaze Co.'. We took orders for the re-glazing of primary schools for which the Germans issued glass permits. The municipal authorities paid double the pre-war price which in the circumstances was comic, as bread had already reached ten times its original cost. However, with some judicious wangling and greasing of palms, one could 'save' almost as much glass as went into the contracted building. These 'savings' allowed a fair amount of private work for which, with no permits and no glass, the pay was sky-high.

Wrapped up to the eyes in our heaviest skiing sweaters and anoraks, we knocked out the remaining shards of glass, scraped out the old, stone-hard putty, pulled out panel pins and cleaned the wood frames. We had to learn it all the hard way. To cut a pane of glass in half is child's play, but to handle ten-foot sheets resting precariously on rocking school desks is not so easy. A slight wobble of the diamond cutter, a trembling hand, or a too hard, impatient knock – and the whole sheet splinters. The new putty, so soft and pliable in trials, hardens into unbreakable lumps when left in the freezing school rooms until one learns to keep big gobbets of it next to one's skin under the sweaters. Then there are the really old windows, the ones opening outwards – these you glaze from outside hoping that your friend's hold on to your trousers is firm, that you will not slip on the ice-covered ledge.

We began by doing it all wrong but, to survive, had to learn quickly and well. We learned to knock in the panel pins low and hard against the glass so as not to tear our thumbs when smoothing the putty. We learned to carry and handle panes without shredding the skin of the hands. But in spite of hard frost, and many trials, we never learned to work in gloves and this was the worst misery.

Late at night we would retire to the warmest place in the building, usually one of the smaller rooms, which we had glazed first. Often we would find it already occupied by some squatters, but we never ran into any trouble, however queer the company. The dirtiest-looking and foulest-swearing tramp turned out to be a Colonel of Artillery passing through Warsaw on his way home and we were glad to help him with food and money. On another occasion, there was a group of dangerous-looking men who never uttered a word and never slept without leaving one of their number on guard. When the draught slammed the door I caught a glint of light on the long barrel of a Lüger in the man's hand. They disappeared silently at dawn and left stuck under the door a thick wad of banknotes. Most frequent, however, were just vagabonds and petty thieves. But we never really knew who our guests were or whence they came.

In a few months of hectic work the windows of the capital changed back from dark, blind holes into merry eyes shining in the winter sun, and our commercial venture came to an end. But there were more changes in the town than mere window glass. Even in the shopping centre the multi-coloured, brightly-lit displays were replaced by hastily painted sheets of hardboard bravely sporting a small pane of glass, behind which one could see one or two utility objects. They were like the crowds, like the individual people. No more the jostling, chattering happy multitude of elegantly dressed revellers, no more slim, silk-clad legs or the staccato of high heels rushing to the late show. Instead, dark coloured, thick woollens of ski-suits, heavy hiking boots sliding and skidding in narrow footpaths dug through deeper and deeper snow drifts. The faces pale and thin, the hurried gait intent and purposeful. But looking closer, observing any of the individuals who formed the drab, subdued crowd, one saw much more. Everywhere there was the will to live, to make the best of a bad job, to win. There still was bright lipstick on the lips and often a conspiratorial, inviting wink. The men plunged heavily into the snow making room for the ladies and frequent collisions or falls were accompanied by smiles and helping hands. There were also the soldiers of the Third Reich, some boisterous, some more subdued, all in immaculate field grey, all looking at and for women. The crowd parted silently, quietly, leaving them all the room. Faces turned away, avoiding eye contact, leaving them isolated like the mediaeval carriers of the plague. Sometimes a single soldier or officer more gallant, or more desperate, than the others would make way or open a shop door for a girl, but no girl accepted the favour. A leper might elicit fear and compassion – a German commanded only the utter disdain of women and the thinly veiled hatred of men.

Our world had changed dramatically, but life went on. My parents' profession was not affected, except for the extra work caused by malnutrition, frostbite and the spread of infectious diseases. On the other hand, some occupations simply disappeared, leaving many people in a vacuum. There were no cars to drive and very few lorries. All universities were closed. Printing was reduced to one 'approved' newspaper and some leaflets, but no books of any kind. Theatres and other entertainment, politics and social work, arts and schools also suffered. But private enterprise flourished. First came the students of chemistry making 'Olde English Marmalade' of turnips flavoured with aromatic esters. The electrical department countered with the 'Electricity Super Saver – recommended by the Führer himself'. It was simply a strong magnet neatly sewn into a leatherette cover. This, when placed on top of an electric meter, stopped it dead. The absolute solidarity of the community was demonstrated by many official meter-readers, who simply reminded the owners to remove the 'Super Saver' from the meter ... for two days a week. My Princess manufactured an 'Extra-Nutritious Spread' which was originally not a bad paste of lard, tomato purée and onions. Later I had my suspicions as there was no more lard but the business prospered whilst she was constantly enquiring for vaseline and any other solid grease. I was not so enterprising and finished as a statistician, employed by the Isolation Hospital for Infectious Diseases. The work was 'guaranteed' and 'safe' as the Germans required masses of figures and brightly coloured graphs.

The passage of time brought some stability to everyday life. It also brought more and more gossip. Listening to foreign broadcasts carried heavy penalties, whilst 'The Rag' (common name of the only daily) printed nothing but new restrictions and a few local news items. In this stifling isolation the word of mouth spread and carried like the beat of a jungle drum. One heard it in the shops, on the streets, the air itself seemed to carry it. There was the 'sure' news about English bombers ready to flatten Berlin, the French Army was to invade Germany next week, Germany was suing for peace. There were rumours ranging from sheer lunacy to utter comedy. The Americans had invented a new magnetic metal which paralysed and imprisoned German tanks; the Maginot line was overlaid with thick rubber which flung the shells back at the attackers ... There was also news from Poland: a blown bridge and so many peasants shot, a derailed train and so many workmen hanged ...

Then my friends began coming for information about explosives, timing devices, sabotage. And Princess again asked for help. This time it was the destruction of important documents in a German-occupied building. So, a fire gutted the place in exchange for her promise to keep out of further activity. One promise, which I knew she would break without compunction.

The fast-rising cost of living, the inadequacy of the food rations and desperate shortage of all basic commodities made life into a real rat race. Thus there was neither time nor opportunity to consider life in general and the German occupation in particular. But during the long winter nights, made still longer by the curfew, I thought deeply about the situation. In spite of their draconian reprisals the necessity of destroying Germans remained paramount. But as it also remained terribly expensive in terms of Polish lives the solution had to be sought outside the country – possibly in the Polish Army in France. That is IF the army existed... IF one could get there. Travel restrictions in Poland, mined and guarded frontiers, pro-German Slovakia, 'neutral' Hungary, Italy ... Suddenly, for the first time, I understood the motto over the entrance to my old school:

> From your thought comes your will,
> From your will your deed shall spring.

When I consulted my parents Stalek was the first to say yes. Mother couldn't speak, but finally nodded her head. Then, convinced that a pair would have a better chance than a single man, I approached Bob. A brilliant scholar, rather staid and unenterprising, but a skier and one of my best friends, he accepted with alacrity. We found out that the Polish Army did exist in France and that travel in Poland, though not prohibited, was rather dangerous as the Germans arrested for smuggling any passengers carrying food. These and many others intercepted on the railways often disappeared without a trace. Information about the frontiers was so vague and contradictory as to be useless, whilst of the more distant lands nobody knew anything. But, at least, we obtained two addresses of 'safe and well-informed' people living on the south border of Poland and decided to go there. Clothing and luggage also required thought as skiing apparel attracted too much attention, and suitcases would be like a ball and chain. We chose to wear quiet sporty suits, thick sweaters, two sets of underwear and heavy shoes studded around with fearsome 'ice nails'. Bob had his old duffle coat and I took my leather coat from which age had removed all shine and elegance. Each of us carried a small attaché case with a few sandwiches and one more set of underwear. Our equipment was completed by a few one dollar notes secreted in the worn handles of our safety razors and minute negatives of reports on the situation in Poland sealed in the heels of our shoes.

Again Princess walked with me to the Central station. Her last, long kiss held all love, all our dreams of the future, and I had my first doubts about leaving her.

CHAPTER 10

PILGRIM'S PROGRESS

At dawn on 5 March 1940 our express train reached Cracow. The few passengers crowded into the waiting room, leaving us inspecting unobtrusively the sleeping station. Ice-bound platforms, darkness and fog masking distant rail tracks, a notice of curfew on a chain across the exit arches. The silence of the deserted buildings was shattered by orders shouted in German and the clamp of heavy boots. Groups of Gestapo in their black uniforms burst from the street and swept straight to the waiting room. Most of the passengers were herded into a closely guarded crowd whilst only a few old men and women with small children were allowed through the cordon. Flattened in a shallow niche we saw it all and spotted also another patrol coming towards us from the far end of the platform. A few steps away a faint light showed through the dirty panes of another door and without looking further we barged into a large dimly-lit room. Deep armchairs, a few reclining figures, one nearest to us in the resplendent uniform of a German army colonel. I saw him first and hesitated, whilst Bob, oblivious of the new danger, pushed me forward and closed the door. There, clearly visible against the lights of the platform, was the large sign 'ONLY FOR THE GERMANS'. But there was no going back and, as quietly as we could in our hob-nailed shoes, we tiptoed to the far end. The door burst in with a kick from a Gestapo man and the colonel jerked upright yelling for his aide:

'Franz! Get that black swine out of here! I want to sleep!'

Confusion amongst black uniforms, some argument, a young lieutenant in army uniform pushing them out, closing the door.

We had a long wait for the local train but at noon we arrived at the little God-forsaken town of Limanowa. With the Cracow adventure fresh in our minds, we left the station quickly and headed for the market square to enquire our way to the manor – the first address obtained in Warsaw. We were hungry and sleepy when, at last, we pulled the wrought-iron handle of an old-fashioned bell. After an endless wait both wings of the huge oak door were flung open by a stooped man in faded livery. Seeing the pair of us he hesitated, and I realised that, unshaven and dirty, we did not inspire much confidence. But a lifetime of service asserted itself and the butler addressed my companion who, with his fuller face and fair complexion, must have looked more presentable than I. Bob gave his name and asked for Marshal Mars who was our first contact. The man bowed and waved us in: 'If you wait here, Sir, I'll inform the Marshal.'

Standing under an enormous crystal chandelier we waited in the shadowy hall. Fierce, dusty heads of stags and boars leaned out of their age-darkened shields. Below them were the closed ranks of life-size portraits in tarnished gold frames. Only the pale faces were visible in the gloom, faces disdainful, suspicious of interlopers. A door slammed shut and an old woman in a black dress approached us floating noiselessly from the far end of the hall.

'I am the Marshal's daughter. I am sorry but Matthew is slightly deaf and did not catch your names, gentlemen.' Bob introduced us both and the old lady raised her hand, stopping him. Her eyes closed, the forehead wrinkled, and after a long pause she smiled: 'I know! Your father ...' she inspected Bob carefully, 'No it must have been your grandfather, he married ... but I shouldn't really gossip. Oh dear boy, I wish I could have met your father. But I am so happy to see you!'

As we crossed the threshold of this house time seemed to skip back a century. During dinner of many courses and wines, I fished gently, but never learned what our host was the Marshal of, or when and where. They lived in the past and expected us to be equally familiar with names and gossip of the Austro-Hungarian Empire. Then, in front of all the retainers, they began to discuss our problem, the matter about which we barely dared whisper. Their unquestionable goodwill clashed with their abysmal ignorance of the current situation. But at last we stopped them sending the footman for the Sergeant of local police, 'a most helpful chap who caught three poachers last year.'

Late at night we managed a quiet tête-à-tête with 'the little niece' who at forty was the baby of the household. Apparently her boy-friend had escaped to the West starting from a Jewish inn some thirty miles distant. Swearing us to secrecy she divulged this address and arranged for a sledge – the only way of getting there.

In the country the curfew ceased at sunrise for which we waited impatiently in the yard. The dark sky paled, leaving momentarily a streaky grey which was transformed into a clear cobalt. Only a few smudges of rose madder hung above the mountains where the farthest peaks lit up like a stage setting showing a winter scene. The blue valleys were full of mist whilst more and more hills blazed with dazzling whiteness.

We perched on a cross board spanning the shallow box mounted on steel-shod ash runners. The driver sat side-saddle on the forward corner with his legs almost scraping the road. The sturdy highland ponies were hitched to the single, rigidly fixed thill. The sledge was rather jerky in its movement but very light and, when its runners froze, it was easy to break off the ice with a slight sideways movement of the horses. They were so used to it that after a stop they always moved sideways before commencing a straight pull.

The deceptively easy trot of the horses tirelessly swallowed mile after mile. The road ran obliquely towards the mountain chain which in the clear frosty air seemed almost within reach. But looking carefully, one saw an endless succession of similar rounded hills stretching between us and the distant mountains.

In the late afternoon we stopped at the inn, a highland building of great, solid timbers and doubly-sloped roof. The timbers and shingles were bleached silver by the passage of innumerable seasons. By contrast with the blinding snows the interior seemed pitch black. As our eyes adjusted we saw spears of sunlight stabbing through the chinks of the ill-fitting shutters and, in the diffused glow of a storm lantern, a man emerging from the shadows. He was twisted and bent under a lop-sided hump which sat on his shoulders like a sack of flour. His face was framed by the long side-curls and beard of an orthodox Jew. After the pastoral sledge ride the eerie darkness of the inn and the grotesque appearance of its host was truly sinister. But our flagging spirits revived with the arrival of huge plates of scrambled eggs and sausage – food forgotten in towns, though still obtainable in these remote regions. Bob ascertained the identity of our host and ordered ale for all three of us.

Then, after a sip or two, he pronounced the password obtained in the manor. The whispered phrase burst among us like a grenade. The innkeeper seemed to rise and float away till he fetched up against the wall with his arms pressed into the timbers – crucified there in his panic. Bob carefully repeated the words and the Jew knelt pleading, calling on the Prophets and the Saints. It took a long time to calm the terrified man and convince him of our bona fides. Only then did we learn the whole story.

There had been an organisation which smuggled groups of young men across Slovakia. The business had flourished and the 'fees' soared from a modest fifty zloties per head to hundreds which had to be paid in dollars or gold. Then, greed and squabbles in this loose federation of the local smugglers resulted in a squeak to the Gestapo and the subsequent slaughter of many members. Those who escaped lay low and would not again jeopardise their lives.

We spent the night buried in the hayloft but returned to the inn for breakfast. A beautiful Jewess with bewitching black eyes served us hot milk and dark rye bread. When Bob went out to check our sledge the girl whispered into my ear two names of smugglers in the nearby village '... they might help but don't let on I told you.' And, though sceptical of this information, we decided to investigate it.

Another sledge ride and a long trudge to the cottage in the forest. There they lived: a highlander with arms and hands like an old, gnarled oak and his son in a town suit. They were smugglers all right and, after one look at us, said so. But that was in the good old days – not now.

'In the soft, heavy spring snows? With the Germans prowling like bloody wolves? You must be mad!' Still, they gave us a good meal, a bed for the night and a vague hope should we come in a month or two.

Next day we found the other smuggler but had to put up with the same negative reply and a cold, hungry night in an empty barn. Then there was nothing to do but try the second address obtained in Warsaw, and in the evening we arrived at the small town of Gorlice. Our exuberant, care-free mood evaporated as we realised the dangers of the border zone and our impotence. But some stubborn streak made us more determined than ever to press on with our quest. We were also becoming more cautious and cunning. Dismissing the driver in the busy market square we no longer dared to ask but drifted with the crowd looking for the address. Even after finding it we checked that nobody followed and, from the darkness of a back garden, observed the house to ensure that it was still occupied by the owners and not by the Gestapo.

Lady Klima, the heroine of the Polish Legions of the First World War, admitted us through the back door. Tall and thin, in a black velvet gown, she wore round her neck an old-fashioned ribbon of the same material so that her hatchet face seemed detached, floating on its own. She identified Bob by questioning him about minute details concerning his family whom once she had known well. Then, on his recommendation, she accepted me and, after a frugal meal, we got down to business. But all too soon it became obvious that, however energetic and patriotic, she still lived in the past. So we retired no wiser though full of promises for the morrow.

The next evening we met many people arriving at intervals and admitted only after a theatrical exchange of passwords. We both felt that their play at conspiracy was as dangerous as it was barren. Still, we had no choice but to play with them and wait for the 'Commander' who came and went, leaving us with more contacts which took several days to check, and were found useless.

During these days of wandering from village to village by dilapidated buses, by sledges and on foot, only one episode stays clearly in my memory especially as it happened on my birthday, 16 March. Between New and Old Sacz we came across an imposing inn which offered us the hope of a meal. It was a forlorn hope as shops and restaurants had not even the meagre fare promised by the ration coupons. We passed through a dark vestibule into a veritable Aladdin's cave: a large hall, empty of people but full of tables laid with spotless linen, bone china and sparkling crystal. A big, portly woman approached and looked us over carefully. She was Jewish with a hooked nose and a large head of hair, once red but now an odd mousy colour. She interrupted Bob's enquiry about lunch: 'I wonder, gentlemen, if you will not be more comfortable in my private room?' Bob, with his slightly anti-semitic views, bristled as she leaned towards me and whispered that the whole show was for the local Gestapo who ate there regularly and were expected at any moment. Later, in the private sitting-room overflowing with nineteenth century furniture and innumerable knick-knacks, she served us with rainbow trout and white Anjou. Mrs Finder, for that was her name, had managed the inn for the past forty years. She showed us photographs and old registers with many signatures of Polish leaders. She shrugged her shoulders, suddenly looking very old: 'I can't help you now. It's too late for the "tourists" and very, very dangerous. But if you want food and a safe night come back to me.' Adamantly she refused payment and wished us luck.

Back in Gorlice we felt at the end of our tether when Lady Klima offered us one more name of 'Eva' adding that 'she was not one of us' – which we took to be encouraging.

Two days later and forty miles further we met Eva. She was small, brusque and as ugly as a young girl could be. She was also very business-like. We learned that already there had been some arrests in Gorlice and that we must lie low for a few days, which we spent in a distant gazebo freezing to death and gnawing dry bread. She came only at night bringing more bread and a thermos flask of hot tea laced with brandy. The third night she told us of another smuggler who 'is in it for the money but jumps well' (is experienced in crossing the frontiers). She added that it was probably the only chance if we managed to strike a bargain and could pay, 'otherwise get out of here – you are bloody lucky to have survived so long.'

It was an early afternoon when we faced the 'good jumper' who was a middle-aged, powerfully-built man with an open, smiling face. He listened to us patiently, almost sleepily, but his dark eyes darted quickly, following our every move and gesture. Only when Bob, who was usually the speaker for both of us, ran out of steam did the smuggler begin to speak. It was the highland dialect, sometimes difficult to follow but spoken slowly, distinctly and rather strangely for a peasant. It was so much to the point, so carefully and objectively balanced – but for the dialect, it sounded more like a lecture than a smuggler's spiel. The snow, deep, soft and heavy, required a lot of physical strength and stamina to cross. But the same snow also hampered the guards, who often suffered frostbite. Yet almost every night 'tourists', some shot, some frozen, died in the mountains. The German patrols were intensified and worked with dogs. Parts of the frontier were already wired and mined. Slovakia was to us enemy country but could be, just could be, crossed by train. The Hungarian border was patrolled on both sides, but if one got through, it was safe to contact the Red Cross Centres which catered for the 'tourists'.

This was the précis of his statement whilst the simple words painted a distinct and most vivid picture of the enemy-held, snow-bound mountains. He paused and added, looking straight into Bob's eyes: 'Take my advice, Sir, do not try it. You will be safe here for the night, but go home tomorrow.'

Silence fell and stretched between us into a tangible tension. The snow, mines, dogs and frost. He did know all about it ... but we were going to France and I asked: 'Will you take us across? We have to go.' Bob wakened up from his reverie: 'We want to go. How much?' The smiling man remained unruffled, expressionless and continued as if there had been no interruptions: 'First we go out' – his gesture towards the window seemed to encompass all the beauty and wilderness of the mountains – 'and when I know that you can walk, run and climb, then you pay me two thousand zloties each, that's a hundred dollars each. I will also change for you another twenty dollars into Slovakian crowns and take you to the Polish border. I shall not go further, but I will tell you how to go and what to do.'

That shut me up as we had between us barely a quarter of this money and far less in dollars. Bob also remained speechless for a long time, till his jaw tightened and, with a nonchalant smile, he started bargaining. I knew it was useless; the man had stated his position and was not going to change it for a chance 'tourist'. But he still watched us both like a hawk and that gave me an idea.

When I left home I could not resist a romantic whim and took my favourite negative out of many photographs of Irka. Now, crossing the room and turning away from the smuggler, I slid it out and held it under my wallet. Then facing our host I interrupted Bob who was not making any headway:

'We have to go, we are going and we have damn all money. Will you tell us the way?' – the little, almost black square slipped out of my fingers and fluttered to the floor. I had hoped that in the circumstances a man of his intelligence and powers of observation would recognise a negative and take it to be a micro-film of some document rather than an old snapshot.

He was out of his chair like a flash, but of course I had known when and where the negative would fall and reached it first.

'What was it?'

'Nothing. Just a scrap of paper.'

He looked at me and smiled. 'All right, it was only a scrap of paper. But you should have told me that you are on duty - not going privately. You have no money, so you don't pay and I'll give you enough Slovak money. If you are sure that you can manage the mountains I'll take you tonight to the frontier.'

When the white slopes lost their sparkle and the valleys filled with shadows, we set out with only shaving tackle, spare socks and some bread in our pockets. The smuggler had spent an hour hammering into us all the details of the route. The frontier we had to jump in one fast run (hence a 'good jumper') and climb two mountain ridges. In the third valley a stream had to be followed to the crossing - 'not a real bridge, but do not try to cross the ice - it's death! Then straight over and along the road to the rails.' He impressed on us that we must be at the station before six in the morning, when the first train was due: 'In the shack speak German and get tickets to Kosicka Bela where the innkeeper will direct you to the Hungarian border.' Without maps, in the unfamiliar mountains, it all sounded like a recipe for disaster and we both worried over these instructions until it was time to go.

We left without supper as our guide advised against full stomachs for the run. Soon we discovered that his fast walk was for us half walk, half run and Bob hissed between two wheezing breaths:

'He can't keep it up!' - but he did.

We passed the little village, doubled up behind some cottages - 'not to leave a trail back' - and spurted uphill along a goat track. It was not only slippery and uphill, it was murder. The track was about six inches wide, just enough for a single shoe. The slightest slip tumbled us into waist deep snow, forcing us to scramble back, to claw our way up and up behind the vanishing silhouette of the guide. There were patches of dark forest, uneven tussocky slopes and tangled clumps of bushes which clutched our legs. Later, one's vision and consciousness shrank till there was nothing around, no up and down, but only the deep footprints which one had to follow on and on in a horrid nightmare. On and on along the track, feeling only the pounding heart, the bursting lungs. On and on, into infinity, till I stumbled over the resting body of our guide and was flattened by Bob falling on top of us. We stretched on the snow in a deep hollow under the trees. Our 'good jumper' was speaking, and before his words penetrated, I heard his laboured breathing. The realisation that he was almost as spent as we were did more than anything for my morale. The frontier ran along the low open ridge only a couple of hundred yards in front of us.

'Bastards' patrol just passed, we rest a quarter of an hour, then you jump. Remember to cross fast two more ridges and be at the rails before six! You'll do all right.'

Then it was time, we shook hands and ran. Keyed up with the night and the adventure, we left the frontier behind, crossed the two high ridges and tumbled down the last precipitous slope. We slid and rolled to the very bank of the ice-bound river. We had been told to go downstream to the crossing, but in the fickle starlight the valley floor seemed flat and the surrounding mountains did not give a clue which way the river flowed. Bob was for tossing a coin or trying to cross the ice, but I had too much trust in the guide's warning and thought of a way to check the direction of the current. Through boulders and bushes we struggled to the edge. Broken slabs of ice were piled high against rocks, and everywhere yawned black crevices and holes. But under the bank we could see the shimmer of running water. We could not reach it, but a third pellet rolled from the pages of Bob's notebook landed on the water and skipped to our left disappearing under the ice.

Half an hour later we were at the crossing – at least we thought that it might be the crossing, and it certainly was not a bridge. From our side of the river a mighty pine had fallen and its tangled crown rested in midstream. From there, but four or five feet downstream, another thick trunk, scrubbed round and smooth by the elements, led to the other bank. Slowly and carefully I climbed on all fours along the downwards sloping bole of the first tree. Even in the dim starlight it was not a difficult passage, though the silvery slabs of ice and the dark water below had a sobering effect. The centre of the 'bridge' was much worse. The other tree seemed miles away and was considerably lower with its shattered end frozen into the river. The polished surface glistened with patches of ice and the stubs of broken limbs were more likely to impale one than to provide a handhold.

Below, the metallic glints of rushing water, the bottomless holes and the craggy slabs of ice did nothing to boost my confidence. But there was no backing out, and with arms and legs extended to grasp, I jumped awkwardly from my perch and landed on the other trunk like a squatting frog. Then, skidding and sliding, I crawled along the glossy, icy pole to the far bank. Bob followed the same way, but his luck or agility did not measure up to the task, and he joined me with one leg soaked up to his belly. In the hard frost of the night he had to undress and change his socks whilst I wrung out his trousers and underwear till the seams crackled and, after all the delays, we set out to climb the next hill. Without further trouble we found the 'road' – a rough mountain track. We followed it downhill at a jog-trot glancing anxiously at our watches. At a few minutes to five, after twelve hours trek, we reached the railway line.

It was a single track coming from, and disappearing into, grey murky hills. Our narrow road petered out in trodden, dirty snow surrounding a wooden shack. On its corner, nailed to the rough timbers, were several metal roundels advertising various brands of beer, and below them, a board with the painted name of the station. We could just read 'Topor', the rest had peeled off long ago. But it was our station of Toporcik and a vertical column of wood smoke rising lazily from the chimney was promising warmth and rest. Opening the squeaky door we were enveloped in a cloud of stinking vapour. In the barn-like room, dimly lit by a flickering oil-lamp, one crudely partitioned corner formed a ticket office. The place was full of men sprawling asleep on the dirt floor or perched listlessly on the benches along two walls. In sombre peasant overcoats or lumber-jackets they all looked dreary and drab, half dead almost, and, after a momentary hesitation, we entered and made our way to a corner where we slumped to the floor. It was cold, draughty and miserable, but I slept until noise and commotion woke me up. The ticket hatch was opened, people were talking desultorily in little groups. Bob got two tickets and a few minutes later we were in an almost empty train speeding south. 'Speeding' is a misleading word as we really crawled in the rickety, jolting, old corridor carriage, stopping at every station. People, mostly peasants, came and went, whilst we sat unobtrusively, feigning sleep or gazing intently out of the window to discourage any attempts at casual conversation. Once or twice we were addressed directly but an abrupt *'Nicht verstehen'* (German for 'don't understand') put an effective stop to it until a tall, swarthy man with a wide face and a nasty grin leaned between us and answered back in broken German:

'You Polish! You pay me or next station I call police, I call gendarmes. You pay hundred crowns now!'

Bob tried to bluff him, but it fell flat and the gipsy speaking louder and louder demanded now two hundred crowns. The other people in the compartment began to take notice as Bob tried desperately to hush him. The squeak of the brakes announced the next halt, and the gipsy struggled to open the window when I cut in with my own mixture of Polish and Czech:

'Shut up! We pay after this station, so nobody knows!' Bob nodded and the gipsy continued, but in a whisper:

'You give three hundred and a watch, after this station.'

The train stopped and some people got out. Others still looked askance at our trio and, on tenterhooks, we sat with pretended nonchalance till the whistle blew and the clanging, hissing train gathered speed.

'You pay now!'

'Yes, outside so people don't see,' I replied, crowding him in to let Bob go first. The man followed quickly, anxious not to be left behind. Bob went along the corridor to the privacy of the platform at the end of the carriage. I glanced behind and saw only the empty corridor. The gipsy turned to me, lifting his grasping, claw-like hands for the money, his back almost against the outer door of the carriage whilst Bob stood in the very corner squeezed against the narrow lavatory door. But behind the back of the gipsy I saw Bob's extended arm, hand resting on the old-fashioned long lever of the door lock, and I winked at him. The door opened slamming back against the carriage wall and I hit with my right, straight to the solar plexus. There was no noise, no outcry, just the two of us left facing one another across the small platform with the wind whistling through the open door. Outside, there was empty space with trees and rocks a long way down at the bottom of a steep valley.

We continued the journey in another carriage till, in the middle of Slovakia, the train stopped at Spiska. As everyone was getting out we realised that this damned train did not go any further and we had to find the connection to Kosicka Bela. We also noticed at the ticket collector's barrier a group of gendarmes listlessly checking papers of the travellers. After a squint through the other window we jumped down on the 'wrong' side, crossed another set of rails and entered the station building through an empty, unguarded platform. It took a long time to find our next connection in the time-tables displayed on the walls. The odd accents over the letters, and words with hardly any vowels, hampered the search for the train to Hungary (which we had been told to leave two stops before the frontier). Having retired to a dirty, deserted washroom we held a council of war. As there was a full six hours to the departure time we decided to walk out of the little town of Spiska and have a badly needed rest somewhere under a hedge. That seemed reasonable enough as the weather was much warmer at this lower altitude and there was more mud than snow. In a quarter of an hour we were out of the town, but isolated farms and single houses seemed to stretch on as far as the eye could see. Then a small newly-surfaced side road opened a vista of vast, flat fields bordered by thick undergrowth. The road curved back and cutting across some drainage ditches we emerged nearer to our target. Suddenly all hell broke loose: an aircraft roared over our heads whilst a couple of soldiers appeared from nowhere firing their guns and shouting like mad. We had stumbled on to a military airfield!

The criss-crossing ditches came in really handy and the patrol did not pursue us for long. But we reached the main road in a sorry state of total exhaustion, not to mention the thick coating of mud and slime up to our knees. Bob suggested trying a small hotel, and seeing no other choice, I reluctantly agreed.

Back in Spiska we entered a dingy hotel and pressed the bell over a little hatch. From the far end of the corridor appeared a middle-aged woman straightening her white apron. Bob produced his well-rehearsed but extremely limited German speech, whilst the woman inspected us from head to toe and beckoned us to follow her. In a large double-bedded room she smiled and became most voluble but almost incoherent in Slovak and Highland Polish. She had a son like Bob, in the army, no – he was more like me, but the Germans took him ... she will help us, help all Poles ... Weeping, she offered to clean our trousers and advised us to leave at the very last moment and board the train when it was pulling out of the station – 'they not stop it and you away!' We checked that the bedroom window opened freely offering an escape route over the roofs of some outhouses and, semi-conscious, we tumbled into a dirty, unmade bed.

After a couple of hours we washed, shaved, and with gratitude pulled on freshly pressed trousers. Then we spent the longest quarter of an hour of our lives. Going too early meant waiting at the station under the eyes of the gendarmes; being too late did not bear thinking about. At last we left with three minutes to spare and forced ourselves to walk slowly, reaching the barrier when the flag fluttered in the hand of a guard, the engine puffed clouds of steam, and the train jerked forward. In a concerted rush we knocked aside the ticket collector and the policeman, raced after the train and jumped on the footboard of the last carriage. We found some empty seats and slumped down feeling relaxed and almost safe. The guard came and, without glancing at us, extended his hand for our tickets. He punched them and suddenly looked again, scrutinising them carefully, whilst I realised that the names of the two frontier stations right across Slovakia were a dead give-away. Then his face lit up with a hearty grin, he stepped back a pace, stood to attention and with the hand touching his peaked cap at a salute, started humming the Polish National Anthem. We sat flabbergasted whilst after a few bars he shook our hands, grinned again and, murmuring something like 'Mum's the word' left the carriage. Other passengers, after stretching their necks or even standing up to observe this pantomime, settled down in glum indifference.

At four in the afternoon we alighted at a little station almost identical to the one at which, ages ago, we had mounted our first train. A minute ticket office and a low platform were squeezed between the rails and a country road, all surrounded by dense forests and framed by brooding mountains. In two miles we reached the recommended inn at Kosicka Bela. But the inn-keeper, scared worse than our hump-backed Jew of the first contact, instead of helping, threatened to call the gendarmes unless we left immediately. Feeling lost, helpless and desperate, we kept on the road. Well past the village we saw three young labourers coming out of the forest. One carried an enormous cross-cut saw, two had big woodcutters' axes strung across their backs. We had only a few seconds to make up our minds, but feeling that, at the worst, we were a match for them we approached casually. Bob talked to one whilst I kept very close to the other two watching their eyes. They seemed like simple, dull peasants, though the one Bob had chosen was rather belligerent and demanded to know who we were. Not losing sight of the axes I crowded my pair until they retreated a couple of steps. The other, deprived of their direct support, shut up and shrugged his shoulders in mute surrender. We then found out that in five or six miles the road went right across the guarded frontier, but we could not elicit any more information. We let them go and watched till, running, they disappeared down the road.

Further on, in the deepening dusk, we met a uniformed forester with a gun on his shoulder. We used the same technique of getting close before speaking, but there was no need for these precautions. He was more than sympathetic and helpful, and told us of a small forest track branching about a mile ahead. He advised us to take it, as the main road was frequently patrolled. Where the track crossed a fire-break the red markings of a summer tourist-route began and led south to Kosice in Hungary. It was only six hours fast walk in summer but now, in winter, he thought that we could not make it. Here, in the high mountains, there was again plenty of snow and the route-markings had not been renewed for years. With the night and the frost he was sure that we would finish like other groups, the corpses of which were dug out now when slowly shrinking drifts began to reveal their secrets. But armed with the new information, with the last frontier within easy reach, we were not frightened or intimidated. Like two overgrown pups we scampered up the road, anxious to be out of the patrol area.

We found the branching footpath and turned into the forest. It was dark under the old trees and the going was rough. We seemed to be climbing a steep, narrow ravine, probably the bed of a dried stream. We could not see much and scrambled up the icy gutter, stumbling over high rocky steps whilst invisible shrubs caught our clothing and threatened to poke out our eyes. The further and higher we went, the worse was the track. From time to time fallen trees forced us to climb the almost vertical sides of the ravine, or, crawling, burrow our way through tangles of broken branches. There was also more ice and we often slid back losing the hard-won height. The once sharp points of my ice-nails had worn smooth and now were more a hindrance than a help. But still, puffed and blown, we scrambled and even retained some sense of humour. On one occasion, slipping, I knocked down Bob and, like a small avalanche, we sailed together to fetch up against a solid boulder. Feeling Bob's body quivering under my weight I asked if he was all right and, with a gale of laughter, came the half smothered reply:

'Remember those moving stairs ... and slide ... in Blackpool? Now it's even better and we haven't paid a penny!'

But at last, we reached a less steep and more open place and sat, or rather lay, down for a well-deserved rest. We found thin sheets of ice which we crunched with the remains of the bread from Poland. Battered sodden lumps were delicious, though heavily laden with muck and dirt. Somewhat revitalised, we went on and soon reached the promised firebreak. It was lighter here and we easily found a tall pine with a white ring cut by a dark band, which in the light from Bob's torch proved to be a vivid red. It was only then, at the first mark, that we ran into more trouble. Good tourist routes have trees, or rocks, painted so that from each mark you should be able to see the two following signs, or at least one good splash of colour. Here, though the night was not very dark, we were unable to spot any signs. When we did find one it was small, faded and almost invisible. Slowly we developed a search system. I stood under the marked tree and, sighting on our own deeply-trodden back track, steered Bob in a general 'forward' direction. When his silhouette almost disappeared, I whistled and he began casting sideways, till with the help of his torch he located the next sign. Then he would stop and direct me on to the next stretch. Sometimes the route veered and we lost still more time seeking round in a complete circle. Soon we realised that the rate of our progress was hopelessly slow, and there remained but one option: abandon the red route and strike straight south. These were not the rocky Tatra Mountains, and we did not expect deadly precipices or unclimbable crags. But the compass course would mean steep climbs and perilous descents, all taking much more time than the easier tourist route. There was also the problem of keeping (without a compass) the right direction in a dark forest. It was a hard and risky, yet inevitable, decision.

We found a small clearing which allowed us a glimpse of the Great Bear and the Pole Star. We looked carefully at the trees and there really was more moss on the north side. But we knew that the moss was unreliable and that a few paces out of the clearing, we would lose the view of the sky and so forfeit the all-important sense of direction. We peered into the murky depths of the forest, trying to find something to aim at. The near ground was falling away in a gentle slope and further on, due south, was a black patch of bushes making a perfect target. At the first glance it had appeared too close for our purpose, but after a few minutes walk in the deceptive blue-grey shadows it receded further and further. After the hopelessly slow progress when seeking the invisible red signs, we were now going like an express train. It was an easy slope with no more than a foot of snow and we congratulated ourselves on the brilliant solution to our problem. But soon the snow deepened, reaching to our knees and the going got tougher. Then, with the snow about my hips I realised that the south-facing slopes had already lost most of their cover whilst the north-facing ones, the uphill for us, had all the winter falls. Nearing the brow of the ridge we were thoroughly exhausted. Each step was like climbing into a high bath-tub filled with soft cushions, hampering and never giving firm support. We tried crawling but became bogged down in soft drifts. We tried jumping but sank deeper. Then it was back to walking and when the leader fell exhausted the other struggled forward. Soaked in sweat, with snow melting on our steaming bodies, we reached the bushes. All our muscles were sore, almost paralysed. The calves, thighs, bellies, even chests and arms ached unbearably. Forcing our way through the shrubbery did not help as our feet caught in the convoluted branches under the deep snow. It was a nightmare of falling and struggling till the bushes ended and there was just snow. Up hill and down dale, crossing ridges and ravines, till totally exhausted we sat down facing each other. The snaking back-trail, almost invisible in the rising mist, was no longer a help in deciding the further direction. There was no moss on the smooth trunks of the surrounding trees, and above the naked branches stretched the uniformly dark clouds. We were thoroughly lost in the alien forest, in darkness, cold and snow. There, half-conscious in my exhaustion, I remembered Princess and knew that she was waiting for me, that we belonged together ... that I should go on – after a little rest.

From long skiing treks Bob was as familiar as I with the insidious white death of resting in snow. But there was no choice, and on our side we had the will and the impudent faith of youth. So Bob set his little alarm clock to ring in two hours and we curled up in the snow like huskies on the Klondike trail. It was cold, wet and impossible to sleep – when I was shaken by Bob grumbling that I had slept like a log. Only two hours had passed but I awakened in another world. From a star-studded sky the Great Bear pointed the way, the light mists were ready to hide us, and heading mostly downhill, we were making up for lost time.

In the grey dawn we reached an exceptionally wide fire-break and saw in the distance the unmistakable shapes of frontier watch-towers. It was the ideal time to cross: enough light to run safely, yet not enough for the guard to shoot straight. We pounded across the open space and into the forest on the other side – the Hungarian forest! When completely out of breath we slowed down to a fast walk but did not stop until in our exhaustion we were both staggering like drunkards. Even then, remembering that people caught in the frontier zone might be turned back, we hid in a narrow ravine. After a good rest we continued our trek south in the glorious warm sun of the early morning. It was only then that we felt thirst and hunger. We could eat and eat; after all, it was more than thirty-six hours since we had left Poland without supper. About noon we struck our old path with the red markings, and saw further, downhill, some movement in the forest. We jumped off the path and, trying to leave no footmarks, hid ourselves as well as we could.

Amongst the tall trees we saw colours – far too much colour for a frontier patrol. Vivid orange and blue were flashing nearer, till round the last bend came a girl on skis. A real tourist – just as we ourselves had been only a year ago ... We tumbled back on to the path, and Bob called out in English asking if it was Hungary. She glanced up, saw us only a few yards ahead and, trying to turn back, skidded and fell.

Bob, always a gentleman, rushed forward to help, whilst the girl cowered, struggled to get away and finished in a knot of skis, legs and sticks. From below, also on skis emerged her boy-friend, and I realised that, after all our adventures, we must have looked like a pair of brigands. Luckily they both spoke a little French and after long explanations everybody was happy. They were overjoyed at not being mugged and impressed at meeting real live 'smugglers', whilst we learned that the Kosice Red Cross place was only a couple of hours ahead. We made it in the afternoon of 21 March, just over two weeks since we had left Warsaw.

CHAPTER 11

IT IS BETTER TO TRAVEL HOPEFULLY...

Just as we were told, there was a little cross splashed with red paint on a dilapidated wooden fence. It was a queer set-up, but they had their priorities right: we were given buckets of sweet tea and bread with orange-coloured Hungarian sausage full of paprika. Only then did we have a good wash which made us almost presentable. Then followed a short interview with the man in charge – a large man in a pin-stripe suit which could not hide the ingrained mannerisms of a professional army officer. He appeared to have a good grasp of the situation in Poland, backed by an encyclopaedic knowledge of pre-war names and life in general. Within a quarter of an hour, satisfied with our story, he concluded:

'Right! Twenty-three hours rail transport ... I mean, we will go to the station and I'll put you on a train to Budapest. Now, to the mess ... you are probably ready for dinner, gentlemen.'

We gathered that sometimes, somewhere, a palm was greased, but mainly the whole thing ran on the goodwill of the Hungarians who for long centuries were staunch friends of Poland. In spite of the German pressure, the Hungarian police and frontier guards did not turn back the wandering 'tourists' and even helped them by a show of strength and fire cover. Also a network of 'Red Cross' points run by the Polish Embassy ensured that the escapers were quickly and quietly taken out of circulation and whisked away.

After a huge meal we rested, ate again and strolled to the Kosice railway station where we boarded a train for Budapest and slept the rest of the night in the comfort of Wagon-Lits. We had been given enough money for a taxi to the Polish Consulate where we arrived before eight in the morning. Early or not, the machinery moved like a high-pressure

American business and not a Civil Service which, after all, it had been. A thorough medical check-up was followed by a session with the passport photographer and a long talk with our Military Attaché. By the time that was completed all our clothing had been cleaned, invisibly mended and pressed, even the shoes were shined and, as two New Zealanders, we were booked into a comfortable 'pension' in the sleepy backwaters of the capital. The negatives of our papers and all the reports had been already enlarged and printed. The latter, judging from the reaction of the Military Attaché, were much wanted and highly regarded. We had been asked what we wished to do and were offered, on completion of the necessary formalities, free travel to France. In the afternoon we rested quietly, recovering from the strain of the past fortnight.

The next day we spent with the Attaché talking of various ciphers which the people of Poland wanted to use in clandestine radio communication. There was quite a lot to discuss as the results had to be passed back by simple and innocuous-sounding code messages. Later we changed a few dollars into Hungarian pengos and set out sight-seeing. We wandered from the heights of the Fisherman's Towers to the banks of the Danube, crossed and re-crossed the bridges, visited the magnificent buildings of the Parliament and attended Easter Mass in the Old Cathedral. In a few days we got our new passports all duly stamped by our Embassy and the Hungarian police, as we were supposed to have lived in Budapest for a long time. But there were still delays with Yugoslavian and Italian visas though we already had French ones. Still, considering the thousands of Poles who had crossed Europe from east to west in the last few months, it was no wonder that some countries were uneasy about the situation. But we were in no mood to consider anybody or anything. The Army in France needed us and we were waiting impatiently for another go at the Krauts. The spring sun shone on the blue Danube whilst the grey waters of the Vistula barely stirred under ice and the yoke of the Hun. At night bright lights enveloped the city but from the dark skies the Great Bear looked down and reminded me of Princess. She seemed to be always with me, just behind my shoulder, so close that I had to glance back, just a quick look round, but there was only an empty street, or some stranger uneasily turning away from my stare. I bought a couple of notebooks and in the long evenings made notes as we gossiped and reconstructed our recent adventures. These notes, later left with Bob, survived the upheaval of the war, and after his death were returned to me, thus helping me to write this story. We also took care to assure our families at home. The mail to Poland functioned normally, but, to prevent any repercussions there, we both wrote to addresses not directly connected with our families. My letters went to the sister of Princess, whilst Bob used the address of good friends of his parents. Of course we wrote obliquely, in what is called 'free cryptic', so that a plain and common message conveyed only to the initiated the real news.

At last came the day when, with passports, visas and tickets, we mounted the train. Just before this we had had our first argument: Bob wanted to take a few days off to see Italy, whilst I thought it to be almost treason and desertion. The quarrel had been settled unwittingly by our Attaché who, handing over our tickets, remarked casually that their validity allowed us to interrupt the journey and, if we could manage financially, it was a God-sent opportunity to see Italy! I gave up grudgingly, only later to realise that they served Athene whilst I was possessed by Ares.

'Doing' Venice we put to shame all American tourists and managed to see in a day more churches, palaces, canals and works of art than the average visitor can cram into a week. We stayed the night in the magnificent and expensive Hotel Regina and had there a strange experience. On the evening of our departure as we waited for the bill to be made up, the Manager, resplendent in full evening dress, appeared on the steps of the foyer and loudly called our names. Appearing unconcerned, but ready to bolt in case of trouble, we strolled over, our well-worn sports suits contrasting with the immaculate uniforms of the staff and evening dress of the guests. He stepped back to be in everybody's view and began an impassioned speech in fiery Italian whilst a lovely red-headed secretary at his elbow translated into English for our benefit. Even without the translation the mood was unmistakable when heroic words rang through the hall ... *Polonia* ... *Fratello* ... *Guerra* ... *Patria* ... he finished by flourishing our bills over his head and tearing them to shreds. When our country was oppressed by the Hun he could not accept a penny from his heroic brothers. The people went mad, clapping and shouting; all the men tried to shake our hands, whilst the ladies fought to hug and kiss us. I was too young and shy to take full advantage of the opportunity, but

Bob was more equal to the occasion and was doing especially well with the gorgeous secretary. When finally rescued, we were taken to the Manager's office, where two older gentlemen tactfully offered us money which we gratefully refused.

Our next stop was Florence where we expected hospitality from an Italian associate of Bob's father. It took us a long time to find the number of the firm and to puzzle out the secrets of the automatic pay-call telephone, but at last we got through to be told in a mixture of several languages that our prospective host had died a month ago. Luckily we had another contact, a Polish lady living in Florence. Unfortunately, we had forgotten her address which we had not dared to commit to paper in Poland. We both agreed that the number was in the teens and that the street name had an association with clothing. There was no help for it but to buy a street plan, and hope that by studying the index we might remember. In the station waiting-room we consulted the new booklet. Beginning with the 'A's we slowly got to the 'B's, and suddenly we both saw it together: Buffalini – but of course, puffed up like the buff-jacket! We were lucky that it was not Ximenes or Zoroastro. Soon after, with the help of the same plan, we were inspecting houses on Buffalini Street from number eleven onwards. Shortly we struck oil at number fourteen. Through a chained door a young lady eyed us suspiciously before denying, in reasonable English, any knowledge of our Polish friend. Nevertheless she asked our names, which she repeated carefully, and added:

'Please, you come back in one hour. Imperative you come back! But I know no lady. I know nothing. Come in one hour!'

The door shut with a solid and final slam.

Even a month ago we would have argued, knocked again, or at least deliberated there and then. But, with minds broadened by travel, we quickly walked away and, in low voices, discussed the matter in the next street.

The girl obviously knew something, but was not telling us and the only thing to do was to stroll around and return after the hour had passed. Though impatient and anxious, we could not resist the quaint charm of the old town with its narrow, crooked streets, and mediaeval houses. The old-fashioned lanterns, throwing small, ill-defined fragments into bold relief, made it into an enchanted world of fairy tales. We passed a little piazza where the open space showed us the velvety Italian sky shining with myriads of stars and amongst them, my old friend the Great Bear, which lifted my spirits considerably. Bob was a little annoyed with my suddenly expressed optimism and the prediction that everything would be all right.

The time was up and we knocked again at number fourteen. The big door opened wide and behind it, against a brilliantly-lit hall, was a crowd of people from which two ladies stepped forward welcoming us with outstretched arms. One was our reluctant guardian of the door, the other, speaking Polish, drew us in. Apparently, in the absence of our Polish lady, her Italian friend, suspecting some fascist ploy, had played safe. Now all of them were delighted to see the visitors from occupied Poland. We got completely lost in the press of friends which she had already managed to mobilise for our reception. They all were more than friendly, they were loving and laughing, and unbelievably well-informed about the Poland of yesterday and today. We understood it only after learning that one of the men present was an Italian professor who had lived in Warsaw and fought on our side during the German siege.

The following days passed like a beautiful dream. It was already spring brought about not so much by the passage of time as by our journey southward. We seemed to live in an unreal world wrapped in a continuously changing rainbow. The delicate pink of almond blossom contrasted with the azure of the sky whilst the mellow reds and browns of the old town stood out against the fresh green of the Tuscan hills. There were the most famous marbles of Michelangelo, bronzes, frescos ... We were not shown these wonders, we were introduced to them, like to old friends, by the man who loved them all and made them vibrantly alive with endless stories and anecdotes about their creators. We went to the best restaurants, where charming Italian girls taught us to eat spaghetti, artichokes and shapeless beasts of the sea. We also met sombre gentlemen from the university staff (some presented only as 'a good friend of ...') who all wanted to know about the Polish Campaign and the Occupation. Several of them were making notes, and none hid their sympathy for Poland and their hatred of the Germans to whom they referred only as 'those northern barbarians'.

We left exalted, drunk with the Italian Renaissance and beautiful girls of the Florentine spring. This strange and heady mixture had been made all the more intoxicating by its contrast with the past dangers and drab, icy winter of occupied Warsaw. Then after climbing the Leaning Tower of Pisa and listening to the echoes in the Baptistry, we crossed the last frontier and rolled to the first stop on French soil. We looked through the train window at the station of Modane and wanted to cheer and sing the Marseillaise. The passport control officials reached us at last and, rather brusquely, ordered us out on to the platform. There were only two of them – just asking for trouble. But as it was France we meekly joined a little crowd of our fellow countrymen. We were taken to a small hotel and found ourselves guarded by the Polish Military Police! Our travelling companions, trying to find out what was going on, clustered around the guard who just told them to shut up. This was too much for both of us, but Bob was first to react and, in his best barrack-room voice, summoned the sergeant of the MP. The man looked round leisurely when I lost my patience.

'On the double!' – I roared, and the man ran.

'Stand to attention!' – and he stood.

Then we slowly learned what it was all about. With all the scum of Europe coming over, the civil authorities forgot their friendship for Poland and demanded that the Army collared and kept everybody under strict control. Obviously uneasy, he apologised to us ('Sir!') and said it would be sorted out immediately – in three or four days!

Facing one another we sat speechless in the little, dingy hotel room. What a bloody finish to our heroic journey!

'*Fraternité, Egalité* ...' and I burst out laughing. We had a long talk and I, used to the Army ways, was accepting things as they were, but Bob would not have it:

'We are not damned recruits! I am going to Paris and you should come with me – we will sort it out there.'

But I always had this law-abiding streak and we agreed to separate.

The next day when we were marched, almost like a group of criminals, to the train, Bob simply and casually strolled away along the platform and when accosted by another Polish MP asked most politely, but in English, how he could help him. The soldier saluted, apologised and walked away whilst Bob mounted the train to Paris. Our group travelled to Lyons where we spent the night in the 'soldiers' dormitory' which was a large stone hall with a few wooden benches and ... a guard on the door.

We were awakened at three in the morning to entrain at nine for Bressuire, right across France in the Vendée district. By then I thought myself immune to surprises, but the continuous administrative chaos of this 'collecting centre' held me spellbound. It took us three days to cross France but in Bressuire I needed nine days to fight my way through the various Commissions for Registration, Medical Examination, and Verification. These were dreary, endless days of waiting in jostling queues and then, inside, keeping just the right balance between whining entreaties, man-to-man plain speaking and downright bullying. The offices adopted 'international' working hours: French late-opening time, English long lunch-break and Polish early-closing. This left us wandering aimlessly the best part of the day, and I spent many hours just outside the town in an old, ruined castle. It was a quiet, deserted place, a welcome change from queuing and pushing in the municipal buildings taken over by our administration. One could sit and dream of brave knights and their paramours, of haughty seigneurs and their mistresses: but the dreams faded and I was always left with Princess, seeing only her golden hair shining in the afternoon sun or glistening mysteriously with the bluish tints of the moon. These were the best memories of Bressuire, being again so near to Her and forgetting the alien crowd, the mindless bureaucracy and our filthy quarters.

We lived in a gymnasium nearly as old as the castle. Its flagstone floor had three longitudinal paths bordered by long balks of timber. The spaces between these paths were once filled with straw, but in my time that had been mashed into a dirty grey mess of dust, sand and chaff, covered with equally filthy army blankets. The daily 'cleaning' was a farce, especially when some newcomers shook their blankets and produced clouds of dust forcing everybody to run from the hall. Even ordinary sweeping of the three paths was a skilled job, as a dry operation was out of the question, whilst a drop of water too much formed a glutinous mud. The motley crowd of inmates was as strange as the accommodation. The prevalent language was Polish, though often spoken with foreign accents, slang and many choice curses. There were Polish escapers from the internment camps of Hungary and Rumania, many ne'er-do-wells and a sprinkling of criminals from all over the world. Some had been forcibly ejected from the country where they had lived, but many were volunteers, though rarely with purely patriotic motives. Lost in this seething mass were pathetically helpless intellectuals with refined manners and academically-flavoured speech. There were even some White Russians of the Old Guard and a few French-speaking descendants of old Polish emigrants.

The local population, after an initial and long-forgotten bout of curiosity, left us strictly alone. It was neither the language barrier nor the cultural estrangement; there simply was no meeting-point between them and us. They were peasants, shopkeepers, rentiers, intent only on the daily toil and family savings, whilst we thought of war, of tomorrow's hope and above all, of today's girls. The girls were another bone of contention when the handsome Romeos took over, leaving the local lads standing or lying flat with bust jaws. The wenches loved the attention and the quick, caveman-like conquest, not to mention the free-spending ways of the newcomers when they 'acquired' any money at all.

I met a few old acquaintances from Warsaw, but now we had little in common except boredom and disappointment. They warned me against some of our crowd, but I was ahead of them. I had established my own system of quiet politeness backed by a military bearing and my heavy, iron-shod sports shoes. The old PT sergeant, who used to hammer into me his maxim of 'Hit first, hit hard and keep hitting', would have been proud of my one and only debut in Bressuire.

Then, unexpectedly, I received a letter from Bob; he was in Paris and urged me to apply for a transfer to the Air Force, as otherwise there was no prospect of any action. He had already applied and, writing in free cryptic, added that, with the help of his uncle who was on the General Staff, success was assured for both of us. Of course I filled all the papers the same day, the day the Germans took Denmark and attacked Norway (9 April 1940).

After ten days in Bressuire came the next step in my military career: a move to the Transit Camp in Partheney which was a similar but smaller town. It took only four days to be 'processed' by the administration and soon we were issued with French Army uniforms which looked like a quartermaster's nightmare. They also gave us Polish buttons, badges of rank and plenty of thread, but no needles - presumably Fred Karno's army managed with less. The uniforms, such as they were, changed not only the appearance, but also the behaviour of the men. The most aggressive villains became somewhat subdued whilst the 'professors' and the 'volunteers' acquired a little more self-confidence.

On the other hand, the 'first timers' were dismayed by the discomfort of the rough and unyielding tightness of the military apparel, whilst the ex-soldiers were disgusted with the inferior type and quality of the uniform. Also the men of the cavalry, horse artillery and signals were issued with bandage-like puttees instead of high boots and spurs, which was adding insult to injury!

The issue of uniforms implied the disposal of civilian clothing as we were now entitled to only one rucksack each whilst there was no provision for storage of personal effects. This must have been a standard occurrence of which the townsfolk were well aware, as they besieged us offering to buy everything. Our quarters suddenly became a crowded one-day sale where the French civilians with newly acquired fluency in the Polish language swarmed over us bidding, shouting, fingering and practically stripping those in better clothing. The only snag was the price: a pair of good shoes was worth the equivalent of half a bottle of local 'plonk', whilst suits were going even cheaper in spite of the multitude of buyers who, with French thriftiness, were not letting their enthusiasm run away with their money. Nevertheless it was the buyers' market and I was staggered to see the mountains of luggage that some of us had managed to convey so far.

The drooping puttees were tripping me up and in the dense crowd I had an illusion of safety only when sitting down and holding on to all my possessions. My flagging spirits were unexpectedly revived by two old French soldiers who came with the locals to see the fun of the fair. From the First World War they spoke a bit of English, and longed for a gossip. After clearing quite a space around us by crude and offensive remarks addressed in French to the stampeding women, they planted themselves by my side to spin their yarns. Not only did I hear of Verdun and the 'Bloody Boche', but I also profited by their knowledge of the Army and its customs. Amongst long-johns resembling a straight-jacket, thin socks and other French rubbish, we were issued with two enormous pieces of woollen cloth. Opinions were divided as to the possible uses of these shawls: some cut them into foot-wrapping cloths whilst others tore them into rifle-cleaning rags. However, my new comrades-in-arms enlightened me that the cloth 'must' be wrapped around the body to prevent chilled kidneys, bellyache and even to ensure sexual potency. Having grasped the supreme importance of this piece of equipment, I promptly sold it to them for about four times the going price of a suit, and, by this simple expedient, gained enough room to stuff my own suit into the rucksack. Also, having filled with mud the hole in the heel of my shoe (where secret negatives had reposed) I sold the much-worn pair. My new friends persuaded a woman that, with the steel nails, the shoes were worth at least double the current price, and we all parted delighted with our gains.

The discipline tightened with daily sessions of square-bashing which also resulted in an odd salute or two for the senior officers! Otherwise it all was like Bressuire: boredom, inaction and doubts about myself in France. France, so completely uninterested in the war; France, secure behind her Maginot Line of impregnable fortifications, and oblivious of the Germans sitting comfortably, behind their own Siegfried Line. They all could sit till Doomsday, while Poland and her people perished. The occupation, Warsaw ... Should I have stayed with Princess? There was a lot to think about and plenty of time to worry. Again I often sat in the ruined castle – there was a castle as in Bressuire. In the dusk, I would climb one of the towers and, in the closing darkness, wait for the winking eyes of the Great Bear ... These were sombre, lonely hours in an alien land. Hours filled with memories of the last years, of home and friends left behind, but mostly of longing and love for Princess.

Then came an entertainment group – the Polish equivalent of British ENSA – and we all trooped, or rather were herded, to the local theatre. The outwardly uniform crowd of khaki-clad men was not enthusiastic. Those with money would have preferred a night with their lady-friends, and the impecunious grumbled that they would rather have the money. The townsfolk from Poland knew the famous names appearing on the bill, but had doubts about 'theatre-going' in the time of national catastrophe. The peasants shrugged their shoulders at another Army imposition. The cold, draughty and poorly-lit building was singularly inhospitable; the subdued crowd impatient and hostile. The curtains parted and the little crowd of actors huddled in bright lights whilst some bemedalled officer introduced the cast: 'Our one and only ... our brave ladies ... our gallant gentlemen ...' An elderly man in evening dress answered with 'How proud we are ...' The audience began whispering, talking, fidgeting. There was a new character speaking, another member of the mutual admiration society. The voice of the next one was completely drowned by the restive crowd and the senior officers in the front row were turning round, hesitant to interfere, unsure of what might come next. The curtains closed and in the brilliant spotlight was left a single girl in a plain white dress. The moving curtains and the changing light gave her one chance and into this lull rang her strong soprano. Standing very still, she sang clearly, distinctly; without a piano, without any accompaniment, she sang of the opening white roses.

The romantic song of the Legions, the song of flowers blooming on the unmarked grave of Johnny, who fell somewhere in a forgotten skirmish and who will return no more to his waiting girl. The old, hackneyed song reverberated through the cold theatre, through the ill-assorted, rebellious crowd, and the crowd changed into individual frozen people, seeing only his mother, his wife or girl. She finished, but the building and the audience remained absolutely silent. There was not the slightest movement, not even a sigh. She curtsied to the audience, turned and parted the curtains to disappear, when the applause erupted spontaneously, not spreading from one enthusiast but exploding throughout the crowd. The egg-heads clapped, the peasants shouted, the vagabonds roared and stamped. There followed monologues and folk dances, choruses and declamations and more songs, but now they could do no wrong, and the enraptured audience clapped and applauded till hands turned red and lungs ran out of breath. The show finished with the Polish National Anthem. It was no longer 'them' and 'us', but all individual people welded into one homogeneous unit, not only patriotic, but somehow good, positive, and lifted up above the daily toil and personal troubles. Surreptitiously I tried to dry my eyes, and saw around me all the men with tears rolling down their cheeks.

We left the Transit Camp of Partheney in French fashion: a railway goods-wagon marked '8 horses or 42 men', attached to some passenger train and shunted frequently on many stations, till, dirty and hungry, we arrived in Versailles. There we marched to the barracks which, enclosed within a perimeter fence, boasted the sign 'ARMÉE POLONAISE' followed by a Polish inscription 'SIGNALS TRAINING CENTRE'.

It was a long-abandoned French military establishment now generously allotted to the Polish Army. We were soon distributed amongst the few companies occupying the long, single-storey huts full of multi-tier cots with palliasses. There was even a sort of dining hall crammed so solid with wooden tables and benches that we had to climb over to get in. Packed like sardines, we quickly shovelled in the food to make place for the next shift. The food was barely acceptable to those few of French origin, whilst the rest grumbled and threatened the cooks with sudden death. Vague considerations of mutiny invariably began at breakfast when bitter, luke-warm fluid was carelessly slopped into our kidney-shaped dixies. This chicory substitute was certainly very different from the weak but very milky coffee served in the old Polish Army. At lunchtime the warriors' wrath exploded over the inevitable stew which resembled well-laundered solids of minestrone soup reinforced with chunks of gristle. Lack of potatoes – the staple diet of a Polish peasant – was not offset by the standard issue of red wine poured carefully into galvanised cups. Those familiar with the fermented grape choked on the first gulp and swore off drink; the comments of the others remain absolutely unprintable. But, unbelievable as it had appeared at first, in a week's time most of the men had learnt to drink, if not enjoy, this black-coloured vinegar.

Three-quarters of the day was occupied by lectures on Army organisation and the French equipment which was unknown to us. The regulations and instructions were ladled out at speed with disregard of the differences in the intelligence and experience of the pupils. We were still not an integrated unit, but just a random collection of individuals, mostly individualists, coming from environments as disparate as remote Polish hamlets, seamy backwaters of European cities and the cloisters of famous universities. The instructors were equally ill-assorted as they had been chosen not for their knowledge, but because they had joined the Army before the others. This unlikely mixture was leavened by personal disappointments and ambitions. Through the filter of many frontiers seeped to France a few of the strong, whilst the weak stayed where the war left them. Thus, the usual ratio of officers to men was reversed. Furthermore, the old experienced NCOs looked with open contempt at young blades of French origin who obtained commissions 'through the bedrooms of old generals' wives' as the gossip claimed. There were also disgusted ensigns like myself, who nominally had already received their commissions twice: an order issued in the first days of the Polish Campaign advanced all ensign-sergeants to the rank of second lieutenant, and the new Headquarters in France confirmed it in similar terms. But the great preponderance of officers over privates resulted in long delays in placing the actual names on the current lists.

There was a fair amount of free time which weighed heavily on most men. Those with money were usually seen with the brightly-painted samples of local talent. The most active were the born businessmen who thrived on some odd transactions in and out of the garrison boundaries. Abstract, esoteric discussions amongst the 'intelligentsia' drifted into pre-war Polish politics and flared up into bitter quarrels. Chess became too slow even for its addicts, whilst draughts and dominoes lost their attraction when played without money.

Exploring the neighbourhood I wandered into the Versailles gardens where, in the unbelievable splendours of the seventeenth century, I found solitude and enchantment. The Grand Canal, the countless fountains, the innumerable statues, all silent, deserted, lost in the endless gardens. Day by day I penetrated further to Trianon and Petit Trianon – names read in a previous existence, views glimpsed in some paintings. Enshrined in the rose- pink colonnade of the terrace, I sat on the marble steps reflecting on this empire of the Sun King and Napoleon. But I also saw my shabby uniform and tasted the bitter wine of the Army. In front of me, the flowing shapes of nymphs and goddesses froze into dead, age-stained lumps of stone: immortal pinnacles of art and culture turning into tombstones of transient glory. The glory had passed, the Empire had been forgotten by its own people, now so indifferent to all but their miserable hoards of a few gold coins. This graveyard of ideals, this barren desert, was no place for me.

Boredom and vexation were occasionally relieved by unexpected occurrences like the compound vaccination administered by the French doctor who talked twenty to the dozen. As we developed high temperatures and endless aches and pains, we assumed that he had been warning us of these symptoms. However, we all turned out for lunch and found that we could not swallow a bite but, gasping with thirst, quickly drank the wine, local water being strictly prohibited. Soon after I felt queer and had to sit down in the middle of the road. Glancing back, I saw shimmering silhouettes of the others collapsing in untidy heaps. My eyes closed and I barely remember the arrival of stretcher parties. Next day the doctor explained through an interpreter that with this particular vaccine one should not touch alcohol. We were then issued with a bottle of table water per head and soon recovered.

Another time, the time of the great odour, was more macabre. It began in our hut with a slight, sickly smell which quickly reached a crescendo of unbearable stink. As complaints to the authorities produced only a shrug of the shoulders and advice to wash more frequently, a few of us constituted a self-appointed committee, and, armed with bayonets, carried out a ruthless search which revealed the source in possession of a volunteer from the French Foreign Legion. He defended it viciously, but somebody whacked him over the head, and the committee triumphantly brought out a jar half-full of pickled human ears! The legionnaire was disconsolate at the loss of his trophies, but we stood him a bottle of plonk and promised that in future he could keep any German ears.

In the meantime Bob arrived from Paris. He had already obtained his transfer to the Polish Air Force but was temporarily seconded to the Signals course which I was attending. Whilst I had wandered through various camps he had toured Paris by day and spent the evenings with his uncle, meeting many VIPs of the Army and the exiled Government. Discussing our recent experiences we began to see our new Army as a merely defiant gesture by a Government with no country and no people. Behind its impenetrable Maginot Line, France opted out of the war whilst our generals, with platoons instead of divisions, and ministers without portfolios crowded the elegant salons of Paris. Stagnation and the passive atmosphere depressed us both though Bob was prepared to wait for his posting to a flying school. But Bob had not left behind a girl who carted explosives around occupied Warsaw.

On Sundays we managed to obtain passes to Paris which we explored thoroughly though, without money, it required miles and miles of walking. Bob also insisted on meeting people of the New Emigration whilst I tagged behind unwillingly. On one occasion we met Bob's friend and my acquaintance, Voytek, who was in a discussion with two staff officers. It was not much of a discussion as Lieutenant Voytek was laying down the law whilst the two portly colonels listened politely but took the opportunity of our arrival to vanish quickly. He dragged us to a quiet corner to explain the situation. He was seconded to the Government to organise the Scouts in Poland into a resistance movement, but was completely stymied by the lack of communication with the occupied country. He complained bitterly that the Army Intelligence, 'like those fatties you have just seen', was giving him endless instructions but could not provide liaison with the country as there were no couriers willing to risk the journey. The hubbub of conversation around us seemed to fade out, jostling figures of guests disappeared, Voytek still talked, but I only saw his mouth opening without hearing a word – this could be my opportunity, the chance of doing something, the way to renew the fight, to get at the Germans and ... and possibly rescue Princess.

I interrupted rudely and dragged Bob away to check with him the standing and integrity of Voytek. Bob vouched for his friend but, guessing the train of my thoughts, tried vehemently to dissuade me. His attitude to girls and love was so academic that I did not argue but simply asked his help. Bob's protests died and we returned to Voytek who was overjoyed at my proposal to volunteer as a courier, though to give him his due he warned me repeatedly of the grave dangers of the job.

CHAPTER 12

LOVE AND FOLLY

In the spring of 1940 Paris was more beautiful than ever, reborn in fresh greenery, full of flowers. But, dashing from one meeting to another, I caught only fleeting glimpses of it. There were interminable conferences at the Second Department - the Polish Army Intelligence, fruitful talks with Voytek and sterile discussions at the various ministries. The last took place at the magnificent castle of Angers which was the seat of the Polish Government. Officially still on the Signals course I was ordered to report 'immediately' here or there. Each time I was issued with a travel order and tickets but no money or rations and was soundly cursed by my commanding officer for dodging lectures. In my ill-fitting uniform and army clodhoppers I dined sumptuously with ministers, shook hands with generals and travelled across France hungry as a stray dog. Of these frantic days it is the irrelevant, chance encounters that I remember better than the ponderous official meetings. Once I missed the connection in Tours and, wandering around the station, I sat to a game of poker with a couple of NCOs, a government chauffeur and a French railwayman. I staked my last few pence (not enough for a meal) on a royal pair and changing only two cards, got a pair of deuces. Smiling happily I chucked my favourite fountain pen into the pot and with the addition of my wrist-watch, bluffed the Frenchman with his full house. After an hour I stood them all a good dinner which, unfortunately, did not restore their spirits. Later, returning to Paris, I shared the compartment with an elderly but fascinating artist and a girl escaping from a convent school. With a little English and lots of sign language we had the time of our lives. The jokes and laughter were sustained by our misunderstandings, by the childish coquetry of the girl, the bonhomie of the gentleman and my own exuberance after my success in Angers. There I won the final battle over the wording of a letter to our Military Attaché in Budapest. The letter now contained the phrase '... to give help and satisfy his requirements pertaining to the mission ...'. Conversely, I had no trouble in exacting the price I put on my services: deposited in our Embassy was the passport for Princess with an English visa and enough money to get her from France to my friends.

I still had my sports suit but to get good shoes I had to sell my Mother's gold bracelet which I had brought from Warsaw. The final insult was offered by the commanding officer who ordered my arrest when the dates on my Army discharge document did not tally. But by then I had had enough and created such a row that within an hour I was not only released but driven to Paris in a staff car.

On 11 May, armed with a Diplomatic passport (a huge sheet of parchment) instead of the ordinary blue booklet, I boarded an express to Turin, Trieste and Zagreb. By chance I chose a compartment in which travelled a Hungarian lady returning from a visit to England. We chatted easily of her memories which were so similar to my own impressions of England. But underlying her laughter there was some worry, the reason for which suddenly emerged from her fur coat draped on an empty seat. It was a lovable Persian kitten which she was determined to bring home. She had smuggled it through France but was terrified of the Italian customs which were very strict. We were talking happily when the train stopped and the Carabinieri, armed to the teeth, began checking the travellers' papers. They had just examined the girl's passport when the playful kitten scrambled out of a silk scarf in which his mistress had wrapped him in an attempted camouflage. After a moment of stunned silence all hell broke loose - it was '*Mama Mia*' and '*Santa Madonna*' with the rifles lowered menacingly at the little creature. Loud cries about '*proibizione*' and calls for the officer of the guard brought in the resplendent uniform sparkling with silver badges and decorations. The girl stopped crying but large tears still rolled down her cheeks and I decided to test the powers of my diplomatic status.

'This is my cat!' I said in English but, affected by their own performance, threw in expansive, theatrical gestures of pointing at the cat and tapping my breast with the index finger. Shouting erupted again at twice the previous volume. At last they demanded my passport and I handed over the folded square of parchment. The bemedalled uniform took it in two fingers and sprang to attention.

'Excellency! We not know! *Scusi, pardon!*' – and two of the gendarmes were despatched immediately to fetch a saucer of warm milk for the cat, whilst I considered giving up engineering in favour of a diplomatic career.

We rolled on through Northern Italy to Yugoslavia which was the end of this comfortable and carefree journey. Apparently, under German pressure, Hungary refused to issue entry visas to any Polish nationals. So in Zagreb, I changed to a local train puffing slowly towards the Hungarian border. As instructed, I alighted at the small village of Virovitica, walked forward past my train and crossed the railway track to a wide, cobbled road, where four dilapidated taxi-cabs waited patiently for non-existent passengers. The cars were infinitely old and well covered with a white dust, but the third one – exactly as in the instructions – showed traces of a vivid yellow paint. I wrenched open the door and got in when the motor roared and the car took off like a wild bronco. The door slammed shut as the rattling, groaning machine careered down the road. It shook and jumped, swayed and bumped but kept on at a good speed. Wedged firmly into a corner of the back seat with legs braced, I survived half an hour's ride until with a screech of brakes the machine stopped, and the driver, still without a word, pointed to the door and forward along the deserted country road. I got out and walked in the indicated direction whilst the taxi made a U-turn and raced away. As I was approaching a small bridge I heard somebody whistling. It sounded more like the hissing and panting of an old shunting engine than a musical production, but assuming that it must be the signal of my future guide, I joined him singing the Polish version of 'Madelon'. I felt that we were in different keys and in different bars of the melody. Nevertheless, the recognition completed, we met under the bridge. He wore long cavalry boots, army breeches and a civilian jacket. He was young and fresh – like the fields around us, like my old friends. Finding out that I was not a real diplomat or staff officer, but an ensign like himself, he roared with laughter:

'We go across the fields, it's only half an hour to our lair. The brass hats we take through the bog route, all of two hours and not half wet, so that they appreciate our dangerous life!'

We soon reached a solitary, ramshackle cottage and joined the little gang of about half a dozen young Army officers of the Polish liaison post. They wanted me to stay a couple of days but realising my haste promised to move fast, and one of them left to arrange 'a quick go'. We talked of the apparent stalemate in the West, of the Occupation, the Polish Army in France and ... of home. We had dinner of a spicy lamb stew followed by black Serbian coffee boiled with sugar till it became a thick tarry syrup. They also produced a case of really old, smooth Tokay – the gift of the Yugoslav border guard with whom they lived in friendship sustained by regular gifts of vodka and a special payment for every person smuggled across the border.

We left in the darkness of the night and in an hour reached a river where two of them pulled out of some bushes a small boat resembling a wooden horse trough. With three of us there was about an inch of freeboard left and, with small planks, we carefully propelled ourselves across to the Hungarian bank where two dark shadows awaited us.

'We have him!' they whispered, hauling me out on to the steep bank whilst the canoe glided away over the black water. Not wasting any time they hustled me away from the river:

'The Magyars are not very friendly here, better step out!' A couple of hours later we had a good rest in the fields silvered with dew. They told me that there was plenty of time to reach the small station. There I was to board the Budapest train as a Liaison Officer on business concerning the local camp, where some units of the Polish Army had been interned after the '39 Campaign.

Our Military Attaché in Budapest examined my credentials, raised his eyebrows at the phrase about satisfying my requirements, and got down to business. He suggested that I join a group which frequently crossed Slovakia and was now preparing to carry five million zloties (some quarter of a million pounds sterling) for the Polish Resistance. The operation was urgent as the Germans were replacing the old currency with the new 'occupational zloties'. As nothing could be committed to paper I had to memorise the names of the Central Bank officials and other details of this operation in addition to the masses of names, addresses and passwords already learnt in France.

In the last month conditions had deteriorated so that there was no chance of using trains in Slovakia, and the eighty miles of mountainous country had to be traversed on foot under cover of darkness. To protect my family from any consequences of my escapade if it went wrong, I proposed to travel under a false name. Also, as there were rumours that the Germans were impressing Poles into their Army, I decided to become younger by a full six years. I chose a permanent address in Warsaw, in a street which had been completely demolished during the recent siege. All this was taken care of and I became Jan Salski, age 17, with a set of well-worn, pre-war Polish identity papers, whilst the newer German documents I was to pick up in Poland. I also insisted that the group would not know anything about me, so the Attaché, instead of the usual orders, gave me a private letter of introduction to the man in charge asking him to take across the 'young boy stranded in Budapest'. I would rather take any ribbing from them than risk so many people knowing too much. My final need was for a pistol, and a young typist took me to the next room where the shelves of a steel cabinet sagged under masses of hand-guns. There were plenty of twelve- and ten-millimetre cannons as well as quite a few six-thirty-fives but, nothing in between. In the end, it was one of the chauffeurs who handed to me his own slim seven-sixty-two FN with a spare magazine. The same night I went by a sleeper to Kosice.

In the old 'Red Cross' place I met the band with their leader the 'Engineer'. In their early twenties, looking rough and tough, they were led by a taciturn middle-aged man who was as put out by my arrival as was his band. After all, I was not only a stranger, but also a youngster and not under his command. I had to listen to a lot of rude remarks of which the most innocuous were about snotty-nosed kids running back to mummy instead of joining the Army in France. The Engineer was further vexed by a telephone call from his Budapest Controller which left him no choice about including me in his party. He was slightly mollified, however, by my offer of taking a share of the load that the group had to 'ferry' across Slovakia. The money was in sealed packets weighing about twenty pounds each but as there were nine or ten of them we broke some and divided the weight equally amongst all of us. In addition there was bread and tinned food which had to last for the three nights of forced march and two days of rest in between. During the packing the Engineer noticed my pistol and, taking me aside, started asking questions to which I replied that he had his instructions and had better carry them out. It was probably my quiet but rather authoritative attitude which gave away my real status and I promised myself to be more careful in future. However, he looked thoughtful, and, though he never asked me another question, he stopped his young men from baiting me. Later he offered me some hand grenades, adding that these were carried only by himself and his senior man as he did not trust the others with the 'bloody things'.

We set out at dusk to cross the Slovakian frontier in darkness and have all the night for marching. From the heavily overcast sky a slight drizzle was falling steadily and the whole band was in high spirits. I was told that it was perfect weather for the crossing as the guards would stay under cover. We marched steadily but fast, soon branching into an unmade road which deteriorated to a cart-track and then to an overgrown path. The route was rising gradually as we approached the dark forbidding hills. We stopped for a short rest but with the ground thoroughly sodden and cold we decided to keep going till the drizzle eased. Somebody whispered that we had already crossed the frontier and were well into Slovakia, but I saw only the low clouds and the steep, slippery slope. The rucksacks were heavy and I was glad of my old leather coat which offered good protection from the chafing straps. The drizzle continued but we stopped for a breather, hoping for a rest, for a good stretch on the soft grass. Somebody sat down and cursed the icy water seeping into his trousers. Others squatted, propping on boulders the rucksacks which, with every passing hour, seemed heavier and heavier. Soon we had to continue our trek to reach, before dawn, the wild heart of the mountains for a day's sanctuary. Then came the feeble light showing heavy clouds racing over the mountains. Some were shredded on the far crests, others billowed wetly around us. We stood dejected around the Engineer who, with map, compass and binoculars, tried to ascertain our position. He cursed the mist and the rain, and declared that we were a few miles short of the intended resting place. There was no alternative but to hoof it fast across the next valley into the more desolate mountains. The remaining climb was short and soon we tried to run downhill. But the slippery clay and the loose stones of a goat-track were too much for tired, heavily-laden men. Somebody stumbled and staggered against the man in front and, in a second, three of us rolled down in a tangle of arms, legs and rucksacks. Nobody was really injured but all had skinned knees, torn nails or bruised elbows, and all were thoroughly covered with soft yellow clay. Then, in a few hours of gruelling march, we reached the 'safe' ground, whilst the rain increased to vicious downpours interspersed with periods of sleet.

At first glance the resting place did not seem any different from the terrain we had been marching through. It was a naked hillside of almost bare soil with tussocks of sour grass, dead heather and bracken. Scattered around were outcrops of rock, loose stones and small clumps of pitiful, twisted bushes. Only when a blast of wind tore a hole in the curtains of rain one saw higher ridges and mountain peaks screening us from the prying eyes of the outside world. It could have been a safe resting place but we did not get much rest. First, feeling cold and hungry, we attempted a meal. The rucksacks had to be laid on the wet ground, and the persistent rain poured into them the moment the flaps were unbuckled. Cold, moist bread crumbled into a grey mess and the tins were the greatest disappointment. The unlabelled containers, instead of solid army beef, held thin vegetable soup with yellow lumps of congealed fat and we did not dare light a fire. We tried the cold salty liquid, and gagged on the greasy gobbets. Only two, big country lads, swallowed it whilst others managed only a few mouthfuls. The best was the wet bread with sugar but we had very little of the latter. After this feast each one tried to improve his bivouac. Men half-covered with bunches of bracken cursed as the ground water soaked their clothes, others twisted and turned to find a less uncomfortable position on hastily-built stone platforms. Rolling on the ground I squeezed myself under the low branches of a few small bushes to discover immediately that this lair was no better than any other place. The same sodden earth, the dripping twigs, the cold ... But for a whole hour I kept my eyes shut though there was neither sleep nor rest. Finally I gave up and, crawling out of my bushes, found the others squatting miserably around. We tried to huddle close together but succeeded only in getting more uniformly wet and chilled.

In the afternoon the Engineer decided that with this weather we could safely proceed through the mountains. It was a slow, heartbreaking start with stiffened muscles, wet shoes and a general feeling of wretchedness. The valley rose steeply into the clouds but before the climb there was a wide stream to be crossed. The water was only a foot deep, but it hissed and gurgled greedily, splashing the surrounding rocks. My companions cursed in utter disbelief, swearing that it had always been a dry valley.

Still, there was no choice and linking hands we walked slowly into the raging torrent. Stones rolled under our feet, bumped into our legs. The water sucked and pulled like a wild beast. We marched on with little yellow jets squirting from our shoes, with dirty trickles running from sodden trousers, whilst the rain continued to fall steadily. The night, our second night, followed an early dusk. We passed one or two hamlets without hearing even one protest from the village curs. When we couldn't march any further we lay flat to rest and moved on when it was too cold to rest any longer. At dawn we had covered only half of the planned distance and had to turn aside into the higher mountains and denser forests for the day's rest.

The second day was like the first one, only this time spent in a primeval forest. The ground was softer to lie on and the water came down in solid cascades with every gust of wind. I slept on and off for a few hours but finally awoke chilled to the bone and had to walk and jump to escape painful cramps in both legs. The other men were no better off. The afternoon provided two more disasters. All our bread disintegrated into a dirty dough full of grit and sand whilst the rucksacks became impossibly heavy. We laughed at the first man who staggered and fell when slinging the load over his shoulders but we soon discovered that all packs were by now unmanageable – the banknotes had become waterlogged. We discarded and buried all extra weight like the foul soup, remaining bread, spare socks and underwear. Even shaving tackle and extra ammunition was dumped. We were left with loaded pistols, all the banknotes and three grenades. Then it was time to struggle on with the next night's march, and it was a grim struggle. But in spite of all our efforts at dawn we were still another night's march from the Polish frontier.

On the edge of the forest we found a new hide. There the Engineer announced that in view of our exhaustion and lack of food we would deviate to a desolate inn leaving the rucksacks under the guard of two volunteers who would soon be relieved. Afraid of meeting Slovaks, I volunteered and was reluctantly joined by one of the men. The Engineer left me his ordnance map confirming that we would be relieved within two hours. I repeated the instructions, concluding that in two and a half hours, 'that is at 1400 hours, we are to continue on our own!' Cheered by the prospect of food and rest they went laughing at my fears and formality. With only two of us left we felt lonely and vulnerable. The forest seemed bigger but not as thick as before. We were too tired to move, too miserable to talk, to do anything but steal surreptitious glances at our watches on which only the second hands crept lazily whilst the other two appeared frozen solid. After centuries of waiting, an hour passed and the rain continued unabated. Two hours lapsed and our passive vigil changed to active anger, to cursing the lazy bastards. But anger soon gave way to apprehension and fear of impending doom. At the edge of the forest we stretched flat in a shallow depression and watched the slope in front. At two o'clock we decided to wait another half hour. But we chose new, well hidden positions with a clear field of fire and dense undergrowth behind to cover a withdrawal. At half past two there was no point in waiting any longer.

Without thinking I took command and my companion was relieved to be told what to do. We repacked, each taking only one complete parcel of banknotes of the highest denomination. The spare rucksacks we carried half a mile up a little stream, walking in the water to leave no footprints. There we hid them between two boulders. Dragging our feet, we milled about the camp site making a maze of criss-crossing tracks. There were several routes pencilled faintly on the map but luckily my companion remembered the names of some villages along their usual way. This route I would be able to follow though, marching in daylight, we had to make wider detours around the inhabited areas. As we had no doubts that our comrades had been caught, the fear and excitement spurred us to new efforts and we moved fast to get away from this dangerous area. But soon the overwhelming pains of exhaustion, hunger and cold returned and we just trudged on like clockwork soldiers with their springs running down. My mission was not directly affected though there would be more difficulties in Poland. Still, I had to concentrate on the present, on fording the innumerable streams, on a decision when and where to descend into the valleys and cross the river. Because the map did show the river of which I was apprehensive in spite of my companion's assurance that 'it's just a bit of a stream'.

At dusk we were trudging over the soggy meadows, wading through the shallow but extensive floods. We scrambled up the steep embankment and there, only inches below our feet, swirled a dark brown torrent. In the fading light its surface was creased with circular whirlpools moving slowly and stopping as if independent of the main current. The uneven, boiling waters were broken here and there by protruding branches which raced downstream, and vanished as quickly as they appeared. Only some fifteen yards separated us from the black shadow of the opposite bank but the space in between looked anything but inviting. I asked my friend if he could swim.

'Holy Mary, Mother of God! Not in this! We are not going any further, I won't move another step and I won't be drowned like a rat!'

I cajoled and encouraged, pleaded and threatened and at last talked him into a trial run. Some straps, a goodly length of stout cord with our own belts and shirts made up a sort of rope which looked long enough to stretch across. The idea was that after I had swum the river he would throw a stone with the rope on which I would pull across our traps and then himself. I stripped naked and sitting on the grassy bank began sliding slowly into the water. To my tired feet the river felt almost pleasant but soon my knees tingled with the chill water and I was whisked round, pulled off the bank and sucked under. The vicious undertow pushed and pulled like a battering ram as I fought back to the surface. Then I saw the near bank rushing backwards as if viewed from the window of an express train. I could just keep my head above water and began swimming. It was odd and frightening as an arm or a leg was suddenly grabbed by some invisible but all-powerful vortex. I learned not to fight but to drift with the current just trying to breathe slowly and to keep going in my own direction to the other bank regardless of the sideways drift. Frequently I went under to emerge spitting and choking, completely disorientated and still I fought forward until aeons later my hand brushed against wet grass rushing by. I grabbed and pulled away great tufts. Then one tuft held as I dug the fingers of my other hand into soft clay and inched myself on to the embankment. Spitting grass and mud I breathed deeply without swallowing more water and would have lain there for ever if it had not been so cold. I stood up slowly, legs wobbling, arms shaking and teeth chattering. Unaccustomed to bare feet I staggered upstream and walking I giggled, giggled insanely at the thought of the whole scene. There was I in the middle of a dark night, lonely lover and heroic freedom fighter, stark naked but striped blue and yellow with cold and clay, perambulating along the banks of a flooding river. It seemed like a mile before I saw, on the opposite bank, only fifteen yards away, the waiting figure of my companion. We had to shout against the whistling wind, against the hissing water. After seeing some of my struggles he was scared stiff and flatly refused to attempt the crossing. I cursed and blasphemed and still he only shook his arms in absolute denial. I tried again, but I knew that I could not convince him and deep inside I felt that it would have been useless anyway - the flimsy rope would never withstand the pull of the current, the weight of the rucksacks ... he would never make it across. My feet and fingers were completely numb, my body shivered uncontrollably and I could have sat down and wept ... But there was no help, just the two of us on the opposite banks of this bloody ditch and I was freezing. The rain stopped, the rising wind parted the uniform veil of the clouds and the pale moon shone on the meadows and on the river. I shouted at him to run with the current to help me out as I slipped again into the water. This time it did not feel cold but the current was infinitely stronger, more aggressive. The water boiled over my head again and again, I was hit by something big and unyielding, and was half drowned in a mass of knotted branches. He grabbed my hand when I could fight no longer. He tugged and hauled till I was out on the wet grass and I lay there till he brought my clothing and started pulling it over me. Clumsily we both jumped, beat our arms and pummelled one another till the teeth stopped chattering and we could talk.

It was a one-sided talk as my friend was silent and dejected, whilst I reacted in exactly the opposite way to the misadventures and hardship. Somewhere in the distant future were the ultimate goals of Poland and Princess, intricately and inseparably connected by youth and love, university and poetry, by life itself. But there and then, right across the road to the future, were a few hills, a swollen stream - I would be damned if I should give up everything because of wet shoes and skipped meals! I did not think logically, did not state and justify the aims and means, I just knew. I knew and told him so.

'Back across the meadows to the road. Four miles to the village and across the bridge!'

He mumbled about the village, the gendarmes at the bridge. I checked the action of my pistol, pulled the grenades from the pocket of my rucksack and blessed prudence which made me take the spare ones from the abandoned loads.

'Check your gun and remember – we shoot anything or anybody trying to stop us. And get your rucksack on, or stay here and drown!'

I did not know that the months of German cruelty and murders had already changed the average 'tourist' or smuggler from a timid creature of the night into a vicious beast of prey – but this change was to work miracles for us.

We shambled along, too tired and miserable to hurry. But nearing the lights of the village our own rising tension, the sense of danger, made us straighten up and step out boldly. Side by side we walked with right hands tucked in, holding the pistols under the folds of our coats. At the cross-roads just before the bridge we approached a group of peasants. Somebody looked round and saw us. The people fell silent and the little crowd disintegrated and vanished quickly, their shadows sucked in by the dark passages between the houses. Fifty yards ahead were the two gendarmes guarding the bridge. They stared straight at us and I sensed movement at my side.

'Don't shoot! Not yet!' I whispered. Slowly, casually, the gendarmes turned sideways and sauntered away from the abutment. The wooden bridge shook and groaned, the boards of the deck vibrated and moved under our feet. Brown water spat flecks of dirty foam over the edge and between the loosened boards. In a minute we were across and on the road rising into the friendly forest. This first hill and the endless climb almost defeated us both. The modern curse of Midas in our rucksacks was so unbearably heavy that, cold or not, we decided to discard our sodden overcoats. We hid them in the roadside bushes when I saw the bulging pockets of my companion and made him bury 'loose change' – the thousands of zloties which he had greedily concealed about his person. We walked and rested, and walked again till, sitting himself on the edge of the road, my friend said simply:

'You go alone, I stay here,' – and I could do nothing to change his decision. He intended to go back to seek rest in a lonely farm that we had just passed. Solemnly we shook hands and I trudged on up the everlasting hill. I walked and walked, no longer knowing or caring whether it was up or down. I walked till I could walk no further. I was out of the woods and, in the pale moonlight, saw the roofs of another farm. This was shelter which I had to have, and, across the fields, across ditches and across wire fences, I scrambled to a corner of a large barn.

Some rotted boards gave easily and I was inside, out of the cold, penetrating wind. The transition from the wild shrieking elements to this quiet sanctuary was miraculous. By touch I found a ladder and climbed up to the top of the piled-up straw. There in the Stygian darkness I undressed slowly and painfully, taking good care not to lose anything. At last, mother naked, I buried myself and all my belongings deep into the prickly and scratchy, but dry straw.

Farmyard noises and men's voices woke me gradually. I knew exactly where I was and sneaked my pistol from the clothing before I parted the covering straw. The big gates of my barn were wide open and in the sun-drenched yard two men were splitting logs. A couple of dogs wandered about, and a woman at the well was drawing water with an enormous sweep. I was safe for the moment and felt warm, rested and ravenously hungry. I took time to dress and felt more and more hungry. When the woman called her men inside it was noon and my mind was made up. I slid down and went straight to the cottage. The woman was at the cooking range, both men at the table and, seeing me, the younger jumped up grabbing a large carving knife. Smiling, I showed them my pistol and waved them back. They stood sullen, eyes darting in search of a weapon. The woman was cowering at the range. With a mixture of Polish and a few, half-remembered Czech words I explained that I wanted to buy food. The older man offered to bring eggs from the hen-house, but I just pointed to a clay bowl half-full of eggs. Slowly we settled down to an almost amicable relationship, though both sides kept a watchful eye on the opponents. I got about a dozen scrambled eggs and as much bread and milk as I could consume. The woman seemed genuinely friendly, but the men were obviously watching for a chance to attack me or to run for help and I only understood it much later, when I heard of a substantial reward offered by the Germans for every Pole captured dead or alive. I paid them in zloties which they seemed to prefer to the Slovak currency. I paid handsomely, leaving two or three hundred zloties - about ten times the occupational value or a hundred times the pre-war price. Before leaving I asked the direction to several villages lying at an angle to the route which I really intended to follow.

It was a beautiful, warm and sunny day and, though I was painfully aware of all my muscles, I kept a good pace. There was no more than fifteen miles to the frontier and in the perfect weather I could not bring myself to stop for a daylight rest. Hours later, only a few miles from the frontier, while crossing an unmade country road I walked straight into the trap. Three gendarmes hidden in thick bushes on both sides of the road covered me with their rifles whilst a fourth one approached to search me. He stood behind me and I felt his hands moving on my back, on my sides, creeping forward. Guessing that they would not shoot for fear of hitting their own man, I lowered my left hand to the top pocket, pulled out my glasses and, half turning, offered them with a silly smile, saying in German, 'Careful, my glasses!' Their excited shouts of *'Hände hoch'* ceased in an outburst of laughter which ended the search, leaving the Browning stuck in the waistband of my trousers. They laughed and joked, marching me back in the direction of their station in the nearby village. Glancing back I saw three of them sauntering with the rifles slung over their shoulders whilst the fourth, the nearest one, kept prodding me in the back with the barrel of his short Mauser carbine. This one had to go. Slowly, imperceptibly, my right hand crept under my jacket. With my thumb I felt the resistance of the safety catch sliding into the firing position. I eased the gun to my left side, round and round till, still under my jacket, it pointed backward. Then I pressed the trigger. Instead of a loud explosion and a kick there was only a sharp metallic click, which in my keyed-up state sounded like the crack of doom. But nobody else heard it, nothing changed and we all kept walking steadily in the bright, indifferent sun. I felt blood rushing to my face in hot waves, tasted salty sweat on my lips and thought only of getting rid of the accursed gun. Stumbling, I began to argue about a rest. They laughed again but, seeing my face, stopped and allowed me to sit on the edge of the road. Bending low as if totally exhausted I pulled large tufts of grass and slowly and laboriously cleaned my shoes. Discarded grass with lumps of sticky clay piled up between my feet and into it I slipped the gun under the cover of my bent body. I desperately wanted to kick the gun deeper into the ditch, into a safer hiding place but, afraid of a noise or a glint of metal, I left it there, on the very edge, and got up slowly. As we marched, a thousand thoughts flashed through my mind. There had been a cartridge in the chamber, the hammer fell, it could have been a faulty cartridge – so rare nowadays; it must have been the gun, which I had never fired. Blast the chauffeur, curse the Attaché ... but all that was now past and I must, must make up some story to tell on reaching the station.

One of them spoke good Polish and at the station I talked, and better talked. I was a poor orphan left in Budapest by a wicked uncle who escaped the war ... hunger and privation in the alien metropolis ... homesickness and loneliness ... the slow trek across Slovakia to get back to my elder sister in Poland. They listened enthralled, brought me some food and told me to rest whilst they typed the report. The station cottage did not have a cell and I stretched on the commandant's bed after slipping off my wet jacket and there, on my belt, was still hooked one grenade! – where I lost the other two God only knows. With my teeth I ripped the back edge of the mattress and slipped in the grenade and a spare clip of ammunition which I found in my trouser pocket. This near mishap brought me down to earth and I realised that, sooner or later, somebody would find in my rucksack the few hundred thousand zloties which did not quite match the character of the poor orphan. Still I had time to think about it.

Shouting and gesticulating they burst through the door dragging in the rucksack, torn brown paper, and waving thick packets of banknotes. I was up, shouting with them, touching the money, crying and cursing. It was a dirty, bearded Jew whom I met on the steps of the Polish Consulate in Budapest! They wouldn't help with travel to Poland, but he bought me a ticket to the frontier for my solemn promise of carrying the parcel of food to his family! I swore not to open it and he gave me an extra hundred zloties! The blood sucker! The speculator!

They listened, but kept fondling the bundles, counting packets, spreading them out on the bed, on the floor ... well, it looked like a fortune, a king's ransom, and only I knew that it was quickly becoming a worthless heap of coloured paper: the last moment of exchange for the new currency was only a few hours away. Still the piles of bright, unused notes represented to them untold wealth, lives of undreamed-of luxuries. They could not take their eyes off the money, could not restrain their hands from touching the treasure and it only needed from me an odd word, a half-spoken thought, before we struck a bargain. They were to keep the 'Jewish' money and, at night, they were to smuggle me across the frontier to Poland – no trouble at all as they knew all the patrols on the other side.

At dusk, after a substantial meal, when we were getting ready to go, the telephone rang. It was their headquarters ordering special vigilance and night patrols to catch, at any cost, the seventh spy of the most dangerous group which had been apprehended with an enormous haul of money. The orphan's fairy tales were blown sky-high and they were too frightened to go on with the swindle. Late that night the special convoy arrived to take me to a proper jail.

CHAPTER 13

PRISON BARS

The last vicious push sent me staggering into a cell, and before my eyes had adjusted to the murky twilight the whole band of the Engineer's 'smugglers' was all around me, shaking my hands, slapping my back. There were no strangers with us and soon I heard about the misfortunes of the group. After leaving me with the rucksacks they reached the inn where they were made welcome. In front of a roaring fire, half naked, they were drying their clothing when, together with a hot meal, in walked the gendarmes. My friends were arrested and handcuffed after a short struggle during which not one of them managed to get at the arms stacked neatly in the corner. In spite of all the shoving and slapping around they held out for three hours before taking their captors to our original resting-place. There, when nothing could be found on the trampled ground, they were really beaten up and it took a lot of time and reinforcements to discover the hidden treasure. The next day, already in prison, they were joined by my last companion who surrendered soon after parting from me. But the most important news was that the Engineer had already started negotiations with the Slovakian Intelligence Service which took over the case. It was really the same gambit as my own but on a much bigger scale: 'split the money between yourselves and let us go quietly.' The proposal was eagerly received, but its implementation was delayed by squabbles about the division of the loot whilst we waited in our cell, which was a large basement under the main building of the prison. Walls and floor were of rough stone blocks, the only light came from a hole high up in a corner of the room. Boosted up by my colleagues I saw that the unglazed, foot high and three feet wide slot was barred by vertical rods. These, though of solid steel, were not anchored in the wall, but just sunk in the thick wooden frame, a frame already rotten to the core. With my full weight on the centre bar I gave a sharp jerk and the bottom of the frame began to crack and split. But the Engineer dampened my enthusiastic efforts: 'I talked to them, I saw them. They are so greedy they won't let the money go - it's another day, or two at the most, and if we break out, there is the town to cross and twenty miles to go. Not a chance!' He was probably right though I felt like having a go. So we waited in our cold, damp cell. With a slice of coarse bread for breakfast and a lukewarm pint of starchy 'goo' for dinner we were hungry and miserable. On the third day, despite the 'independence' of Slovakia, the German Gestapo from Poland arrived to take back with them the money and all of us.

Guttural shouts of the Germans in black and silver uniforms, narrow slots of the prison van and railway coach with closely-barred windows. We were again alone but now frightened to the edge of panic. Hoarse whispered questions without answers, and waiting, anticipating the unknown future, the investigation, the questioning. The questioning to which I had to have simple and immediate answers, answers which must be remembered exactly and for ever. Jan Salski, born 1923, yes twenty-three because I am seventeen. Born in Bialystok, that's Russian zone now - impossible to check ... But I lived in Warsaw, address in a street demolished by bombing, house and flat numbers as our old address so I'll not forget. Parents' forenames, mother's maiden name just as they are, but I'll be an orphan so nobody looks for them. Background: apprentice in a garage, I know enough for that, but uneducated, a bit stupid or just simple ... And to stick to it whatever happens ... Escaped to Hungary in the first days of the war, lived in Budapest - this might be difficult, but it is the only way. The railway carriage, the agitated, frightened whispers, all faded as I repeated over and over the new story of my life. I added more and more details borrowed judiciously from my real life to ensure that I remembered without hesitation, without mistakes. It was the truth, the whole truth and nothing but the truth, truth to which I could swear and which could not be changed in the smallest detail.

The local train puffed and jolted from one whistle stop to another and in no time came to rest at the border station. Our group and some twenty other prisoners were herded across the main road to an elegant villa guarded by sentries with machine pistols. I hurried along, careful to be in the middle of the crowd, never first and certainly not at the end where slower men collected all the kicks and blows. We were pushed into a small cellar. At the top of the narrow steps was a door from which the guard called one or two names at a time and a prisoner or two ran to disappear upstairs. Then my new name was called and a man in civilian clothes led me to one of the rooms opening from the ground floor corridor. A uniformed Gestapo officer began barking questions in German: name, date of birth ... Stammering and bowing (I am seventeen, I am stupid) I murmured in Polish that I did not understand. From behind me the civilian spoke in excellent Polish asking my name and date of birth. As I answered he dictated in German to a typist sitting in a corner of the room. The officer kept strolling across the room passing me back and forth. Suddenly, turning fast, he hit me in the face and kicked as I staggered backward. The kick missed but, bumping into some desk or chair, I felt my legs swept from under me. The interpreter, hauling me up, whispered: 'They kill you if you resist!' - only then did I see behind the typist's desk the half-open door, and beyond it another German with a Lüger pointed at me. The first one started again: '*Name? Geburtstag?*'

They used whips, canes, heavy walking sticks and hobnailed boots but I knew that any change in my story would make it worse ...

The interpreter poured a jug of water over me and when my eyes opened said distinctly: 'You stupid bastard! The name on your identity card is a new one put into a washed space! They know it as well as you do. If you don't tell them your real name you will die here!'

'But Sir, this is my name! In Budapest, in the consulate, they gave me the card but I could not remember another name so they put my own on. So help me God, it's my name! How could I remember another one? Joseph and Mary my witnesses!'

The interpreter's mouth opened wide and he roared with laughter, staggering around the room in bursts of mirth. It took him minutes to translate whilst he coughed and laughed till the tears ran down his cheeks. And the Gestapo roared with him. The rest of the story - life in Budapest, trying to return and carrying a sealed parcel in exchange for guidance across Slovakia - all went quickly and without any more questions. The interpreter took the typewritten report and, giving me a pen, hissed: 'Sign here but not your real name!' - which, in the triumph and the release from tension I had almost done. Bless the man whose magnificent performance lent some verisimilitude to my otherwise unconvincing story.

I was thrust into a small cell which was already crammed to capacity with prisoners standing shoulder to shoulder. The barred and boarded windows did not give much light but one could see the motley crowd of unshaven individuals in dirty, often torn, clothing. There were many black eyes, split and swollen lips, as well as dark brown stains of dried blood in matted hair. In the corners, along the walls, small close groups held whispered conversations. Then I saw a tall figure pushing slowly towards me with quiet apologies whispered so politely that in the circumstances they sounded utterly bizarre. The voice and especially the almost Victorian turn of phrase were unmistakable: George from my own old form of Batory's College. I looked at him, caught his eye and turned away slowly. He kept pushing through the crowd and apologising profusely till, almost touching me, he continued in a stage whisper:

'I beg your pardon, Sir, from a distance I thought I had met you before but I was mistaken, I am so sorry. My name is Livsky and I beg your pardon for intruding like this!'

So he was at least under his own name, in good fettle and still used his habitually archaic language.

'Never seen you in my life. I'm Salski, a mechanic from Bialystok.' We chatted awhile and I learned that he was caught on the frontier as a 'tourist', that is, one attempting to escape westward from Poland. Every day dozens of them were arrested and locked up or sent to concentration camps. But at least they were not often interrogated and George had escaped the attentions of the Gestapo. I mentioned my new age and enquired about conditions in Poland as I had lived in Budapest since the beginning of the war – one couldn't be too careful in this crowd. I also asked how I looked and was told, to my surprise, that except for swollen lips and ear I was quite presentable. More detailed inspection revealed a lot of bruises and very wet trousers, but again there was nothing serious. This 'check up' and the chance meeting lifted my spirits considerably: I was Jan Salski, I was all right and no longer alone.

In the evening we were given some bread and water. With a lot of shoving and pushing we organised ourselves for the night. Two men with gun-shot wounds and three severely injured during interrogation were given enough room to lie flat whilst the rest, sitting or crouching, dozed fitfully.

Next morning we were handcuffed and loaded into army lorries where a long chain was passed through the cuffs and padlocked at both ends. A heavy escort delivered us to the prison in Nowy Sacz where a villainous-looking guard distributed us in pairs to already overcrowded cells. I kept sneaking through the crowd to be just behind George so that we both were pushed into one cell. After the frontier lock-up the accommodation was palatial, with only eight of us in a cell which even boasted three beds. The six inhabitants confronted us swearing and cursing – 'stupid tourists' spoiling the good life for honest people. Their leader, a big rough yokel, advanced towards me:

'You don't get food today, and the beds are ours! You kip on the floor!' – he gestured towards the corner and swung his hand to hit me in the face. I did not think or consider – my left hand grabbed his wrist whilst my right arm shot under his armpit in an elbow-breaking lock. He screamed in a high-pitched yell until I let go and he staggered back hugging the strained arm.

'We take this bed and we get food today!' I said, wondering what would happen if they rushed us. But they did not and we became friends, whilst their leader watched that we got a fair share of the bitter, black bread issued once a day.

In the morning the door opened and 'trusties' under the supervision of a heavily armed guard ladled out warm, tasteless herb-tea. They also filled with fresh water one bucket and emptied the dirty one. Then there was the long day of sitting on the beds, gossiping and listening anxiously to the sounds of the prison: the heavy tread of wardens, screams of beaten prisoners, shouted names when the guards tried to find a particular man, as nobody knew who was locked up and where. The noise of revving engines was always followed by arguments whether a new transport had arrived or departed. In the evening the door opened again and the same 'trusties' ladled out thin soup and handed over a loaf of bread. There were no towels or soap, no blankets, and we all wore the clothing in which we happened to have been arrested. Some, especially the 'tourists', retained a surprising amount of private possessions, like handkerchiefs, glasses, safety razors, sometimes pencils or even notebooks, though, of course, no valuables which had been looted long ago. Here I must do justice to the Germans and admit that the Gestapo pocketed only the best watches and gold, leaving the shoddy goods for lesser fry.

Soon I heard about George's short travels: trying to escape from Poland he had been arrested even before reaching the frontier. The sins of our cell-mates were more diverse. There were smugglers, petty thieves, a black marketeer and a murderer who was most indignant about his imprisonment because he had never touched his 'stupid bitch' and only 'done the lover'.

A week later, long after all the internal traffic of the prison had ceased, shouts echoed along the corridors and my new name was called repeatedly. I pounded on the door as was required and when it was unlocked, there, behind the warders, stood two SS-men. They marched me across the empty street to a building with the ominous sign of Gestapo District Headquarters. Our steps reverberated loudly in the deserted passages. With the muzzles of two Bergmanns poking into my back I was again feeling utterly alone, a few seconds away might be more questioning and torture ... or just the end in the stutter of pistols. The prison, with the company of George and even that of the local evildoers, suddenly seemed a home from home. Stairs, more heavy doors and a brilliantly-lit room with a young Gestapo officer at the desk.

'You took your time, didn't you!' he barked at my guards, in German of course, but then turned to me and in broken Polish asked my name. Satisfied with my answer he turned to a large door, like that of a built-in wardrobe, except that it was of steel plate and secured with two transverse bars. Unlatching the bars he opened the door and pointed:

'In you go.'

A moment of hesitation and the rising guns of the escort – I went in. Once it had been a wall-cupboard. Now it smelled horribly of urine and blood. There was enough room to stand; probably a few people could have been squashed in. The door shut, the bars dropped into their sockets, and I heard the click of padlocks. It was pitch dark and stinking. But I saw rows of light points at the top and bottom of the door – ventilation holes so that at least I would not suffocate. Sounds of steps and the holes disappeared as the light in the room was switched off. Then the slam of the outer door and dead silence of the grave. It took a considerable effort to remember that it was not the grave, at least not yet. The floor, when touched, felt sticky and I recollected that it had looked dark, coated with blood and filth, but leaning against the side wall I could squat almost comfortably. Then I went over the story of my 'new' life, examined all details again and again making sure that all fitted together coherently, and that I remembered everything. I think I slept for quite a time.

Some noise woke me up and I was standing by the time the steel door opened. I was scared, but remembered to look even more frightened and helpless than I felt. It was the young officer of yesterday but with only one SS private. He looked at me, laughed, and began to talk in German, but seeing my dejected expression and gesture of incomprehension, told his soldier to explain.

'Herr Sturmbahnführer' – his heels clicked here – 'is going on holidays and on the way will deliver you to the Cracow prison.'

In front of the building was an open, black Mercedes with the stiff, celluloid-framed SS flags on the front wings. I was put into the back and handcuffed to a solid ring fixed to the front seat. The officer got in by the side of the driver and we were off. The blue sky and the sun reflected in a thousand sparkles from each drop of the morning dew. The open road and the fresh greenery of the hedgerows. Empty fields, dark mysterious forest ... They drove very fast and, taking advantage of potholes, I pretended to slip off the seat, and with my full weight jerked the ring holding my handcuffs. I succeeded only in bruising my wrists whilst the anchor held fast without the slightest give. I must have rocked the front seat because the officer turned back to look at me. Luckily my simulation of the 'accident' was good enough and he told me to hold tight, supplementing his German with eloquent gestures.

My suit was considerably worse for wear and in spite of the sunny day I felt frozen stiff by the time we reached Cracow and stopped in the courtyard of the enormous red brick building of the Montelupi prison. Steel gates, concertinas of barbed wire crowning the surrounding wall, barred and screened windows, made plain the purpose and nature of the place. It was my first 'proper' prison with its long corridors and offices where I was searched thoroughly, listed in great, heavy ledgers and led to a cell on the second floor. However, before I could take in the new surroundings there was more commotion; a new guard unlocked the cell and took me down to another office and more questioning. There were two desks: a typist near the door and further, a big, fat German in 'civvies'. On his desk were several files and scattered papers which he appeared to study whilst I stood in front of him. After a few minutes which seemed like hours he told me to sit and began questioning me in atrocious but understandable Polish. Having obtained preliminaries of name, date of birth and address he got up, and leaning over me he started a tirade:

'You truth must tell! I everything know. I real German-born but expert on Poland and Hungary am! Live Poland, speak Hungary.' He stopped and I, judging his intelligence and expertise by the language, risked the only sentence I knew in Hungarian to the effect that I am a Pole but long live Hungary!

'Yes, yes,' he answered in Polish, 'but you must only Polish speak!' – and now I knew he did not have a clue. The interview lasted a couple of hours with only two dangerous moments when I was slapped about a bit, but luckily inexpertly and not seriously. The first problem arose from his question about my crossing point from Poland to Hungary at the beginning of the war. He had a map and I knew neither the area nor the roads.

'But Sir, I don't know. How could I? I told you that our best customer was taking his family and wanted a mechanic to go with him just in case, so I went for a lark. But he was scared of the crowded roads and made me drive. He said, from a map, where to go. I'm only seventeen but I drove for two days. Never a scratch on his Chevrolet through all the jams and the rush! I can work for you! I drive perfect, never stopped, never a bump, and I wash the car too!'

He repeatedly shouted: 'Where you frontier cross?' and I replied: 'I'll work for you!' till at last he gave up in sheer exhaustion. Later, to check on my claimed stay in Budapest, he asked me to describe in detail the uniform of a Hungarian policeman whilst I could not even recollect the colour:

'Sir, policeman – nothing, they are a stupid lot! But have you seen their firemen? Aren't they comic with their brass helmets and all the medals – everyone with medals!'

He slapped me but I kept on fast and furious about anything at all, losing him in obviously unfamiliar language, throwing in all the idioms, school slang and crudity of an uneducated, simple garage mechanic. He asked about prices of bread and butter. I replied with a detailed description of Hungarian confectionery and especially the marvellous cream cakes. But at the end I got away with my whole story when he patted me on the head:

'You talk too much, but you good boy!' – and we both signed the lengthy statement. I had planned late but carefully; even when outflanked I had stuck to my guns; I had done my best and it was just good enough.

The eighteen by twelve foot cell was to be my home for the next six months. Whitewashed walls, scrubbed wooden floor, two large windows, deal table and bench. In one corner was a brown painted contraption resembling a telephone booth and containing two dirty buckets emptied by ourselves twice daily. We all stood to attention with one guard at the open cell door whilst the other warder, shouting 'on the double', supervised two prisoners who ran with the buckets to the 'wash room' at the far end of the corridor. They returned with the dirty buckets emptied and two 'clean' ones full of water which had to last the next twenty-four hours for ablutions, washing of eating utensils and drinking. In the cell, by the side of the 'convenience' was a galvanised tank over a washing trough, all mounted on four rickety legs. Further on was a shelf on which the enamelled bowls, one per head, were neatly stacked. On the same shelf was also a glass meant for drinking water but used exclusively for honing a single razor-blade which served all of us once a week when, on Saturday, we were required to be clean-shaven though no official provision was made for the execution of this order. Along the wall were stacked straw palliasses, four of them, as the cell was designated as a four-men unit though it housed up to fifteen of us for long periods of time. The coarse sacks had been once filled with straw but in my time they contained only a fibrous dust which, if shaken carefully, could be spread into an even layer of an inch thickness. There were also four blankets, thin, worn and moth-eaten but still highly desirable in spring and autumn, whilst even during summer nights it could be miserably cold in the unheated building. The windows opened inwards leaving in the frame a heavy grating of thick steel bars. Outside this was the 'basket' – a topless box of heavy sheet metal with slides sloping out to provide light, but shutting off all view and preventing signals to the outer world or other cells.

The prisoners were a chance cross-section of the occupied country where already the 'respectable' were found in prison as often as the dregs of society and more often than the 'professionals' who were adept in avoiding capture. The place was not unlike a hotel with 'casuals' dropping in for a couple of days just like commercial travellers. The permanent residents like myself welcomed them, feeling pride of ownership and responsibility for the tone of the place – after all, it was our cell.

My own entry into this little group was facilitated by the Gestapo interrogation which commanded the unreserved sympathy and help of everyone, as they all knew only too well what it implied. Thus the first questions were not concerned with my name, origin or crime but simply how badly was I hurt and how could they help. I was offered a drink of some cold 'coffee' saved from the morning issue as well as the real treasure of a cigarette. I was grateful for the coffee and, as a non-smoker, refused the 'gasper' to the great relief of the three joint owners. No, I was not hurt, as after an interrogation a swollen ear and a split lip could not be considered an injury. I gave my name and, in turn, they all introduced themselves. There was a little podgy butcher and sausage-maker expecting for the last three months to be released any day. He had been incarcerated for just one little pig that somehow died without proper permission from the authority. As a master of his trade he liked nothing better than to talk of all the intricacies of his work with lips smacking at detailed descriptions of cold meats, bacon and various smoked sausages. With unlimited time at our disposal I often listened to him, learning the innermost secrets of the trade like 'watering' of sausages for village feasts and weddings. The 'heavy sausage' was only served after the company was well in their cups: 'and never leave any lying about for the buggers to taste next day – they would break your head and refuse to pay up.' As a prosperous shopkeeper he avoided the two pickpockets locked up with us: 'Don't talk to this scum, boy. I'll find a place for you in my shop when we get out of this here.' This pair of thin, half-starved individuals – the master and his 'herder' (one who bumped into people or created a 'crowd') were swept into prison from the university where they pursued their trade on one unfortunate day. 'You just can't trust anybody these days! Damned professors have no money in their wallets and an honest man gets picked up for being near them!' There were also a couple of students suspected of communist sympathies and considering themselves far above the uneducated plebs. These I gave a wide berth as they might have spotted any incongruities between my supposed background and an odd sophisticated word that I might let slip inadvertently. There was a strange man in the uniform of the Polish army but claiming to be a

Czech. He was suspected of being a Gestapo informer and had a hard life in the cell without much chance of finding out anything about the others. There were also two Ukrainians, both seriously injured in repeated Gestapo interrogations. Both were dark, uncouth and silent. They spoke little Polish and their Ukrainian speech reminded me of my war in the east. But in spite of my prejudice, after seeing their battered hands with torn nails I tried to tend their wounds though, with lack of materials let alone disinfectants or other medicaments, there was little I could do. They were pathetically grateful and I felt really sorry when, a fortnight later, they did not return from the next session with the Gestapo. The last inmate at the time of my arrival was a young man with mousey hair and staring blue eyes, a silent man wedged hard into a corner, immovable and completely mad. I was told that he had been just an ordinary man till a month previously, when he was carried back in his present state from an interrogation. Soon he was taken out at night and that was the last we knew of him – there was not even the name to scratch on the wall.

Days passed slowly, monotonously. New people came and went, some so colourless that, a week later, one could not recollect them at all. Others had personalities which remained etched for ever in one's memory. The first of these was an old lag of a housebreaker, a grim man who taught us a lot. On arrival he half undressed and slowly began to extract from various seams of his underpants and shirt objects of immense value. There were about six safety matches, a piece of friction pad for them and two pieces of pencil lead. His dilapidated shoes gave up a razor blade, one lighter flint and a needle which I was to inherit later. The needle was especially valuable on Saturdays when the scrubbing of the floor resulted in several splinters which we had great difficulty in extracting from our fingers. With the blade he proceeded to unpick various patches sewn on his underwear and these yielded a crop of cigarette papers and relatively clean rags. All his pockets, jacket lining and especially trouser turn-ups carried an inordinate amount of fluff which he sifted and winnowed until he was left with a few ounces of tobacco. After this auspicious beginning he ingeniously hid all the treasures around the bare, inhospitable cell so that they survived intact the periodic searches carried out by the warders.

'And if any of you bourgeois-intelligentsia think of telling the screws, think again; I would get it in the neck, but I would sure do you in later!'

But later we became friends and he greatly advanced our education. He began with the windows which we, the rank amateurs, dismissed because of the covering metal baskets. He pointed to us cracks between the surface of the outer wall and the basket flange. Then, instituting a door-watch for wandering guards, he proceeded to tap on the metal cover till a light drumming answered his signals. Now, calling through the cracks in a stage whisper ('Project your voice, you stupid clot, don't just yell!') he conversed with inmates on our sides to the left and right as well as with those above and below. Similarly he showed us in the 'telephone-booth-convenience' the little opening of a ventilation shaft which, after the removal of a grid, allowed not only talking 'up' and 'down' but also sending small objects tied to a thread unravelled from one of the blankets. Though I still did not smoke I also learned from him how to 'make fire'. First, all matches were soaked, so that each could be split longitudinally in four without crumbling the head. After drying, one quarter-match was used to ignite and char a piece of linen rag which was quickly extinguished and stored in a small tinder box. The flint was set into a minute board broken off from the washroom when the guard's attention was momentarily distracted by a put-up fight. From the same source came a few shards of a broken window pane. With a glass fragment scraped along the board one struck a spark from the flint and caught it in the tinder which was nursed by blowing till a cigarette could be lit. Much later, when all the matches and tinder were used up, I gained fame throughout the prison as an inventor and public benefactor! I managed to steal a clear electric bulb of spherical shape, and with great care hammered the back of it till only the plain glass envelope was left. This, when filled with water, made a lens good enough to concentrate sunlight on the tip of a cigarette till it smoked and lit. The gossip about the end of this invention reached me long after I had left prison. The contraption worked satisfactorily in summer and autumn but with the weak winter sun it did not provide enough heat and the smokers tried to improve it by using hot coffee instead of water. As the murky brown spot of light did not even feel warm on the hand it was decided that the magic failed soon after my departure from the scene!

On 25 June the quiet silence of the prison was broken by the distant blare of martial music from the loudspeakers in the streets. We all froze, listening intently to the joyful dancing notes – somebody breathed softly the incredible word – 'Marseillaise'. Somebody shouted, a few picked up the melody: '*Marchons, marchons, formez la bataillon ...*' There was noise on the corridors, snatches of words from the yard, from the adjoining cells. Somebody called that the French had broken through and were entering Cracow. My heart beat wildly but I could not believe it, I knew it was some trick of the bloody Krauts. Then louder than ever erupted the most hateful tune of 'Germany over all, Germany over the world ...' And soon, through the windows, through the walls, through the ventilation shafts came the news: the French have surrendered, the war is over. But I did not believe it any more than I did the first joyous shouts. The war was going on and we would win whatever and whenever, and I would survive and be there. Hatred of the Germans and my love of Princess fused into a fanatical obsession with survival, the idea which was to stay with me till the end came many years later.

The same evening shouts echoed again when herds of new and already well-beaten prisoners were distributed throughout the overcrowded cells. These were the people who had reacted spontaneously to the tune of the Marseillaise and we got our share of them in the bloody but unbowed figure of a young university lecturer. It took me a month of surreptitious study before I was sure of his bona fides. Only then we became good friends. He joined me in the physical exercises that I practised daily in spite of the constant hunger and inadequate food, and I was delighted to learn chess which as a 'master of Cracow' he played at tournament level. We began by laboriously scratching a chess-board on the surface of the table and then thought of the men. Here our 'old-lag' offered all the necessary advice. Hunger or not, we had to save enough bread, work it into a soft pliable dough and beg or steal some soap to add to the mix – 'otherwise some greedy bastard will eat it at night!' Slowly, gradually we manufactured a full brown-grey set and started on the dark one which had to be chewed as this process turned it ebony black in a couple of days (even today I still don't know whether it was a chemical reaction or just dirt licked off our own fingers). Still, in a few months of daily 'tutorials' I became good enough to play with him on equal terms, especially as I concentrated better whilst he was often distracted by the unpleasant itch unavoidable in the filthy environment with millions of lice crawling in everybody's clothing.

My own suit was becoming more and more threadbare and I decided to make a new one. As there was, of course, no fabric available I settled on combining two existing garments. The long-vanished Czech left behind a good tunic of the Polish uniform and from another cell I managed to scrounge a torn and blood-stained sports jacket of orange-brown colour. I cut away the high collar of the tunic and replaced it with the open one from the 'bookie's' jacket including the extremely wide lapels. Other bits of the fabric provided facings for the pockets and cuffs as well as covers for the military buttons. The most laborious job was not the actual sewing but unpicking the machined seams to unravel the old threads without breaking or tangling them too much. The resulting creation was somewhat gaudy with the violent orange-brown decorating the spring green of the Polish khaki. But the garment fitted me well and was much warmer than the old suit.

I also spent a considerable time in engraving intricate designs on a plastic soap-box which I had been allowed to keep. As the needle was too precious for this task, I used a small shard of glass and covered all sides of the lid before leaving the prison. Later the box went into the 'prisoner's effects' bag, which, with usual German thoroughness, was sent to my next-of-kin when the stores became too full. As it was posted without explanation it was taken as a sign of my death and caused a lot of unnecessary sorrow and heartbreak to Princess and my family.

The time flowed slowly but these diversions allowed me to live almost normally without endless brooding and despair. I also slept well when most of the prisoners tossed and turned on hard floors listening with dread to the frequent noise of the lorries taking away to the place of execution those no longer required by the Gestapo. In my time at Montelupi very few men were released, as once the German machine seized a political suspect he was usually shot at the end of the investigation, or, if found innocent, then, in the company of small-time criminals, was disposed of to a concentration camp.

Through surreptitious gossip, I learned more of my smuggling colleagues. Apparently, for a long time they maintained that the money was for the Red Cross but under unrelenting questions, to avoid more beatings, one of them mentioned the name of an already dead man from the Polish underground. This, of course, only increased the pressure and soon he admitted all sorts of anti-German activities whilst the investigation picked up new momentum, spreading wider and wider. However, my own performance must have really been good as I was never again questioned.

The prison was overflowing when a new man was brought to our cell, a tall, blond Finn with almost black eyes and a quiet, retiring disposition. He was the most enigmatic figure of all that I met there. He was supposed to speak only Finnish and Hungarian and never betrayed any knowledge of even single words of other languages. On the other hand his exceptional intelligence allowed us to have long and complex 'conversations' using only signs and gestures, rarely aided by diagrams drawn on the floor with a wetted finger. It soon emerged that he was a tailor returning from a visit to his relatives in Hungary. He described his own detached house in Finland and 'told' me a lot of his single but merry life there. He was obviously a good skier and we shared memories of snowy adventures. The thoroughness of these wordless communications was best illustrated by the story of the purple birth-mark on his forearm. This was supposedly the result of a mulberry dropping unexpectedly on to the forearm of his mother in pregnancy. The mulberry caused us both a lot of problems but going through China by pulling the outer corners of his eyes, and ladies' dresses which as a tailor he demonstrated brilliantly, we finally arrived at caterpillars, silk and mulberries. Tailoring he knew, his Finnish origin seemed likely, but the education, knowledge and intelligence which he displayed seemed far in excess of that expected of a provincial tailor. Of course I observed him for a long time before making any approach and was doubly careful as he had never been roughed-up by the Gestapo.

It was possible, though always difficult and dangerous, to pass a message to the outside world, and I was not prepared to risk my life for a chance of receiving food parcels. But 'the Finn', always sure of his ultimate release, seemed to provide an opportunity which, after several months with him, I decided to take. We never talked in the real sense of the word and I was not going to write anything, but 'the Finn' was released and some time later an unsigned message was dropped through Princess's letter box. It was a scrap of paper with pencilled words in capital letters:

'YOUR CAT CALLED SALSKI SEEN RECENTLY IN MONTELUPI.'

But by then I was already in a transport dreaded only a little less than the one to the place of execution.

CHAPTER 14

THE BOTTOM OF THE ABYSS

The increasing frequency of transports affected us all as night after night we listened to the revving engines. The convoys leaving before midnight went to the place of execution whilst the later ones rolled to Auschwitz - the place of ultimate horror and slow death. Then came the night when I was called before dawn. In the yard there were forty of us, and the warders, always so rough and brutal, for once looked on us with compassion and offered gallons of herb 'tea'. Then, handcuffed and chained, we were herded into two trucks.

In a few hours the trucks stopped, the tail-boards were dropped and the raucous shouts of *'Raus! Alles raus! Schnell!'* were followed immediately by the sound of blows and screams. I jumped down from the high deck on to a pile of squirming bodies and ran to the main group of prisoners. Kicking and shouting, more SS-men waded into the heap of bodies. The first lorry was already empty except for four prisoners who slowly and ineptly were dragging out the last two men. They tried to lower the bodies gently but the limp bundles slipped through their hands and flopped to the ground like soft, wet rags. One was an emaciated young Jew with red hair and sideboards framing an almost transparent face. The other, smothered in tattered black robes, was a priest, and a new shiver of horror ran through our group whilst the guards roared with laughter. Somebody whispered that the two men had cut their wrists during the last journey.

On a strip of grass we stood to attention facing a blank wall. Behind us a pair of SS-men strolled to and fro talking desultorily. The first hour or two they walked close to our line hitting anybody who moved, but now, tired or bored, they paid us little attention. Here and there I heard subdued whispers: after an inordinate amount of early morning 'tea' we all were in the same predicament and I, for one, certainly could not hold any longer. A quick glance behind – the uniforms far away at the other end. Careful not to move my body I undid my fly and – oh God, what a relief – took care not to make a pool in front. Angry whispers hissed around me asking what I was doing and did I want us all killed, but I finished and stood quietly. Relieved after hours of intense concentration to contain the rising pressure and pain, I felt tranquil, again capable of thought and of observation. Blank wall in front, wide road behind, barbed wire fence on the left. To the right were brick buildings surrounding a large empty square. A few silhouettes flitted like ghosts at the edge of my vision. Before I could see more all hell broke loose at the far end of our line. Shouts, blows, screams and the burst of a sub-machine gun. We were ordered to turn about and the red-faced guard roared in Polish with a hard Silesian accent: 'You filthy Polish swine! I'll teach you to piss here! I'll let all the water out of you, you bloody bastards!' – his automatic pistol traversed our line as if seeking the next victim – 'About turn!' And we stood very still for hours, for ever more.

In the late afternoon, carrying four corpses, we marched to a drab building where we were ordered to strip and wash under the freezingly cold showers. There were no SS-men but brutal German prisoners supervised, kicking and beating more effectively than the SS thugs. In the next room our heads were clipped to the skin and all body hair shaved off whilst we were drenched with some de-lousing fluid which felt like living fire. Then we got new clothing: a pair of socks, a thin shirt and underpants, a pair of trousers, a jacket and a cap of grey and blue striped fabric. Of our own possessions we were allowed to keep shoes and belts, and, those who had them, spectacles and spoons. At last we were listed on various cards and exchanged our names for numbers stamped on two strips of white fabric with a red triangle which were to be sewn on the jacket and on the trousers. We were now the 'prisoners in protective custody' of the Concentration Camp Auschwitz. I became number 6643 which I was never to forget.

Clutching our numbers, we were led to one of the brick buildings surrounding the square: 'Block eight, and don't forget it, you scum!' The 'block-elder', the prisoner in charge of the building and all its inhabitants, welcomed us with a short speech about working hard so that we might live for some time, and 'don't steal' he finished. Then, to drive home this point, he ordered his minions to bring the thief. Two well-fed prisoners with black arm-bands dragged in a thin, miserable looking man and handed to the boss a pick-axe handle. 'He stole bread and bread is life. He should hang, but we are merciful to a young bugger on his first offence. Stretch him across the stool!' – and he laid into the man's behind. The terrible screams faded into gurgling moans whilst the blows continued with a hollow sound as if he were beating an empty cardboard container.

We were allotted to one of the rooms and, as there was no bread for the newcomers, we were given as much thin soup as we could drink. Then there was just enough time to sew on our numbers, using the two communal needles, and to prepare for the night our palliasses of straw dust which were spread all over the floor. We lay down in rows packed so tightly that all had to lie on the same side and on command turn round together. Sleep in these conditions seemed impossible and I tried to marshal the memories of the day's events.

There had been so much of the bizarre and unbelievable. The slack, dead bodies, the freezing showers, the screams of the thief, all remained vague and mixed up. Somebody pounded my back growling: 'Turn! Turn you stupid git!' Later, after all the soup, I had to go to the loo, treading carefully, but still trampling on the sleeping bodies that cursed and hit out blindly. The loo was all wet and stinking, the return journey was just as difficult and there was no place left to lie down. I lost my balance and fell on top of the tightly packed row. More curses, ineffective fists flailing around me and I sank slowly between two squirming men. Still later everything was moving and heaving in time with the measured boom of a distant gong, the harsh, bright bulb lit up the centre of the ceiling. The next day had begun.

Trying to pull on my trousers, I blessed the man who last night had taught me to roll my clothing into one tight bundle and to tie the shoes round my neck: some of the newcomers from my transport were already barefooted and could not find a trace of their shoes! Then the shouts urging us to get out and wash were followed by the sound of blows and I was swept out with the surging crowd. The people streamed out of the block and scattered into milling groups which disappeared in the pre-dawn darkness of the camp streets. I tried to follow those around me, lost them, and with another group barged into a dense mob surrounding the big hand-pump: the only well for some five thousand people because the other one was reserved for the use of the kitchen. Somebody finished rubbing his face with a handful of water thick with dirt: 'Want it boy? Where is your dixie? – Oh, have it like that!' – and he poured the thick liquid into my outstretched palms so that I could 'wash' myself with this tenth-hand water. Individual shadows, and small groups flowed back into the barracks and I followed, finding my way as I had remembered to look over my shoulder and to memorise the direction for 'home'. I had just made it to my room as the black 'coffee' was ladled out, a litre per head. We stood sipping the bitter fluid, choking on the scalding mouthfuls but trying to get it all down before the gong began beating again.

In the grey light of dawn the flowing crowd elongated into a rectangle ten ranks deep, with the tallest men on the right and the smallest on the left. Our block-elder stood in front whilst his second-in-command with the help of hall-bosses pushed and pulled, shouted and kicked, moulding the mass into a perfect geometrical pattern. Then the block secretary began counting carefully the front men, ten for each file. At the very end laid out neatly were three corpses from the last night. The secretary checked the numbers with the figures on his pad, called to the elder and together they counted again whilst from the gate and the offices approached slowly an SS-man, the Block-Führer in charge of several barracks. The elder came to attention and, when the Block-Führer approached, began barking commands: '*Achtung*! Caps off!' No, the caps, flapping against the thighs, did not make enough noise, begin again ... Only when nothing more could be faulted did he report the number of prisoners in his barrack – it did not matter whether they were dead or alive, only the total number of bodies was important. The SS-man counted us slowly, carefully, and from his frowns and curses it was obvious that the numbers did not agree. He started again, his fingers twitching till both fists were clenched and another mark was scored on his clipboard. At last the count tallied: '*Alles stimt!*' (all fits), and the man moved away to count other barracks. We stood to attention waiting till all the sums were laboriously gathered and reported to the Lager-Führer, the NCO in charge. The morning roll-calls usually tallied correctly and the gong sounded again. With the first stroke the orderly ranks exploded and in a free-for-all everybody rushed to form new groups – the working detachments – '*Arbeits Commandos*'. Most of the prisoners of our block belonged to the demolition group and soon I stood with them in a column of a few hundred men marshalled now five abreast and again counted over and over by the foremen and the capos. As the block-elders ruled inside the camp, so during the work time the capos were the absolute masters of the men in their charge. Bewildered by the last rush I just managed to keep in step when the column started its progress towards the camp gates, past the orchestra playing German marching tunes. The capo reported the 'commando' at the gates, the duty SS-men counted the passing hundreds and so we went to work.

After long months inside a prison cell I suddenly stepped into another world. There, only a few yards from the edge of the road, was grass, some bushes, real trees. The grey of the grass was splashed with mud thrown by the passing columns, the leaves were already shrinking and falling in the cold November morning. I saw this new world, the free and living world, which I had almost forgotten. But between us and this other world were the hated field-grey uniforms and the cocked automatic pistols.

We stopped, collected tools from a solitary hut standing amongst the piles of broken brick and uprooted trees, the last remaining fragment of a large manor now razed to the ground. A foreman led us through an orchard to a neat little cottage. Another detachment was already hacking down old trees. The red bark of cherries, the smooth grey of the apple branches and the vivid orange wood of the pears, all was mown down. We, with pickaxes and heavy sledge-hammers, set about the house. The newly painted window frames and carved oak doors splintered easily and were carted away by the unending stream of prisoners. A few hundred yards away roaring bonfires consumed frames, shingles and furniture. We were just the spearhead of hundreds who carried away bricks and rubble, and others armed with spades, who left behind only a churned sea of mud: the miles of desert into which the growing camp spread further and further, like a cancer devouring the quiet countryside. With the army training and the pioneering experience of scout camps I swung the sledge-hammer in a full circle and hit unerringly the chisel to the intense relief of the holder. I soon discovered that with a bit of common sense, let alone knowledge of structures, I could direct others so that the work became easier and quicker. I kept my eyes open and, without asking, learned about the set-up. The foremen were no experts at demolition, but, like the capos, held their rank because they knew German and enjoyed beating up other prisoners. The SS soldiers in passing kicked or hit any prisoner who did not get out of the way, and, strutting about, looked for anybody who could be faulted. It was prohibited to walk, as one was expected to run smartly; it was prohibited to talk; it was prohibited to be idle. One could be had for not working hard enough, or accused of damaging tools by working too fast. Prisoners were beaten up for relieving themselves in public or shot for 'attempting to escape' if they tried to do it behind some bushes. Beating could be anything from a single, casual backhander, to an 'official' ten, or a hundred, strokes delivered by foremen, capos or the supermen of the SS. Still, there were a few dozen of them and thousands of us so that with a little foresight, care and a pinch of luck, one had a good chance to avoid the fatal attention of the authorities.

At noon we marched back to camp for another roll-call and a litre of soup per head. Then back to work till dusk. The evening roll-call was always the worst. There were changes of numbers caused by the addition of new transports and subtraction of corpses dispatched to the crematorium. There was endless waiting for working groups delayed by a long march. So we stood in rigid formations, often to attention and without caps for long hours whilst 'tea' or evening soup was cooling ... But my first day passed well with the roll-call lasting only an hour. I was called from the ranks by the block secretary, given my bread ration and a slip of paper: a transfer to block five, the one for 'juvenile delinquents' - after all I was only seventeen. But, if I had expected any privileges to be accorded to the young, I was sadly disappointed. The unbelievable German love of perfect order called for such classification, but once the distinction was made it was enough. The new block was the same as the other only more crowded. The rules, the discipline, the functionaries appointed from the German professional criminals, were exactly the same as in other blocks. Ten or twelve hours of continuous work was hard enough. The additional hours of standing to attention at the three daily roll-calls was exhausting. The totally inadequate, often cold food and appalling sleeping conditions were unbearable. But on top of it all there was the unceasing threat of punishment, the need for constant vigilance, of watching out for soldiers, the capos, the block elders. At meals, such as they were, you had to look sharp or lose your portion to unscrupulous prisoners who responded first to the call of your number. The lack of space and privacy in the milling crowds created more stress and strain. There was no time, no circumstance in which one could get to know and befriend individual people. Individuals ceased to exist: it was just 'them' and 'us'. But here 'they' were not only Hitler's heroes of the super race. The division encompassed all Germans and especially those in uniforms like ours but clean and pressed. Whether they carried the red triangles of the 'politicals', the green of the professional criminals, or pink for homosexuals, they were rosy cheeked, well fed and ruthless sadists. On the other side was the terror-stricken mass of numbers without names, without distinguishing features in grey, exhausted faces, bowed heads and shuffling gait. On their breasts the red triangles with the black letter P, P for Poles.

Cruel, identical days followed one another. With no watches, no calendars, the passage of time was marked only by the shortening daylight and the falling temperature. Without these signs of approaching winter one could believe in a still worse hell of only one, same day repeating itself over and over for ever - like the gramophone needle stuck in the same groove and replaying the invariable pattern of roll-call and cold, work and hunger, rain and mud. Only the nights provided a short, uncomfortable respite from tension and fear.

But somehow, slowly and unbelievably, one began to adapt, to get acclimatised. Guarding one's meagre possessions became automatic, just tie everything into a compact bundle and hit hard if an anonymous hand gropes for it in the darkness. Get up quickly with the first stroke of the gong and run to the pump to secure a dixie of third-hand water. Swallow the scalding tea and get out before the hall-boss starts laying about with his rubber hose. Find your place and stand quietly for the roll-call and kick any blunderer disrupting the ranks. At work secure the tool with a smooth handle, hang on to it and don't argue but hit first anybody trying to take it off you. And always, but always, watch out for the SS-men, for the capos, and work harder under their gaze. Be submissive, helpful, be NICE to them, don't ever let them see what you know, because you know that they are shit, manure which you will plough under when the time comes. And don't think 'when' - in a year, in two, in ten, but it will come. Now just live through this day.

Survival became harder with the colder weather and the incessant rain. The cold was bearable and not worth the risk of stealing an empty cement bag (thick tarred paper) which some prisoners stuffed between their underwear and outer clothing. The paper helped but, if discovered, caused draconian punishment for theft of government property. At work we were guarded by a ring of watch towers with machine guns and alert crews.

As our demolition progressed, the towers had to be shifted further, and even a hundred men allotted to this task had a hell of a job made more awkward by the barbed wire wrapped round the tower legs. All the 'authorities' would gather round shouting contradictory orders and laying into the crowd of prisoners with whatever came to hand. On my right, a powerful man on his first day in the camp strove hard to lift and carry but, felled by the blow of a foreman's spade, was left to die in the mud. I saw that the harder one worked the shorter one lived, and so I concentrated on acting. Holding my breath I would become beetroot red, puff myself up and emit a series of heavy grunts. The next time the tower swayed dangerously and stopped, the SS-man in charge pulled me out of the crowd and, patting my shoulder, yelled at them that, if they worked half as hard as I, the job would be finished in no time; then he ordered me to sit and rest as I had done enough! From then on I specialised in looking as if I were working when doing hardly anything. But about hunger I could do nothing, though I realised that it might be the factor in deciding between life and death. Looking and learning about the camp, I became aware that in some working groups, like those in 'agriculture', there were chances of stealing food, but this was infinitely far away from my occupation and position. The immediate problem was my blistered hands which after six months in prison had become soft and did not take kindly to the rough work. Without a chance to rest, the blisters spread, became infected and very painful. One could try the hospital but there were rumours that even going near it one could be caught and sent to the crematorium. However, two men from our barrack went there in despair and from them I learned enough to investigate further. The idea of a hospital was similar to that of the young offenders block. Like the latter it stemmed from the inanely Germanic 'order must reign'. Thousands of men locked up and worked to death, deprived of food, freedom and self respect - they were given a hospital! But a hospital with hardly any means of curing people. On the other hand, the hospital required doctors, whilst the German members of this noble profession, like the rest of the nation, supported Hitler and so were not in the camps. Inevitably, Polish doctors were given the posts and soon almost all the hospital crew was Polish. In spite of the close supervision by the SS, the hospital became our stronghold and, in a small way, a glimmer of hope in this ocean of misery. The rare admissions were controlled by an SS NCO, but out-patients were cared for by our personnel. With a few bandages, iodine substitute, and some jars of ointments, there was little they could do for the dozens of seriously injured prisoners. The overworked orderly attending to me shrugged his shoulders, painted my hands with the vivid red mercurochrome disinfectant, and put round them a few turns of a paper bandage which lasted a couple of hours.

The incessant labour was interrupted every seven days for half a Sunday. The 'free' period was not given to idleness. Mud had to be scraped off shoes and uniforms, hair longer than a quarter inch had to be shorn again and everybody had to be shaved – woe to him who did not pass the evening inspection. With a couple of needles for a hundred prisoners, with a few barbers shaving the whole block of inmates, one had to queue for interminable hours and either pay with a precious crust of one's own bread portion, or be scraped without soap by the bluntest cut-throat razor. At intervals of four weeks the prisoners were allowed to send home a postcard obtainable from the camp shop for tokens issued instead of the real money sent from home. The impecunious, like myself, had to give for a postcard a daily bread ration. We could write only to the next of kin, and true to my assumed orphan state, I had given Irka's address. It was compulsory to write in German, in large script, and say that one was well. This cost more food for translation as very few of us knew German. Even with all these restrictions it was easy for me to identify myself with the new name by a few words recollecting some fragment of our courtship. And, in occupied Poland, even a child would understand the new name and the reason for it.

Heavy clay sodden with continuous rain was kneaded by countless feet into deep mud. Soon, in the cold winter of south Poland, it set rock-hard in uneven, convoluted ruts. Heavy falls of snow covered the earth, the camp and the ranks of prisoners standing motionless for long hours of roll-calls. The authorities acknowledged the winter by the issue of sweaters, overcoats and gloves. But the sleeveless rayon pullovers provided less warmth than a shirt, and the 'overcoats', fashioned like loose dressing gowns, were as thin and cold as the basic uniforms. The gloves, or rather mittens, were really important in preventing frost-bite. Mass-produced from old rags, they disintegrated in a few days if used at work, but if one did not wear them continuously, one's hands became chafed with the skin cracking and splitting into deep wounds.

Last summer I would not have believed that anybody could live in the conditions of the camp. Last autumn I would not have believed that prisoners could suffer more, could become more apathetic, could reach the point when blows and kicks were not avoided, sometimes not felt. The number of corpses laid out daily at the left wings of the roll-call formations increased from one or two to a dozen or more. In the darkness of the early mornings, when the masses surged towards the well, there were more and more individuals heading in the opposite direction. They approached the brilliantly-lit ten-foot strip of no-man's-land separating the camp from the electrified fence and stepped over the single strand of warning wire. Some tried to reach and grasp the high-tension fence, but most just stood still to ensure that the shots from the dark towers above would bring an immediate and final release.

It was after the worst of winter that I fell ill. The catarrh and cough were just normal and nobody took any notice of a sore throat or a headache. I had them all but also felt hot, so hot that I could not bear the tightly buttoned uniform. My eyes refused to focus, and darkness crept from all sides. Then I woke up in a hospital bunk with everything around me looking foggy and senseless. I did not know what was happening nor where, but vaguely remembered that name and age had to be watched. However, details of the secrets eluded my muddled mind so that I just clamped my teeth and did not speak at all. Somebody tried to take my bread and I fought silently, somebody tried to ladle soup into me, soup I did not want, so I fought again. Grey time, not divided into days or nights, dragged endlessly. Then my whole body erupted in boils and sores. It was all pain and unbearable itch. Big boils and small boils, baths in filthy overheated water with permanganate of potash. And hunger, growing hunger. The hospital room filled solid with three-tier bunks, narrow, hard and uncomfortable, but real bunks with no more than two of us per bunk of almost two and a half foot width. There, from the dim, unrealistic background emerged Uncle Edmund. He could not walk and two orderlies half dragged him to see me. After the Gestapo had smashed his kidneys he was dying slowly in spite of all the help that our people could give. Edmund died soon and some time later I was discharged, a staggering skeleton less than half my normal weight, with large ulcers on both legs.

Thin, emaciated prisoners in the last stages of their life were always cold and so weak that their attempts at keeping warm were ineffective slow movements, half bowing, half shuddering. These cadaverous figures and their unco-ordinated movements were likened by the semi-literate guards to the dried-up desert nomads at their Muslim prayers – hence the nickname 'mussulmen'. These mussulmen, people completely destroyed physically and mentally, no longer quite human, were despised, shunned and rejected. Now, I too was a mussulman and, like the others, was automatically allotted to the 'light work'. Day in, day out, I cut and split logs, getting weaker and weaker. After a few endless and hopeless months I made a superhuman effort and, claiming to be an expert gardener, bamboozled some foreman to take me into the agricultural working group. There I consumed masses of seedlings: cabbage, beetroot, anything I could safely lay my hands on. Unfortunately, my inability to push a wheel-barrow or carry heavy cases of seedlings proved my undoing and soon I was kicked out to another group where we were just knocking mortar off old bricks. Like other mussulmen I suffered from continuous diarrhoea and, time after time, contracted scabies which was unavoidable in the filthy, overcrowded conditions. When walking, I tended to stagger like a drunkard, even standing up I was likely to collapse in a heap, but deep inside I was still utterly determined to survive. 'Determined' is not the right word, it was no longer a logical thought and the will to carry it through. It was a vague memory of the infinitely distant past, of home, of Princess's golden hair: the memory of some irrevocable decision taken long ago and now crystallised into fanatical belief. It was not just love and faith, but also my overpowering hatred of the German race and the inflexible need of resistance and revenge. Not really revenge – just the necessity to kill them all so that there would be no more rows of corpses, no mussulmen, no camps. But the camp continued unchanged. The late autumn brought longer and longer roll-calls when we stood unmoving a whole night, to go back to work next day without food or sleep. The second winter covered with snow the living and the dead. On the roll-call square, by the side of a gibbet with swaying corpses, was erected a large fir tree to celebrate Christmas. There, between the gibbet and the tree stood the camp commandant. He wished us all a Happy Christmas and finished his speech with a stern reminder that the camp food and work allowed six months of life: 'He who lives longer cheats and steals or has others stealing for him!' My own six months had already lasted over a year, but now the end seemed perilously close. The longer survival could only be thought of by those with really 'good' work.

A few lucky craftsmen were engaged in their own trades. Cabinetmakers produced beautiful furniture for the camp commandant and other SS officers. Electricians, like the plumbers, maintained the camp services, whilst the 'garage-men' serviced a fleet of SS cars and lorries. All these men were massed in the 'workshop' group. They were not only tolerated for their skills, but were also considered necessary for the smooth functioning of the camp. So they were allowed to work at their own pace, and in the camp their soup was thicker and ladled out with considerable largesse. Initially only the prisoners of German nationality were allotted to these coveted jobs, but now the camp was slowly changing. With the growing demand a few Poles found their way into the good jobs and then the SS bosses saw that the Polish craftsmen were more resourceful in the circumstances of inadequate supplies. But far more important to all concerned was the fact that the Poles caught in any 'unofficial' work or transaction suffered their punishment with gritted teeth but never 'sang' and never implicated other prisoners or SS men. Thus the 'workshops' now employed Poles and very few Germans. Of course these groups were always fully staffed whilst hundreds of excellent craftsmen would have given anything to join the privileged few. Still, I believed that this type of work was the only way to survival and decided to appeal to the Chief Labour Leader of the camp. He was a German prisoner, small, thin and spruce – the second highest in the whole hierarchy of camp functionaries. He was the one deciding all the allocations to work.

First I had to obtain permission from my block elder whose sense of humour saved me a beating. At the hilarious idea of me, a miserable mussulman, going to see the Labour Leader he could not contain his merriment and, slapping me on the back with a blow which flattened me to the floor, bade me go and tell him what's what. On reaching the exalted Labour Office I was of course kicked out by one of the clerks. But I persisted night after night, often forfeiting my food ration. I saw the great man a week later when I had refused to be thrown out and he came out of his sanctum to see the unprecedented row. He even listened, but politely refused my request, pointing out my physical weakness. That night I thought the time had come to give up the unequal struggle. I would only exchange the unbearable pain of spreading ulcers, the constant gnawing hunger, the fear, the endless blows, for the quiet Nirvana of death. It was a good bargain, the sensible one, with only one 'but' – my word given to Princess that I would return to her. Ulcers or no ulcers, I would go again to see the Labour Leader. I was kicked out, I was beaten up and I persisted. He began to know my ugly, shrunken face and sent me back to sawing and chopping wood with the other mussulmen. But still I persisted. To this day I don't know why and how, but a long time later he laughed and allotted me to the workshops.

CHAPTER 15

WHEEL OF FORTUNE

Nobody who was anybody lived in the overcrowded mussulmen's blocks and I was promptly transferred to the barrack occupied by the workshop crew. There were three-tier bunks, as in the hospital, but we slept one to a bed. It was one of the newly refurbished blocks with proper washrooms, running water and clean lavatories. After the average camp accommodation this was magnificent luxury. Unfortunately at my new work things did not go well. I knew what to do and how to do it but in my debilitated state even a light hammer was almost too heavy to lift and it never hit where I intended. A file was no better: instead of smooth long strokes it rocked erratically in my feeble hands. Fellow workers pityingly shrugged their shoulders, the exasperated charge-hand told me over and over to buckle down to it, but it was no good. However hard I tried, the hack-saw stuck, the hand-drill jammed, even the spanners slipped off the nuts skinning my knuckles and impotent tears trickled down my cheeks. Nobody hit me, nobody kicked me, but in a week the foreman reported me to the almighty capo of the mechanical workshop. He was not even nasty but simply told me that I was no bloody good and had to go. It was like a renewal of the death sentence after a reprieve. Knowing that it was useless, I half-heartedly asked for another chance. He just shrugged his shoulders and I, with nothing more to lose, risked all on a last try.

'Herr Capo' – we all had to address them as Sir Capo – 'have you seen WHO signed my transfer chit?'

There was a long, long pause as I stood in front of him looking straight into his eyes. I knew that the little transfer chits with clerk's initials and the stamp of the Labour Office, were usually destroyed by the clerk-of-works after he had listed the new men. But the capo could not be absolutely sure that there had not been added initials – initials of

... here the mind boggled: after all, clapped-out mussulmen were never transferred to tradesmen's groups like those of the workshop. He was still looking at me, beetroot red and now furious, but still hesitating. The simple dismissal had turned into a dangerous problem. He could chuck me out, he could kill me on the spot – but somewhere behind me there might, just might, be an unknown protector, the Labour Chief, possibly even the SS NCO above him, or ... it could be anybody who might demand an account. The capo surrendered, transferring me to the small unit manufacturing wire netting as used around tennis courts. It was light work and, with my mechanical experience, I could deal with the problem of home-made machinery which frequently caused the new net to buckle disastrously. Soon, as the machine-setter, I was well ensconced in the 'factory'. Freed from constant maltreatment and fear, fed on full measures of thick soup, I felt much better, though the physical recuperation was discouragingly slow. And then we ran out of wire, the delivery of which had been getting more and more irregular for some weeks.

The threatening redundancy was a calamity and I was casting about for an alternative job. Inordinately weak, still new to the workshops, I had no friends, nothing to offer in exchange for a favour, so I decided on a bluff even more risky than that which got me into the netting factory. My choice fell on the capo 'Johnny' who was in charge of a small elite group known as 'The SS Garage Service'. He was a big, solid man of whom it was said that he was a Pole, although he did not wear the telltale letter P on his red triangle. It was also said that before the war he had been the chauffeur of the Polish President. But the only facts I really knew were that he spoke the perfect Polish of an educated man and was the only capo referred to by his Christian name. With considerable difficulty I managed to see him during working hours in the garage when there were no SS men about. Making sure that we could not be overheard, I simply said that I wanted to work in his group and that it was most important for me and also for some people whom he once had known. Such a direct approach seemed to flabbergast him and, after a long, silent interval, he asked my name which I gave him, adding after a moment of hesitation '... as long as the camp lasts'. His questions as to what it had been 'before' I answered shortly to the effect that I had already said too much. Again he thought, and I saw his mouth open slowly for more questions and close again at the vehement negative shake of my head. Then he made up his mind:

'Tomorrow I'll square the SS bastard in charge. Come in the evening – I'll have the official transfer for you!'

I came as instructed and ran foul of a hall-boss with a length of rubber hose:

'Where do you think you're pushing, you lousy beggar?' – and somewhere from the far end the quiet voice of capo Johnny calling that he wanted to see me.

'Yes Sir! Of course Sir! I beg your pardon Herr Capo.'

So I entered the Elysian Fields of the spotless barrack, a barrack without any vermin where we changed underwear every week instead of every few months. My threadbare striped uniform was exchanged for a new one whilst twice daily there were one and a half or even two portions of soup. In civilian life one could compare my position with a top ministerial appointment. But in reality there was no comparison: it was a chance of life against the certainty of a slow and painful death.

I was allotted to the repair shop which serviced old, disintegrating bicycles issued to many SS men. Cleaning, oiling and straightening buckled wheels was simple enough, but missing spokes and worn bearings presented difficulties as spares were almost unobtainable. However, when a broken part could not be mended, the charge-hand usually produced an oddment which could be adapted to fit. After a week or two of these sleight-of-hand miracles he took me into his confidence. Having locked the outer door he opened a well camouflaged panel leading to an unsuspected underdrawing. There, neatly laid out, was a considerable number of spares: '... what's left of the bikes that we nicked from the bastards!' Thus I began to learn the business side of our job.

Only a year ago the guards were young and blond, all of the new generation which Hitler had 'educated' in murder, torture and pillage – the typical Aryan nation of the Austrian paper-hanger. But now more and more of them departed to the East Front to practise their skills on the captured Russians. These guards were replaced by older men, unsure of themselves, frightened of the camp and the system. But in their fear they often over-reacted, making our job still more difficult. When such a 'customer' arrived we would get out our repair book and the work sheets and proceed to assess the problem and the man. The ones that cursed and ranted we treated with cringing respect, but would point out that they must see the SS sergeant-in-charge as, on pain of death, we were prohibited to touch anything without his orders. The more they threatened and threw their weight about, the less they liked the idea of reporting their trouble to an NCO, and soon were ready to discuss the matter sensibly. It was a prolonged discussion and a delicate one when, after explaining the lack of spares, we would intimate (though never in so many words) that there might be a chance of obtaining the required part for which we would have to pay dearly. Then it was just plain haggling about the amount of bread, sausage or just money. Of course, these deals covered only 'accidental damage' and 'lost' equipment whilst the ordinary maintenance had to be done anyway without payment. Once we got into trouble when a vicious whippersnapper hit the charge-hand and sent him for our capo whilst I was told to get busy immediately on the slightly buckled wheel of his bike. Capo Johnny arrived soon, but not alone: he was far too wily for that. With him was the SS sergeant in charge of the garage group and our bully ran to meet them with his complaints. The sergeant's roar stopped him dead.

'You barge into my workshop! You beat up my prisoners! I'll see you posted to the Eastern Front!' And the offender, instead of apologising abjectly, tried to explain that we were cheeky and did not want to do a two-minute job. So the sergeant inspected the bike and began smiling wider and wider. By this time tightening the spokes on the wrong side of the wheel I had it in a nice shape of a figure eight and had managed to tighten the bearing so that it crunched horribly.

'Sabotage! Soldier, you wilfully damaged SS property and tried to terrorise my men to cover up for you! That's a matter for the Gestapo! Come with me!' The young bastard was dispatched to the East the same day and the bike, 'mislaid' in the upheaval, provided us with more spares.

But usually negotiations were completed amicably as we would settle quickly for almost anything. And even with the lion's share going to the capo for distribution throughout the group, we were not doing badly. I was getting more and more familiar with the magic idea of 'organisation'. In the camp jargon 'to organise' meant to acquire illegally food, goods or favours. To the authorities it was equivalent to stealing and cheating and was punished severely. But to the prisoners it was a positive, honourable and highly commendable enterprise which kept alive the 'organisers' and many of their friends. Sneaking a crust of bread from a sleeping colleague was theft for which the authorities hanged and the fellow prisoners just killed. To 'borrow' a whole loaf from the central magazine, or to 'divert' a lorry-load of bread from the bakery was 'organisation' which in our eyes testified only to the ingenuity and virtue of the organiser.

Only a few yards away, separated from the workshop complex by a fence, lay the territory of the agricultural group. There were the pigsties, the cowsheds, the poultry runs supplying the SS and Gestapo whilst stores of sauerkraut and turnips fed the prisoners. There also were potatoes, which we craved as 'solid' food, so different from the endless watery soups. It was possible to bribe some worker and catch the spuds chucked by him over the fence. This was a risky and small scale operation whilst we favoured a 'wholesale' project which began with a theft of everything that could quickly be removed from a bike belonging to an elderly SS NCO. The stolen parts reached us by an 'underground' route, even before the expected visit of the owner worried to death about the loss of the SS property. When he arrived moaning that he could not afford the price of spares, we suggested a simple solution: we would pay for the required parts if he would escort two prisoners out of the closely-guarded gate of the workshops into the equally well-guarded agricultural yards. Horrified, but forced to cover up the loss of the SS property, he escorted two 'electricians' with a handcart full of cable and tools. They were soon back with the same cart which, underneath its deck, carried some two hundredweight of potatoes. We hid the loot whilst he wobbled away delighted with the 'new pump', bell and even a full tool-bag. The death penalty for stealing food applied to potatoes as well as bread, and cooking was even more dangerous especially as fires were also prohibited. But a fire in a cast-iron stove was frequently authorised by our SS boss for heating soldering irons, enamel drying or other excuses invented on the spur of the moment. Nobody in his senses would risk a pot on the stove, but there were other means of cooking of which 'rosary' and the 'french sliced' were the most popular. The former was made of a wire on to which the potatoes were threaded and the whole string of enormous beads was lowered into a rusty chimney pipe. This called for various subterfuges like a bucket of water (ostensibly carried up to find a hole in the leaking roof) from which the rosary, screened by the investigator's legs, slid unobtrusively into the chimney. Alternatively, thinly-sliced potatoes were loaded into two enamel bowls wired together and suspended inside the stove for a few minutes. Even with these precautions we were almost caught by a flying patrol from the Headquarters (our 'own' SS bosses half knew about the practice and avoided finding out more about it). The first time the officer walked in just when the bowl had been filled but luckily, somebody managed to pour over the potatoes a can of almost black engine oil which, indeed, saved our necks but broke our hearts. A more terrifying episode happened with another guard who peeped into the stove and, seeing the flat round top of a bowl, sneeringly enquired what was cooking there.

'Cooking, Herr Wachmeister? Oh! You mean this flame-arrester, power-saving-ring invented by Herr Captain Otto-Gottlieb-Daimler? We were told to check if it works with a wood fire, Sir. Magnificent fuel saving for the whole Reich, but we can dismantle it and report that you wanted to see it!' He assured us that we must not dismantle Herr Captain's invention on his account and walked out.

Looking objectively at this period one sees the hair-raising risks that we took for a potato, for a loaf of bread, sometimes for the satisfaction of humiliating the SS supermen. But these risks were taken voluntarily to ensure enough food and maintain some illusion of our own power. Also, however dangerous and hare-brained the efforts, many of them were really necessary to retain jobs which gave us a chance of survival in this death camp (*vernichtungs Lager*). But whatever the death rate, the size and frequency of the incoming transports far exceeded it, swelling the camp population to astronomical proportions. Relieved from the insatiable hunger and the unbearable strain, I began to see and to notice more details of the camp life. By chance I found my old friends – the Engineer and his merry lads who also had been shipped to Auschwitz. But here and now the old adventures seemed remote and insignificant. We had nothing to say to one another and parted with meaningless wishes of good luck whilst around us the camp grew ever larger. In 1941 Russian prisoners of war were brought in and confined in a small compound. Our own meagre rations looked like gargantuan feasts in comparison to the food flung or spilled into their midst. It was small wonder that in just one year from the original ten thousand only a few hundred were left alive.

A corner of the camp, partitioned by a concrete wall and the inevitable electrified fence, served for women prisoners till they, and many others, were transferred to Auschwitz 2, newly-built a few miles away and referred to as Birkenau (the birch-tree wood). The actual wood, or rather a spinney, screened an old barn used as a gas chamber. There mussulmen too weak for work were herded. There some new transports arrived, bypassing the camp gate. By the side of the spinney was the squat building of the crematorium with its ever-active chimney. Further away, the thick columns of black smoke rose from the pits where more bodies layered with wooden beams sizzled and burned, spreading for miles their characteristic, sickly odour. But inside 'our own' Auschwitz 1 we, the Poles, were no longer the most persecuted group. The Jews, with their yellow stars of David, became the chief objects of kicks, blows and torture, whilst the Russian 'Commissars' were simply starved and clubbed to death. Also the type of our guards again began to change. The young and enthusiastic, as well as the older SS murderers of 'pure' Teutonic blood, were being slowly replaced by the dregs of the population from the conquered countries. These were the Volksdeutsch people (men claiming allegiance to the Reich) taking over the camp functions from the Reichsdeutsch (the born Germans) who were needed in the endless plains of Russia. Some of these guards quickly reached new heights of cruelty and bestiality but they also showed hesitation and doubts about the invincibility and sempiternity of the Third Reich. The increasing number of prisoners, the motley guards and the sheer size of the camp began to eat into the neat perfection of the whole organisation. The maltreatment, hunger and death prevailed, but from a certainty became more a matter of chance. Thousands starved but dozens ate their fill. On the other hand, to all the dangers and hazards of camp life, was now added the plague of typhus brought from the east by the Russian prisoners. From their compound it seeped out and exploded in our camp 'releasing through the crematorium chimneys' most of its victims.

In spite of the relative cleanliness of my surroundings I caught typhus. My head began to burn and pound with a persistent intolerable ache; my body, hotter and hotter, was ready to burst into flames; my eyes kept closing whatever I did. Then there was no point in doing anything and I curled up in some dark corner after a few days of misery.

It was still dark when somebody tried to steal my cold comfortable pillow. I awakened ready to defend what was mine. The trouble was that my arm would not move and they had almost wrenched the pillow when the hand of the thief touched my face. I bit it as hard as I could and was rewarded by an ear-splitting scream. Somewhere far away, they all shouted and argued and I could not make sense of it.

'You said they were all dead!'

'Well they are.'

'I just pulled that one from the edge and the other bit me!'

'Don't be stupid!'

'Well! Climb up and see!'

There was more light and they slowly moved me from the third tier of the bunk. Then I was in another room and they gave me delightful, cold tea and all of it sweetened, and I slept the deep, restful sleep of the just - a fortnight of my life had disappeared without a trace.

The hospital was getting rations for all its patients, but as most were incapable of absorbing food, the few survivors had as much as they could stuff in. I was weaker and thinner than I had ever been. But the hospital people warned me of the grave risk of prolonged convalescence: it was rumoured that the Germans might gas all the patients to stop the spread of the disease which attacked the SS men with equal ferocity and without any respect for their god-like Teutonic origin. It was not very surprising as those who lived through typhus, and so became immune to it, collected the lice off the sick and flicked them at any soldier within reach. After long talks with the friendly personnel of the infectious ward I asked for discharge as soon as I could stand up and walk unaided.

I was automatically allotted to a mussulmen's barrack and 'light labour'. There was no return to the workshops without the Labour Chief's order whilst with my deeper knowledge of the camp I would not venture again into the campaign which had once saved my life in an unheard-of miraculous transfer.

There is no point in describing again the hunger, the agony and dehumanisation of a starving prisoner in the concentration camp, though I had to suffer it anew for days, for months, for ever, whilst my ulcers spread into bigger and bigger wounds of raw flesh. However painful and debilitating, these were not enough to gain admission to the hospital and warranted only some ointment covered with a paper bandage which sometimes one could obtain in the out-patients' department. Even that was risky as the long queues were often assailed by the dreaded SS NCO in charge of the hospital. It was on a Saturday that, dead tired, I missed his approach till he poked me in the back with his thick walking stick resembling a medieval mace.

'You lazy swine! What's wrong with you? I'll help you to the crematorium without a hospital!'

I pulled up my trouser leg to show him the ulcers above which was an insignificant, though very red, small boil and suddenly he backed away:

'Erysipelas! Contagious!' and turning away to an orderly who controlled the queue of the out-patients roared again:

'Immediate admission! Move, you bloody doctor!'

Inside, the orderly looked at me with unmistakable admiration: 'If you can bamboozle *him* with a sixpenny boil, you can do anything, mate!' – but an order had to be obeyed and I was again in the relative safety of the hospital, this time in the 'dirty surgery' ward.

It was 1943, my third winter in the camp and the first stay in the hospital whilst in possession of all my faculties. It was a magnificent life: two to a bed, warm, nobody hitting you, no roll-calls as we were counted in our beds. The whole Sunday was now a rest day, and my little boil burst on its own. On Monday the ward doctor examined me, laughing at the little boil and the German diagnosis. Then, looking at the ulcers, he remarked that they were really serious but he had nothing to help me. 'Stay a few days, but we can't keep you long.' And this was the moment I decided to stay long, very long indeed. I was extremely weak but fully mobile and I offered help to anybody working near me. Clad only in underpants and shirt I washed and scrubbed the floors which had to be done four times a day; I carried and emptied dirty buckets, and cleaned up after the patients with dysentery. The overworked personnel welcomed my willing help and at night they often slipped me a second helping of soup. Within a week I was 'promoted' to removing old dressings from festering limbs whilst in the little, crowded surgery, doctors and orderlies cleaned and dressed the wounds. I also began to realise the strange hierarchy of the place. At the top was a German block-elder, the master of life and death but completely remote from medicine and even administration. Below him was the whole gamut of doctors, Polish of course, responsible directly to the SS medical officer. Then there were orderlies and auxiliaries, practically at the bottom of the ladder. But it was only they, the 'old' prisoners, well entrenched in the safe environment, who could 'organise' more and better medical supplies, they who counted the patients and attended to all administrative problems, and ultimately decided who was in or out. It was an incongruous and delicate balance which everybody tried to preserve in spite of frequent quarrels and skirmishes. The orderlies tolerated the doctors who had access and could talk directly, though never on equal terms, to the top SS god. The doctors suffered the orderlies without whose knowledge of the camp and 'organisation' they could not survive. Both parties equally hated the German 'elder' who carefully avoided friction with either group as he knew how easily one could fall into deep, deep sleep in the proximity of various drugs, however scarce.

All patients had their numbers written in indelible pencil on their forearms and mine was noticed by Joseph, the orderly from the surgery.

'Hey! You are from my transport!' – and I saw his number, only a few digits removed from mine. We began chatting and the next day I asked him straight how to get into the hospital crew.

'Not easy, boy. Not easy at all! But Christ! We must stick together, we – the old numbers. I'll tell you: doctors don't matter much, but they could help. Old Foggy is the easiest touch, though the top sawbones would be better.'

We talked a long time, sorting out the best strategy. I kept working hard and being helpful while Joseph, with his friend Marian, persuaded the senior doctor to interview me as a potential orderly. He did not actually breathe fire but certainly showed his contempt for 'ruffians with low prison numbers'. First he asked me to bandage somebody's severely damaged calf and with a grim face watched me do a perfect job of it. After observing some more dressings applied in a most professional manner to the more awkward parts of the body he questioned me at length beginning with anatomy and going further and further. I silently blessed the extensive knowledge picked up in school, scouting and civil defence as well as from the library of my parents. He stopped suddenly and barked at me:

'You pretend not to know Latin but you must be a medical student ... or ... not a bloody mechanic. All right, I don't mind you staying,' and we shook hands. Then I only needed the support of the ward quartermaster whose unlimited influence could push my appointment even through the German block elder, who, like all the others, needed an extra supply of choicest food. To reach and maintain his position in this hard-bitten crowd, the quartermaster had to be a clever and ruthless man, who, unfortunately for me, had a number over thirty thousand and resented prisoners with lower or, as the saying went, 'older numbers'. He had, however, one weakness which was a comical preoccupation with the future of his little, provincial shop. Whilst most of the prisoners were doing their utmost to survive the day, and the privileged few worried about the morrow, he thought only about his piddling business and still dreamed of expansion, of a whole chain of shops after the war. In this situation I became his willing listener as I had decided on another gamble. Swearing him to secrecy, I admitted to being an American of Polish origin, caught by chance whilst visiting relatives. Then I suggested opening a shop in my home-town in Iowa which in my ignorance I pronounced 'Yova'. Spellbound, he listened to my description of the mid-west wilderness and the need of shops and services. But he hesitated until I demanded 20% of the profits for my knowledge of the local conditions. This convinced him of the awaiting bonanza and having settled my commission at 10% he set out to ensure a 'good job' for me as his future partner. About a month later I officially became an 'auxiliary' of the surgical ward.

It was a safe, good life. So safe that we even had time to be bored and to grumble. It was good because we were relatively free from hunger, from fear; after the hell that each of us had passed through, we were hardened enough to shrug off the pain, misery and all too frequent death of our charges. The hospital day began, as in the whole camp, with the sound of the gong, when we herded the patients to the new washrooms fitted with rows of taps above the long, tin troughs. Hardly anybody was excused, and they all dragged themselves painfully and stood wetting a hand, a face and, in the near-freezing temperature, pretending that they were thoroughly washed and cleaned. In the grey dawn, with the yellow glow of the inadequate light bulbs it was always a scene from Dante's Inferno. Some stripped to wash, some to give an impression of washing. Many had discarded their soiled underwear because of the uncontrollable diarrhoea and, in this peculiar light, the whole surging crowd was made up of green-blue angular planes and dark shadows. Individual bodies were cut and dismembered by the white bands of paper dressings so that the crowd resembled more a heap of discarded human parts than a collection of people. Sometimes the uncoordinated, jerky motion and constant shivering, gave the impression of one mortally wounded beast twitching its thousand limbs in the throes of death.

Then the individual people, if they still were people, staggered and hobbled back to their beds. The ward occupied half of the first floor in Block 21. The three-tier bunks were divided into five groups, each holding some thirty patients in charge of one auxiliary. There was barely enough time to swill and swab the floor, each of the auxiliaries doing two groups, as half of us had gone to the kitchens to bring back barrels of morning 'tea'. This we distributed quickly, giving more to those with high temperatures, omitting those who were supposed to fast for three days because of diarrhoea. The place always stank to high heaven. It was an all-pervading, everlasting mixture of stinks from festering wounds, excreta and various disinfectants – the only medical supply in abundance. So even in winter the windows were wide open whilst we proceeded with the head count for the morning roll-call. A miscount meant that the whole camp, the thousands upon thousands of prisoners, stood to attention till the mistake was found and corrected. On a more personal plane, he who was guilty of a mistake was punished unmercifully. Thus one climbed to the top bunks counting heads and pulling off the thin blankets to make sure that no additional body was hidden between the legitimate ones. We tried not to be rough, not to tread on injured limbs, but we had to be quick as already from the stairs resounded the roars of the block clerk calling for the numbers and urging us on in no uncertain terms. We reported the numbers of each group and waited in line till the whole barrack was ready and the SS man accepted the final tally. Then, taking advantage of a valued hospital privilege, we dispersed to our work, not waiting for the rest of the camp and the gong. And work there was aplenty. For one man with only two thermometers and a borrowed watch it was a time-consuming job to take the temperature and pulse of his patients. The dirty buckets had to be emptied and washed, the windows had to be spotless, the breakfast bowls needed rinsing and stacking whilst at nine we began surgery with its long queue of minor operations. Some doctors were good and did their best but many could not cope. An old country practitioner, who for decades had delivered babies and doled out aspirin, was not much use when faced with the wild press of still-moving cadavers, begging, shouting, weeping. This called for the squat, powerful Joseph whose raised fists, each the size of a ham, stopped the riot before it developed.

'Line up here! Sit on these stools! Now, first one, what's the matter with you?' The first mussulman pointed to his foot with blue-black toes and Joseph lowered his voice with more sympathy for the man's feelings than anybody would give him credit for:

'Will you amputate now?' and, seeing the hesitant face of the doctor added: 'By tomorrow the whole foot will be dead!'

The next man had a forearm swollen like an enormous vegetable marrow. Further were carbuncles, boils and more of severe frostbite ...

The surgery was separated from the ward by a row of lockers and closed with a curtain. In the centre stood a folding operating table flanked by two stands. One supported a steriliser and trays of tools whilst on the other were laid out bottles of ether and pressurised phials of ethyl-chloride. Novocain was in very short supply and required too much time so that it was either a light general anaesthetic or, for small though often painful incisions, just nothing! For some obscure reason the latter was known as the 'Hungarian anaesthetic' and Joseph was a past master at it. His apparently callous brutality saved many a patient some pain and much fear. In one lightning move he wrapped a towel round the victim's head and held firmly whilst one of us hung like grim death on to the leg or arm which an experienced surgeon opened up before the patient had time to shout or struggle. Then there was just a new dressing and a shout for the next one. There were no rubber gloves and we all worked elbow deep in the stinking pus of suppurating wounds and deep abscesses, just wiping our hands on wads of cellulose used as towels and as cotton wool. We all developed unbelievable resistance to the streptococci, staphylococci and whatever other bugs swam around. We thrived on the double portions of soup and some extra bread, portions issued for those who needed them no more but were not yet subtracted from the total numbers reported. We consumed all we could get, to keep going hour after hour, day in, day out. There were windows to clean, dead to carry out, food to bring in. In spite of all the grim and brutal experiences I found it hard to devour two basins of soup under the hundreds of starving eyes following each spoonful. But hard or not, I ate all of it and went back to the surgery for the next two hours of dressings. Wipe and clean with peroxide, paint with mercurochrome, smear with the appropriate ointment, cover with gauze and wrap up with the bandages of crinkled paper. The worst were wounds with spreading necrosis when one had to cut away bigger and bigger lumps of dead and decaying flesh ... Then back to wash floors, take pulses and temperatures and be ready for the evening roll-call as now the original three daily counts had been reduced to two thus lengthening the work time and 'increasing productivity'.

I had seen the camp life as a 'new boy' and labourer, a mussulman and craftsman, and now observed it anew from the exalted position of a hospital orderly. With the others, I witnessed daily the misery and pain of our patients whilst every few weeks we were involved in the 'selections'. The SS camp doctor, the Lager Arzt, ordered the 'hopeless cases' to be prepared for inspection and dispatch to the gas chambers. It was then that we no longer envied the privileges and the easy life of our ward doctor who did not wash floors but now had to choose which of his patients were to be killed. A hero would choose the gas chamber for himself rather than condemn to death some of his patients. But after a few weeks, let alone months or years, of camp life there were no heroes, just old prisoners fighting for survival. Also, whatever one doctor did or did not do, the more debilitated, half-starved patients would anyway go 'up the chimney'. It was possible, likely even, that without the list many more would be taken including some not so hopeless. So the ward doctor asked each of us to suggest patients from our own groups. But when we all refused and told him to do his own dirty work, I realised how empty was our gesture. Was it really the matter of our honour and the sacred trust of the healers, or was it just the way to survive without making enemies or tempting the justice of Jehovah? The long line of stools was occupied as for operations or dressings. When the SS doctor came, glanced at them and snarled, *'Only* twenty today?' - they knew where they were going. They knew, and we had to load them on to the waiting lorries.

At longer intervals similar 'selections' were carried out throughout the camp and again we had to supervise and load - hundreds at a time.

The typhus epidemic increased and the authorities declared an all-out effort to eradicate the disease. In strict rotation the whole population of each block was stripped naked and deloused, whilst their clothing was baked in specially imported mobile ovens. The theory was all right, but frequently the dirty clothing arrived back barely warm, with its original livestock not even incommoded. So the war was stepped up: the whole barracks were disinfected whilst naked thousands were kept outside or piled into the adjoining buildings on top of their already crowded inhabitants. Prisoners with lice were beaten up, and all patients of the infectious hospital block were sent to the gas chambers. During this upheaval we were ordered to inspect for lice thousands of prisoners and their clothing. This gave us quite unexpected 'fees', offered by the block elders who wished to keep clean their own records if not their own blocks. Luckily for us, whilst the bribes paid were quite substantial, there was no attempt at intimidation. The 'social' position of the hospital staff, as well as the fact that we were ultimately responsible only to the almighty Lager Arzt made us safe from the hands of the capos, block elders and ordinary SS men. On the other hand even a dirty floor, if spotted by the Lager Arzt, could lead to 'a hundred strokes on the arse', which often resulted in death. But, we in our white uniforms of the hospital staff, could stroll negligently through the camp, respected and envied.

The hospital held other sinister secrets. Sometimes the Lager Arzt in a casual inspection noted just a few unfortunate patients and when the small number of victims did not warrant a lorry, they were simply transferred to Block 20. There an SS NCO, the 'Sanitary', injected phenol straight into their hearts causing blood coagulation and death.

There were also incidents of which only the participants knew. Such was the case of a German capo, a murderer with one hundred victims to his overdrawn account. He was also a hypochondriac and paid some doctors for a check-up after which he expected to get 'good' medicine. On one occasion a series of intra-venous calcium injections was prescribed but the third injection was given from a half-empty syringe causing an air-lock in the heart. The verdict at the post mortem was heart failure.

The hospital crew formed a close-knit group: an exclusive society with a strong sense of loyalty to the caste. This was caused more by the necessity of self-preservation than real friendship. Except for a very few couples with homosexual bonds the rest remained as a group of separate individuals, cold and distant rather than friendly. The orderlies in our ward were a mixed bunch. There was Joseph, a young peasant from a small hamlet; 'Black', a schoolboy from Warsaw; Zygmunt, a medical student from Cracow; an opinionated provincial shopkeeper as the quartermaster; and others of equally diverse age, origin and education. Maybe the inhuman environment prevented normal relations, maybe we lost the capacity for friendship, for compassion, for any decent feelings. Even the very few postcards (no letters allowed) received from Princess seemed vague, tenuous, like some ghostly communications from another world. They came pawed over by a thousand hands, smudged with censorship stamps, couched in the enemy tongue. Only the handwriting was hers and references to some unimportant details of the distant past identified these cards beyond doubt, but even our own endearments translated into the accursed language were no longer ours.

Except the staff, nobody was allowed to leave or enter the hospital and after the evening roll-call there was often a small crowd near the entrance. Some waited, hoping for a bit of extra food that an orderly might bring to an old friend, others tried to get news about a patient. There I once saw a familiar face though now so gaunt and pale as to make recognition uncertain. But it was Little, the boy I once taught skiing, the boy who had later become my best friend of snowy adventures. Now he was a far-gone mussulman and I could only smuggle to him an extra bowl of soup. Then he stopped coming and though I looked and searched I never found him again.

It was later that at the same entrance a prisoner peered short-sightedly at the number sewn on my uniform:

'You are Salski? I have a message for you' – and as I confirmed my identity he rattled on: 'The Engineer said to tell you that he and the boys are dead now. Last week the Gestapo recalled him and the others, and he said it meant that the investigation had been completed and they would be shot. I swore to tell you and now you know.'

He turned and disappeared into the crowd before I could stop him. I stood alone, sorry about the others, terrified of my own future. There was nobody to talk to, nowhere to run, nowhere to hide. The straight streets, the square identical buildings, the hospital no longer a safe haven. And all the suffering, all the efforts and struggles for nothing. My Princess waiting forever in the other world. I had to try again, I had to do something. When the first shock wore off and my panic subsided I went to the senior orderly of our block - a three figure number, a 'founder member' of the camp. He listened quietly and promised to find out more about the Engineer. The same night he took me to the deserted washroom.

'They were all shot here in the camp last Thursday, I checked their cards in the main office. Now about you' - he pointed to a dark corner - 'there is somebody you can safely talk to.'

He left the empty room whilst from behind the washing troughs a vague shadow of a man slowly rose:

'If you want, you can go sick and be transferred tomorrow morning to another hospital block. There is a corpse which will be marked with your number and then you, with his number and name, will be discharged from the hospital. As he was here for black market offences you will be safe from the Gestapo which is concerned only with the 'politicals'. But with your new identity you can never return here, or to the workshops, where you might be recognised. I would advise you to stay here with your present identity - you must have lied better than your friends so that you will probably be left alone now and have a better chance of survival here. Don't say anything - it's your decision to be sick tomorrow or not!' He pushed past, leaving me with a million chaotic thoughts. Immobile, paralysed with fright and doubts, I was mentally flinging myself against the bars of the cage like a maddened wild beast.

I did not sleep that night. I could not possibly talk to anybody about my case and still less about the washroom conversation. The more you knew, the less you talked - this was the only way to survive. I tossed and turned on my bed sweating, in terror of the Gestapo reaching back for me. I weighed the chance of a bullet in the back of my head against the 'safe' anonymity of camp life with its slow equally deadly end of a mussulman. Nobody knew the odds on the Gestapo shooting me the following day whilst the probability of survival in the camp starting again with a new identity was infinitesimal. Logically the choice was fairly obvious. Still, it was not easy to take the final decision with one single stake of one's life. But in the greying dawn, though really feeling ill, I went on with my duties as if nothing had happened the previous day.

Our attitude to the patients evolved in an unavoidable manner. First, we did our duty and tended to identify with individual patients. We cheered them up, hoped that their injuries responded to treatment; we tried to scrounge or 'organise' more Prontosil (the precursor of sulphonamides), more Dutch *'Leber Salbe'* which seemed to help with ulcers. But, as half-healed men had to be discharged, as many cases developed complications, as we ran out of medical materials and carried out corpses, the personal involvement had to be avoided. Otherwise, one sat and wept or cursed whilst there was no time or place for either. And, like Joseph, we did our best and, handling men like fragile pieces of broken machinery, we avoided meeting their eyes – they all had to die anyway. The worst were the very young and, in spite of all our experience, the few twelve- and fourteen-year-olds we tried to shelter, to feed even. But after the Lager Arzt had sent one to the gas chamber and had taken another for his 'experiments' we had to give up and, sending other young ones back into the slavery of the main camp, tried to avoid meeting their eyes.

The dreaded Lager Arzt flitted through the hospital wards faster and more frequently. He now had some civilian 'helpers' (addressed as 'doctors' and 'professors') who picked out Jewish prisoners for castration and sterilisation which were soon followed by the post-mortem. He also brought for training a younger SS officer, a newly-qualified doctor who spent a lot of time in our ward. This young man, called Rhode, I got to know as he frequently asked me to demonstrate dressing and bandaging. I would not speak German and he knew no Polish, but he learnt.

The camp grew fast but the numbers of incoming prisoners were such that more and more transports left Auschwitz for Buchenwald, Mauthausen, Dachau ... and among the crowds of mussulmen there were also craftsmen, doctors and orderlies. With our own cushy jobs no longer safe, I volunteered for a transfer to Birkenau where we were to organise and staff a new hospital in the Gipsy sector.

CHAPTER 16

THE GIPSY CAMP

Clad in white denims our small group of doctors and orderlies left Auschwitz 1 with its brick-built barracks and smoothly paved, spotless streets. A couple of miles ahead, at the end of a pot-holed road, sprawled Birkenau, officially designated as Auschwitz 2. Its sheer size was staggering: as far as the eye could see stretched roads, wire fences and innumerable rows of low huts. On approach the first impression was one of mud, dirt and misery. The huts, with narrow windows in their roofs, were prefabricated wooden stables. Perfectly aligned, they faced the camp street with wide doors at their gable ends. Each of these streets, transverse to the main road, formed the backbone of a sector which was enclosed by an electrified fence and housed some twenty thousand prisoners in its thirty-two huts.

We entered the fifth sector marked 'E' as the sun broke through the overcast skies streaked with smoke from the four crematoria. In front of the huts were men, women and plenty of children in colourful, civilian clothing. The people swarmed along the camp street, gathered in little groups and gossiped, pointing at us with obvious disdain. Some younger men, led by one in a Luftwaffe (German Airforce) uniform, shouted abuse and began throwing mud and stones as we reached our destination – barrack 32. We were received by a block-elder, a small, thin Silesian with the green triangle denoting a professional criminal. As a matter of fact he was a safe breaker of international repute, and immensely proud of it. He was also an 'old number' though not nearly as old as myself and this tempered considerably the difference in rank. Furthermore, though a mighty block-elder, his rule over orderlies was strictly limited. However, all this remained rather academical as, from the start, he became a good friend and 'one of us'. Noticing how confused and shocked we were with the attack by a crowd of fellow prisoners he laughed:

'The Gipsy scum? They still think themselves to be of the superhuman German race - but don't worry, they will soon come to heel and we'll outlive them anyway!' - his friendly tone hardened, his easy smile faded and the narrow face contracted into a vicious snarl:

'But if you saw the bastard in the Luftwaffe uniform - lay off, he is mine! I'll have him soon, very soon. He will eat his fucking Iron Cross and before he goes he will regret bombing Warsaw ...' Passion and fury spent, he continued quietly:

'Forget all that till you settle down. You won't have food problems - kitchen and stores are all staffed by our boys from Auschwitz and for you there will be enough good, thick soup. Anyway, am I glad you have come! Now you will fight for the corpses. Damn stupid Gypsies - they steal corpses!'

With no more Jews in the Third Reich the Germans found new sport in hunting Gypsies. Wandering vagrants were arrested first and soon whole clans followed them to Auschwitz. Then individuals whose blood lines could be impeached were also rounded up. In this last category was the valiant hero of the German Airforce decorated for the massacre of Polish refugees. When on home leave, he had been arrested by the Gestapo because his grandmother's name sounded more Romany than German. Similarly, somebody decided that the primadonna of the Viennese Opera was too swarthy for an Aryan, and so she too was interned. Because, for the time being, the Gypsies were only interned, they were allowed to keep their clothing, valuables and money, and lived in family groups in the E sector of Birkenau. Now large transports were still arriving from Czechoslovakia and Hungary. Most of the inmates spoke German and despised the 'foreign scum' who did not. But almost all knew Romany, apparently a poor language of a few words and no grammar. For example, an adjective *'lachee'* was applied equally to a beautiful girl, a tasty morsel or a good deed. Other words like *'moolo'* denoted death, corpse, malevolent spirit and a curse. But if twice repeated it would indubitably cause the death of the speaker and the listener. It was also connected with funeral rites which were necessary to avoid the vengeance of the departed. Hence the stealing of the corpses from the hospital morgue and secret burials, which were unacceptable to the SS as the roll-call did not tally.

The 'hospital' consisted of two adjoining huts – dark wooden shells full of three-tier bunks. In number 32 were a few dying men, whilst number 30 held some equally moribund crones and a group of pregnant women. In charge was a 'Sanitary'-SS NCO, who, on our arrival, was sleeping off his hangover in the block-elder's bed. We were told to call him 'boss' and warned that he had to be paid for doing anything at all. But high above hovered the shadow of the dreaded SS camp medical officer, Doctor Mengele, who descended periodically to sign innumerable requisitions for hospital equipment. These finally brought a box of paper bandages! And we, the non-human *Untermensch* had to create from this void a real hospital relying only on our camp experience and the bond of the 'old numbers'. This bond, almost a mafia, began slowly with individual Poles gaining positions of responsibility in the camp hierarchy. They supported and promoted their friends and soon most functionaries were the prisoners with low numbers ('old numbers'), either Polish or with Polish connections. Then came to the gas chambers millions of Jews bringing all their possessions. Ultimately some four and a half millions perished in Auschwitz. The diamonds from Holland, gold from France and Greece, currencies from Belgium and Czechoslovakia, all destined for the Reich, were being stolen by the SS and by the prisoners. These clandestine treasures brought corruption on a vast scale. Relations between guards and prisoners were further affected by the growth of the camp and its technological complexities. The semi-literate SS men were incapable of administering or maintaining the necessary services which were in fact controlled by the prisoners. Mengele cursed and threatened the Sanitary for the lack of facilities and the Sanitary came to us. Then we, from the camp kitchen, obtained quantities of margarine, partly for the promise of good medical care, but mostly because we, as well as the kitchen personnel, were old numbers. With this starting capital, escorted by our Sanitary we quartered the camp, bribing and cajoling prisoners and SS men to give, sell or lend us hospital equipment. A trip to a well-guarded 'Canada' (the group sorting out the possessions of the gassed) yielded surgical instruments and drugs by the suitcase. From the workshops of Auschwitz 1 we 'organised' beds. The laundry and disinfection department supplied blankets and sheets – at a price. Soon the hospital was established, several SS men were commended, the Gypsies had their hospital and our position grew stronger and, possibly, more permanent.

At that time not one of us thought of the invisible price that had been paid. After all, spreading corruption in the ranks of the SS was to our advantage, and our skills in achieving it were certainly meritorious. The fact that, in the process, we frequently paid in food from the camp kitchens and continuously ate our fill – this was natural and virtuous. It is only now that one might question the morality of a small group filching the already inadequate food intended for the starving masses. But there such thoughts simply did not exist: the unwritten law of the prisoners sanctified the 'organisation' from the stores and kitchens, the theft of a carton of margarine per week worked out (if anybody ever did work it out) at a sixth of a gramme per head per day, and anyway, the Gypsies still had money and food of their own.

The first weeks were filled with hard work. Cleaning the horribly filthy hospital; long marches under escort to bring beds and equipment from Auschwitz 1 and from other sectors of Birkenau; building partitions and laying concrete floors for surgery, pharmacy and labour ward. Imperceptibly, the relations amongst us, the old prisoners from Auschwitz 1, began to change. The small size of our group pitted against the continuing enmity of the Gypsies, the adequate diet and our communal involvement in swindling the world around us rekindled some human feelings and real friendship amongst individuals. Four of us drifted close together. There was Black with his thirty-nine thousand number, young and 'couldn't care less', drooling at the wide sensuous mouth and ogling anything in skirts. By far the youngest was twelve-thousand and something Bohdan, fair, short and powerfully built. Whilst we all stole and lied without hesitation, the older ones knew that it was acceptable only there and then, but Bohdan, locked into the camp in his early teens, had forgotten the ethical values of the outside world. He lived from day to day by the code of the camp: never stealing from a colleague and despising the weak, he kicked out of his way any mussulman. Bohdan believed only in his own cunning and in the loyalty of the old numbers. Like Black, though even less sophisticated, he existed for the immediate, tangible pleasures: a better and larger meal, a lazy snooze in a warm, safe place and now – women. The last of the four was Teddy and though his twenty-two thousand number fell in between the other two he was completely different. His father had once been the owner of a building firm which had collapsed long before the war. Teddy, blaming the Jews for his father's misfortunes, had become a vicious anti-Semite. With the help of his mistress he had struggled hard to become a building technician and had just begun to make his mark when the war wrecked his world. Of us four he was the only one who, before the war, had known hardship, toil and complete independence. Reserved and self-confident, he stood tall and slim with hatchet face and a polite but meaningless smile on his thin lips. In spite of the gregarious nature of the first two and the almost mean behaviour of Teddy, I became his closest friend, though his unflagging devotion to his Sophie worried me slightly. In my naive and unworldly way I classified young women into two groups: the beautiful 'girls next door' who wouldn't think about it before marriage and ... prostitutes! But, knowing Teddy, I began to suspect that there might be exceptions.

Our relations are difficult to explain to those who did not live there with us. The crowded living conditions excluded any possibility of privacy. We all slept, washed, dressed and ate not only together but on top of one another. Mental contact was also restricted as, with hard work and squalid surroundings, we had neither time nor desire to discuss philosophy or art, and if one tried, the others might not even know what it was all about. Also, pre-war lives, like previous incarnations, were almost forgotten. So the talk was restricted to gossip, the next meal, the way of 'organising' more medicaments or food. Our origins were as diverse as our social class, background and education. We did not have a common cause or ideal, except survival of the individual and hatred of the Germans. But in spite of all that, we did become friends, joined by a bond of absolute loyalty to one another.

It was only with Teddy that I exchanged some memories of the past though, of course, I did not mention France or my real name. 'Of course' - because no one could withstand torture indefinitely and so, the fewer people who knew your secret, the safer it remained. He often talked about his Sophie of the black eyes and raven hair, and I told him of my Golden Princess. Teddy knew perfectly well that I skirted around my own background but he never asked a single question. Once we did drift into abstract fields revealing our opposite views on life: mine, epitomised by Jack London, postulated the infinite power of man's will, whilst Teddy, denying the existence of any conventional deity, believed implicitly in predestination. The heated argument over these ideas got us nowhere as, whatever examples of heroic achievements I quoted, he discarded on the ground that the outcome had been preordained aeons before the birth of the heroes. Soon we both realised that however wrong was the other there was no convincing him.

With the passage of time the SS ceased to be polite to the Gypsies. They shouted, expecting instant obedience, which they enforced with expert use of whips, canes and jack-boots. The food brought in by the internees was running out and the first pangs of hunger resulted in a stream of thefts, robbery and prostitution which soon changed into an irresistible flood. Imprisonment, hunger and the mixture of nationalities completely broke the free and lawless character of these people, leaving a seething mass of individuals without any restraints of morality, culture or custom. Thus, when the father and mother still clung to their golden trinkets, the flesh of their daughters became the only commodity to be traded for food. The 'law' couldn't care less what the Gypsies did, but it prohibited sexual intercourse to us, the prisoners, under penalty of death. For the same offence the SS faced reduction to the ranks and posting to the Eastern Front. But all that did not stop a single man; SS men indulged in fornication anywhere and everywhere. But there were so few of them that there were more than enough opportunities left for us, especially as, unlike the SS, the prisoners always recompensed the female partner. Also, our boys tended to combine the physical pleasure with some kind of love, care and, usually, monogamy – if this word applies in such circumstances. However, that last aspect did not matter a hoot to the ladies concerned.

There were sporadic cases of typhus and many ambulatory patients with diarrhoea, ulcers and injuries aggravated by inadequate food and filthy conditions. The barracks with their earthen floors were bad enough but the sanitary arrangements defied imagination. For the whole sector of some twenty thousand men, women and children, there, behind the last of the inhabited huts, were two more stables for ablutions and defecation. The one on the left of the camp street had a full length tin trough and above it a pipe with a tap every few feet. The men washed on one side of the trough, the women on the other, with the single water pipe dividing the sexes. During the day one or two SS men would frequently enter the washroom barrack bringing some girls. They would then order everybody out and shut the gates for a few minutes to emerge red, breathless and satisfied. The stable on the right was similar but, instead of the tin trough, a concrete channel about six feet deep and three feet wide ran its full length. Three horizontal wooden spars were arranged over the channel providing a bench-like seat on which the users perched precariously. The only concession to bourgeois prejudices were two arrows at the common entrance: these directed men to the right and women to the left, though naked backsides touched and overlapped in the rush hours.

We did not know or care what Gypsies had been like in their previous existence, but here, in the camp, they were incredibly dirty, and so afraid of the hospital, that our patients were either brought unconscious or staggered in when their complaints became absolutely unbearable and often incurable. But the numbers of patients mounted so that we were relieved to hear that additional orderlies were coming to join us. They came the next day but, to our disgust, all with 'millionaire's' numbers of over a hundred thousand which meant untrained and inexperienced new prisoners. Our bitter disappointment was sweetened by the appearance of a second group, this time, unbelievably, girls and most of them Polish! They were to staff the women's ward in Block 30. We met them 'socially' after the evening roll-call when embarrassment and shyness prevented me from seeing the comic side of the introductions. The girls, square and shapeless in their sack-like striped uniforms, with grey kerchiefs covering their shorn heads. The men, solid, hardened by labour and camp life, but now blushing, bowing and scraping. It was Teddy, debonair and, as always, completely at ease, who broke the ice with his burst of laughter:

'If you could only see yourselves, you great baboons!' – and turning to the girls continued:

'Never you mind them! They are house-trained and quite tame ... in ladies' company.'

Within a few days most of the crew, new and old, paired neatly and permanently into happy couples. Very few remained 'single' like Teddy, myself and one of the older doctors, a family man who never came to terms with the reality of the camp. Some prisoners stayed with their Gypsy mistresses, the latter not only beautiful but also most exotic. The exponents of this last group were three friends nicknamed the 'carrion-eaters' as they were responsible for removing, guarding and sending to the crematorium all dead bodies. The carrion-eaters were a strange lot who, probably owing to their grim work, formed a close, exclusive group. Recently they had become the centre of the most fantastic gossip, as it was rumoured that they, together with their paramours, had planned an escape. Escapes had been occurring since the camp was built. In spite of concrete walls, electrified fences, guard towers and machine-guns, prisoners tried to get out. Very few succeeded, and most of these were recaptured to be tortured and hanged. But even so, others were ready to try, and the Germans resorted to executing families and neighbours of a successful escaper: for every one, ten people were brought into the camp and publicly hanged after the evening roll-call. When that did not stop the attempts, the policy changed and ten prisoners belonging to the escaper's working group swung on the overloaded gibbet. But now, that was also past history and a tryer staked only his own life. Still, it was so unbelievably stupid even to mention the word 'escape' that all who heard the gossip shrugged their shoulders, as one does in response to an offensive and humourless joke. It was against such a background that one evening, just after the roll-call, two of the three Gypsy girls of the carrion-eaters shot out of a crowd and ran towards the camp gates calling at the tops of their voices for the SS to stop the escape of their lovers! The result was pandemonium. Half of the Gypsies ran after the girls to learn more; the other half surged in the opposite direction to seize the escapers. These two waves met, trampling over children and fighting one another. The already closed main gates were unlocked and a detachment of SS ran into the camp and became bogged down in the fighting crowd. At the far end, we stood near the hospital, too stunned to move. In this fantastic riot, the three young men with the third girl ran to the fence which separated us from freedom. They grabbed parts of bunks stacked against the last barrack. They piled the timber against the fence. They scaled the barricade, dragging the girl between them. From the adjoining towers the soldiers opened fire and the girl tumbled back. Two boys jumped over and ran for cover, the third hesitated, began to back down, but thought better of it, scrambled up and over and pursued by machine-gun fire, disappeared into the undergrowth. About a dozen SS men forced their way through and reached the place of the escape to join in the fusillade. The real sting of this humoresque was in the end: this *was* the end! Of the three nobody ever heard again. The girl, claiming abduction, was left alone and soon recovered from a superficial wound. She told us that it was all a mistake! The boys wanted to escape, but the girls had it too good and did not wish to go. On that day, the argument had become overheated, two girls threatened denunciation and were told, in the crudest camp slang, to 'publish and be damned' - and they did! It was only then, under the threat of hanging for an attempted escape, that, without any preparation, they had to run to save their necks. We all got off scot free and did not grudge the extra duties imposed on us by their escape. We were used to death and corpses, but loading dozens of them in the middle of the night was a new experience. We had to sling the unresisting, flaccid flesh over the high boards of a trailer and, until we learned how to do it properly, they tended to bounce and come back. Their arms twined round our necks as we fought off the cold, bluish bodies. Equally grotesque were the loud hissing sounds of breathing they made when we climbed up and walked on them to check that nothing would slide down on the way to the crematorium.

Bohdan, who hated the hospital work, obtained a transfer and became the keeper of the clothing and blanket store with responsibility for the laundry and de-lousing. This suited us as our uniforms were worn out, and in Birkenau most prisoners, because of shortages, wore ordinary civilian clothing marked with stripes of red oil paint. Soon we sported the best available suits, each to his own taste. Black appeared in a garish tweed jacket, and I in cord riding breeches from Hungary famous for such wares. Teddy, who also disliked the ill and the deceased, dressed in a pin-striped English worsted suit, became the clerk of the hospital, and was now concerned with reports and roll-call tallies. In theory, all the hospital work was closely supervised by the SS masters, but in practice, it was only ourselves who kept things going. Most of us worked hard, some, especially women, were doing it from a sense of duty; others realised that we were well-fed and well-clothed only as long as the job was done properly. Of the SS, our 'Sanitary', a Mr Bara of some Silesian village, was either drunk or busy 'organising' goods and treasures for himself. We often helped him in this last activity whilst he would stand us a bottle of vodka. Asked about his own nationality, he answered in his Silesian dialect:

'I'm no bloody German, but I'm not really a Pole. I am just Bara, the thief!'

The infamous Mengele became a frequent visitor since the castration of Jews had palled, and he found a new interest in Gypsy twins of which there was a large number in the camp. He measured, photographed, took blood samples and, when one twin died, he killed the other to dissect both at the same age. Between these amusements he strolled through the hospital whipping and trampling patients, orderlies and doctors for a dirty dixie, for a missing button or for nothing at all. On one occasion, I was sorting drugs at the counter of the hospital medical store, whilst behind me Teddy, who suffered from corns, was soaking his feet in one of those awkward hemispherical bowls. This was a serious crime and I became petrified when from outside came a shout warning us of Mengele's approach.

'Teddy! Chuck out the water and get busy rolling up these bandages! quick!'

'I'm damned if I throw away this water, it took me hours to heat it up.'

'Teddy! Mengele's here! Do something!'

'I will not waste hot water because of one lousy German doctor. What's written is written!'

And through the wide open gate marched the dreaded man in his shiny black cavalry boots and immaculate uniform glittering with silver. I sprang to attention reporting two prisoners at work. I was used to his careful and detailed inspection of our uniforms, the slow glance sweeping the shelves in search of dust. But this time, with eyes absolutely fixed, he stared past my shoulder. Like one seeing a ghost he passed his hand over his eyes, looked again and, suddenly shaking his head, he turned about and left the barrack. Behind me, with both feet squeezed together in the small bowl, Teddy just managed to stay upright swaying from side to side like one of those wooden rocking dolls that won't lie down.

In addition to sorting thousands of proprietary drugs brought from all countries of Europe I also worked with the out-patients, though by now we had no love for the thieving, traitorous Gypsies. This work was rather difficult as they were afraid of us, terrified of being hurt, and most suspicious of modern medicine. They usually tried to show their injuries from a safe distance and wanted only verbal advice resulting in an immediate cure. Once, there came a wizened old woman struggling with a thin girl wrapped in a blanket. The little one had an extensive and badly infected burn on her left forearm and I tried to calm her. She stopped fighting, but when I gently reached for the injured arm she twisted like a snake and bit my hand. It was so utterly unexpected that I jerked back and, as her teeth held, she was torn from her mother's arms. I must have yelled, because two of my helpers were already around us, and I just stopped them from hitting the child. With my right hand I forced her jaw open and picked her up off the floor. She was bigger than I thought, at least seven or eight, but starved like a skeleton. Her dark wide-open eyes never left mine as I stroked her dirty, black hair. She relaxed partly and now, holding on to me, asked in a whisper:

'You won't kill me?'

'No, little Kalo Benk, I won't kill you,' I answered this little 'black devil', and her thin arms encircled my neck as she snuggled closer.

I finished with other patients and sent to Block 30 for one of our girls – 'Don't bring me a Gypsy, I want a Polish girl!' The Gypsy auxiliaries helped us a lot, but they were rough, dirty and hated their own kind. A tall, fair, young woman came, asking what I wanted.

'Take her to your block and wash her thoroughly, all over – she is solid with dirt. And be careful – she bites like hell!'

I showed her my freshly-bandaged hand. The little girl clung to me until I promised that she would not be hurt and would come back to me. Her arm healed in a few weeks and I managed to feed her up till she became again a healthy, laughing child. She was the only Gypsy I knew who remained grateful, trusting and honest – at least with me.

This little 'Black Devil' had also brought into my life the tall, fair girl who had come to help. Later, when she enquired about the Gypsy child, we started talking. Fairly new to the camp, she smiled easily and brought with her the freshness of the outside world, the news of Warsaw, of lilac which still bloomed somewhere in masses of heavy, scented sprays. Her name was Sena, and once in the dim past she had worked in the Scouts' Headquarters where we both knew people, though I carefully avoided giving away any clues about my old self. Slowly our friendship grew deeper and stronger. And then, suddenly she collapsed with typhus. Luckily, the prevailing circumstances were very different from those of my own illness: she was already in a hospital and, most important, she had friends. Teddy and I maintained her two hospital charts – one at her bed proclaimed ordinary influenza and was changed frequently to show the short duration of the illness; the other, hidden from the SS, monitored the real course of the typhus. We chose the best doctors, obtained heart stimulants and other medicine, not to mention sweetened drinking water and constant care and attention. Though the disease had lost a lot of its original virulence, it was often fatal. At the crisis, Sena, appearing entirely conscious, peremptorily demanded poison. With tears in her large, blue eyes she refused any help and begged only the final release from this living hell. No amount of argument and pleading affected her decision to die, till I brought her three black pills – some fancy vitamin preparation. Weeping quietly she thanked me, swallowed the pills and after a long drink went into a deep, untroubled sleep. From then on she began the slow climb to recovery. There were other problems and complications like bed sores and mastoidal trouble leading to an operation, which Teddy and I supervised closely. We provided Evipan, scrubbed twice the little surgery, and made sure that all instruments were available and sterile. We did not interfere with the surgeon, though we made it plain to him that unpleasant things were likely to happen if anything went wrong, or if the final scar was not hidden behind the jaw bone. But, in time, she recovered fully and the tripartite friendship was further cemented by her ordeal.

In the meantime the typhus, from endemic, became epidemic and the Germans, as in Auschwitz 1, gassed all patients suffering from it. Luckily the strain fell on Teddy and me while Sena knew little of it. She was in charge of the children's ward and had enough trouble with noma to which there was no answer. This terrible disease spread, rapidly devouring, like some invisible beast, the lips, cheeks and whole faces of the little ones who died like flies. They died, and Sena wept bitter tears mourning each one as if it were her own.

In early summer our relations changed dramatically. We were chatting one evening, but she seemed subdued, uneasy, and suddenly, blushing furiously, interrupted me in mid-sentence:

'I ... I know that men want from women more than just talk ... Teddy said that you will never ask, and I – I don't want you to go to a Gypsy girl! If ... if you want something ... anything from a woman ... it must come from me.'

We met unobtrusively and heavy wooden bars locked the gates of Bohdan's store behind us. The store, with its piles of soft, clean blankets, was out of bounds to all, and, shy and constrained, we were alone in the silent darkness.

Late the same night, I was back in my own bunk, but I could not sleep. There was the recent memory of the soft arms, of white breasts which I still felt pressing against me. There was also the void of broken faith, of my own broken promises ... I had betrayed the Golden Princess. Yet faith and promises can exist only in a fixed universe, and relate to real time. Here, in hell, suspended in the limbo of today and the doubtful morrow ... but these were excuses, mitigating circumstances, and even if it were for today only - I still had to live with myself. At last, I knew that it had been a mistake which could not go on.

Later we talked, but did not find a way out: there was no return to our previous easy camaraderie and I could not bear the sad, hurt look in her eyes any more than I could forget her pliant, wild body and the rapture of our love.

Most of us, when first thrown into the horror of the camp, dreamt of, or prayed for, the miracle of German defeat and our freedom. In the early days of Auschwitz the inhuman conditions and complete isolation from the outside world killed these thoughts as soon as they were born. Later, with increasing numbers of newly-arriving prisoners and guards, gossip spread and German newspapers were sometimes seen. By then, however, the bitter and repeated disappointments of Dieppe, Greece and Crete, as well as the shattering Russian defeats, produced apathy, and lack of interest in the war news. Stalingrad was played down and British victories were ... in Africa! A fat lot of good that was to us. But in the Gypsy camp, though working hard and involved in our own affairs, we began to notice indefinable undercurrents. The Russian prisoners were now treated better, no longer isolated and slaughtered. There were no more mass executions. Somewhere, somebody heard SS men worrying about the outcome of the war. Then our scoundrel Bara switched his activities and, through his contacts in the crematoria, began to obtain good suits. These he sold to the SS men who stashed away the civilian outfits - just in case. Once he brought, and gave us to hide, four big suitcases full of the choicest clothing whilst on his heels two Gestapo officers came to enquire into his affairs. However, nothing was discovered and everybody was satisfied. That is, until Bara demanded back his merchandise which could not be found! The 'Boss' stamped, raved and

threatened us with his pistol when Teddy produced a bottle of vodka:
'Come on Boss! Have a drink and forget it - we must all live together!'
'You bloody bastard! You stole my own things! I'll ... I'll ...'

In the end he did not shoot Teddy but went into partnership with him to the great satisfaction of both parties. Four of us lived exceedingly well and there was plenty for Sena and her friends. Never did Teddy convert stolen goods directly into food but kept exchanging suits for vodka, vodka for gold and currency, which in turn bought cigarettes - the most universal commodity. And on each conversion his margin of profit never fell below several hundred per cent. Of us four only Black smoked and, as we regarded all assets as common property, he helped himself freely to the stocks. On one occasion Teddy and I noticed a considerable shortage in our supplies and jokingly decided to try a cigarette so that Black would not be the sole beneficiary. The smoke stung my eyes and tasted pretty foul, but also gave a strange feeling of satisfaction, and this first cigarette of my life started a dirty and expensive habit which has remained with me ever since.

Work with Teddy opened my eyes to another unique feature of the Gypsy Sector - namely its canteen. Most concentration camps had a sort of shop, staffed by prisoners but controlled from the SS headquarters. These 'shops' sold toothpaste but no toothbrushes, shoe-laces but no shoes, cards or envelopes and postage stamps. Very rarely indeed there arrived small consignments of synthetic salad oil, an odd barrel of sauerkraut or other pickles, and cigarettes at exorbitant prices. All these goods were exchanged for tokens issued to prisoners for money sent by their families. But the Gypsy canteen was different. The 'internees' possessed valuables so the shop was permitted and encouraged to sell for cash, gold or other treasures. Also, as the Gypsies were most unlikely to part with their heirlooms in exchange for toothpaste, the SS took care to stock the shelves with an inexhaustible supply of tobacco, cigarettes and other commodities like synthetic honey and even a vinegary wine. The cigarettes changed with time. The German 'Josma' were succeeded by French 'Gauloises' and later by Herzegovinian 'Dravas', thin and black, with the punch of dynamite. There were also large transports of 'Players' which the SS stole from the Red Cross supplies intended for British POWs. But the most interesting aspects were the takings because, however generously one estimated the wealth of the Gypsies, the shop accumulated monthly many times its value. The SS, delighted with this goldmine, closed their eyes to the fact that practically all of the treasure had been stolen by the prisoners from the crematoria and smuggled to the Gypsy sector in exchange for cigarettes and other goods. So everybody was happy though only a fraction of the takings reached the headquarters, the larger part having been split between the canteen personnel and the SS NCO supervising them. Unfortunately, they omitted to share their profits with the local Gestapo, known as the Camp Political Department. Thus, one day the real masters of Germany, the Gestapo, descended on the canteen. Some of the treasures I saw with my own eyes and Aladdin's Cave looked in comparison like a pawnbroker's den. There were jam jars full of huge diamonds, rolls of toilet paper laminated full length with green dollar notes, long, heavy 'sticks' of wrapping paper glued neatly over stacks of gold dollars. The haul was so enormous that the Gestapo preferred to keep it quiet. There were no reports, no punishment except slapped faces, the treasure disappeared as if it had never existed, and the culprits ordered to carry on as before, but with a proper share for the Political Department!

In spite of our 'good jobs' and highly successful trading, life was no bed of roses. We worked hard and were constantly reminded of our status as inmates of the concentration camp. Just across the wire, in Sector D, we saw from a distance quite a few hangings, some for attempted escape, others for possession of gold. On the other side, only a few hundred yards away, the four crematoria smoked continuously, whilst the long trains kept rolling into the camp siding and along the dusty road flowed endless crowds. To our left marched smaller groups of able-bodied men and women – the camp's new slave replacements. To the right, shuffled the endless procession of other people, mothers with children, infirm, aged ... They walked and staggered all through the long summer days, often through the night. The front of the endless column reached and filled the courtyard of the first crematorium, overflowed and, redirected, shuffled further, to crowd into the courtyard of the next one. By the time the fourth yard was filled, the first one was empty and ready for the next batch. And the marching column was continuously replenished from its source – the camp siding into which screeched, grated and jolted trains full of Jews from Greece, Czechoslovakia, Holland ...

There was little time for watching the slaughter of the unresisting masses and, superficially, their fate had no connection with our hectic lives. But, in reality, despite our puny works and intrigues, we were just as vulnerable, balanced precariously on the invisible edge dividing life and death. Ironically, it was Teddy, the coolest and cleverest of us, who slipped and retrieved his balance brilliantly, though at a price. Somehow, with the growing numbers of admissions and discharges, accounting for the dead and the internal transfers, Teddy made a mistake, and the Sector roll-call was one man short. The fault was found and rectified in a quarter of an hour but simultaneously came, shouted from block to block, the call for the hospital clerk to report, and Bara, slapping Teddy on the back, shook his head:

'Run and report fast because they don't like waiting! They won't kill you, but you'll get at least fifty on the arse.'

And Teddy who, like all of us, saw and tended many broken bodies, ran to his doom.

It was a long distance from the hospital to the open square between the two kitchens where the figures of the roll-call were received by the Sector Rapport Führer. At the time this position was held by a particularly nasty SS sergeant, who delighted in floggings and beatings which he always administered personally. We stood still, shaken and immeasurably sorry for Teddy. Sorry and terrified, as each one knew that it could have been any or all of us. Suddenly, unexpectedly we all heard an unearthly shriek, and after a momentary silence, a real cacophony of shouts, wails and cries. From the beginning of the camp there was a custom, an unbroken tradition, that Poles, and especially old numbers, never cried and just fainted or died silently under the lash. Now we stood glancing at one another as if to confirm that we really had heard and not just imagined the unthinkable. But soon the noise ceased and, dismissed by a shouted command, we ran to see, to collect what was left of Teddy. We met him heading back to the hospital, very red and rather stiff but little worse for his experience. Once inside, Teddy asked us to remove his clothing and do what we could. His backside was swollen and criss-crossed by abrasions and weals which we covered with a soothing, antiseptic cream and applied cold compresses. Only then we asked what had happened. The sentence had been fifty, but unbelievably, for the first time in the history of the camp, it was not carried out, and Teddy only got nine strokes.

'Look! Why do they beat people? – mostly for their own pleasure! You grit your teeth, shut your mouth and they kill you. But shout, roar, moan and cry, and they are satisfied, they are happy: they have inflicted more pain than the man can bear, and they stop. But change this compress and get me another of these pain-killing pills of yours.'

Though unorthodox and mistaken in his belief in fate, he was a genius.

Time moved in its own mysterious way. It almost stopped and stretched its seconds into hours when Teddy had been flogged, then, anxious to catch up on itself, it rushed by, clipping short our sleep, jumping over moments of tenderness and secret meetings. Behind the wires the trains rolled slowly, the people of Europe walked endlessly to their death, and the camp grew. Between us and the crematoria they built one more sector. Behind the railway siding the women's camp sprouted more and more barracks, whilst across the main road stacks of materials piled up and thousands of prisoners began building another extension for the culture of the Third Reich. Prisoners' numbers were slowly climbing towards the two hundred thousand mark. Some Jews, temporarily reprieved from the gas chambers, had their own series of numbers prefixed by letters, the 'A's and the 'B's were already used up. Our Gypsies had also been numbered but with the prefix 'Z' for *Zigeuner*. In this international jungle, where every creature, dead or alive, was counted and accounted for, the masters no longer knew who was still there, who had died, who had discarded the yellow star for a red triangle, or had undergone some other metamorphosis. And this could not be allowed by the victorious nation so proud of its orderliness. So, the prisoners were tattooed with their numbers on the left forearm. Branded like pigs and cattle, marked forever as German slaves, men, women, and children and new-born babies. Because babies were still being born in the Gypsy sector.

We got used to beatings and hangings, we accepted the shorn heads of women. But when we watched the girls being disfigured by the tattooed numbers, saw the tears in their eyes, even the most resigned of us thought of the day of reckoning. The reckoning with the German people, because the names like Hitler, Himmler, or Mengele, did not matter – it was thousands of Gestapo, millions of SS and Wehrmacht backed by all Germany which had created this hell. On one occasion the four of us discussed this matter. Teddy and I maintained that whilst, of course, the Germans would have to be exterminated not even they should be tortured. Tempers began to fray, when the entrance of Bara caused a dead silence. But Teddy, smiling pleasantly at the SS man, continued:

'Look at our dear, tame Boss! You wouldn't pull out his teeth, his nails ... just shoot him quietly' - and turning directly to Bara, added:

'You wouldn't feel it, even.'

There must have been something in our eyes, in our faces, which stopped the man for he just turned and walked out, silent and pale.

During the years of starvation we all saw the kitchens as an unattainable paradise, and even now looked at the chefs as special beings set apart from the rest of us. So I was speechless when two of them proposed that I should join the kitchen staff. Their SS master, known as 'Toothy' for his buck teeth, agreed that help was needed in the bread magazine, whilst they were delighted with the prospect of extra leisure. But now, with more food than I could eat, and all the friends in the hospital, I did not go till Teddy pointed out the advantages of growing influence and widening scope for 'organisation'. Also if things went wrong in the hospital the spread of our employments offered more safety to our group. Therefore I agreed to join the kitchens. The chefs told Toothy that 6643 was the man for the job; we instructed Bara to agree to the transfer and the camp Administration (which had to be on good terms with kitchens and hospital) had the papers signed by the SS supervisor. I started work in the bread magazine as assistant to Adam, the storekeeper. But before I learned the job properly, Adam was transferred to another sector of Birkenau, leaving me in charge. Only then did I realise that the whole transaction was inspired by Toothy who coveted Adam's 'permanent' Gypsy mistress.

After the morning roll-call I received long lists of the huts with the numbers of inmates. These were copied into our ledgers with the corresponding sums of loaves and microscopic portions of margarine or beetroot jam. Then, with the carriers from each hut assembled, we proceeded to issue the food. I stood by the open hatch calling out hut number and quantity of bread due. My two Gypsy minions threw loaves straight into the large box waiting outside whilst I kept count with Toothy hovering in the background and 'supervising'. We never gave short measure though the speed of delivery was such that neither the recipients nor Toothy could keep up with the count. In the afternoon we gave out margarine or jam, cleaned the magazine, unloaded and stacked new deliveries. The real problems arose from the unofficial issues. Toothy used to take several loaves for his mistresses and SS cronies, kitchens required extra bread for their hard-working crews and I had to feed my helpers. Thus at the end of the day I was some twenty loaves short before I even considered supplying my own friends. I received and signed for the bread delivered and was allowed for 'spillage' fewer loaves than were squashed and crumbled in transit. The solution to the problem was made more difficult as the driver and the escort of the transport were new SS men freshly posted to the camp. Terrified of the beasts and evildoers confined behind the wire, they never stirred from the lorry and Toothy refused to approach them on the dubious business, though he was more and more frightened by the possible discovery of our shortages. At last I took the matter into my own hands and told Toothy to bring the escort man into the magazine. When they entered I gave Toothy a Player and asked the other if he smoked. His eyes darted to my boss already puffing clouds of smoke and, hesitantly, he took one and after the first drag examined the cigarette:

'English cigarettes? The best tobacco in the world!'

I extended the packet, telling him to keep it, at the same time ostentatiously flashing the Swiss chronometer which, as a store-keeper, I was permitted to wear. His eyes nearly popped out, and he stammered that he, an SS NCO, did not have a watch. The rest was simple; after a few quick glasses of vodka I explained: extra bread on the next delivery and he would have a good watch. Of course, watches and vodka had to be paid for in something better than bread, which was too bulky for such transactions. I paid in margarine which was clipped off prisoners' rations, but the process was so hallowed by time and custom that it never occurred to any of us to question the morality of it. The goods were usually delivered by Lalik, a young Jewish prisoner employed as a clerk and runner in the Political Department of the camp Gestapo. The next delivery of bread we counted as 6,500 loaves, and after signing the chitty for 5,000 I gave the escort man a gold watch. From that time we never had a bread shortage in the store.

Getting bread out of the store was easy as most of it went to my hospital mates. Giving out their nominal rations, I would begin counting thrown pairs - one, two, three ... but, after say ten, would switch to calling out units, so that the next pair became twelve, fourteen and so on. Toothy never caught on and ten loaves above the nominal number were already in the box. For smaller gifts or payments, I had my own, 'unofficial', key to the 'tamperproof' magazine door which always was carefully locked by Toothy.

There was a lot of hard work but also satisfaction, and many distractions - some rather hilarious though always on the edge of a disaster. Once there arrived at the kitchen a young Jewess in a smart costume barely marked with the regulation red paint. She carried a large ewer and asked for sweetened white coffee. Of course nobody was allowed near the kitchens, and the coffee was sweetened only once a week whilst the milk was reserved for small children. After a moment of stunned silence the chef, who disliked Jews and spent half his time chasing away beggars and thieves, erupted with a string of vituperation and the girl walked away. But soon the Gestapo of the Political Department arrived and proceeded to compare the actual kitchen building with the official plans. But the kitchen had been built just as we had built the hospital and, within a few minutes, they had a long list of unauthorised partitions, windows, doors, fittings and equipment. When the Gestapo chief remarked that the prisoners and SS men responsible for stealing and installing state property would soon be dealt with, I noticed the quiet Jewess just behind him. There was no time to lose and I approached her quickly:

'Look, you've made your point with a vengeance! I can promise all the coffee and other better things, but call off these bastards now. I don't mind paying, I don't mind giving, but this is going too far and even you might find life difficult and ... short. Accidents can happen when too many old numbers are stepped upon.'

'I know about you from Lalik and nothing will happen to you. Anyway,' - she gestured towards the Gestapo chief - 'he is easy to set upon anybody but difficult to recall.'

'Stop him now; ten kilograms of butter, not marge, but butter, for him, and I'll see that you don't lose on it either.' Unobtrusively she sidled up to her chief and in a few minutes they walked away. Within an hour she brought me the long list torn across, and I delivered the butter which was a standard issue for children. The children had to do with margarine which was intended as an addition to a thousand gallons of prisoners' soup. Still, we had to live, and a war with the Gestapo was not the way to do it.

I often met the coffee lady. She 'lived' just across the railway siding in the women's concentration camp, but was escorted by SS men to spend whole days in secretarial work for the Political Department. Her name was Eva and, for the time being, she had a good life, as the SS were mighty careful in the treatment of any property of the Gestapo even if she were merely a Jewish slave. Eva negotiated with her boss on my behalf many times. I had to pay well, but it saved several lives.

An inevitable feature of the Gypsy sector was fortune-telling. We were fascinated by the smooth, rolling phrases of 'journey over the water', 'beware of the dark woman' ... But soon the patter palled even for the most superstitious of us. On the other hand, just for something to do, I learned the phrases, the traditional meaning of various cards as well as palm-lines. I also learnt to watch the face of a listener for the satisfied smirk of 'I knew it!', or a bewildered expression which warned me to switch quickly from a 'dark woman' to a 'fair one'. I became good enough with cards and palms to entertain our girls and, unbelievably, to be asked by some colleagues for a 'reading'. In the kitchens we just shrugged our shoulders because the matter was not even worth a thought. But one day, to my amazement, the senior chef asked whether I had ever had my fortune told by Manchi. The more I scoffed and laughed, the more he insisted and, not to offend him, I agreed. He brought a few friends and an old, swarthy woman. Small and wrinkled like a dried-up apple, she had deep-set eyes as black as I ever saw. Manchi looked at me with her disconcerting eyes and, whilst the company was settling down, she pretended to have forgotten her cards. She went out for them making a gesture for me to follow her. Outside the door she took a pack of cards from her voluminous skirts and leaned close, almost touching me. She spoke in a jumbled mixture of Polish, Czech and Romany, but I had no difficulty in understanding, and no doubt about the meaning of her quiet whisper.

'You not really you, nothing true about you, but not to worry. I no tell others. Don't say aught – I know and you know.'

Though it was such an unexpected statement, I did not hesitate and answered that I just did not know what she was talking about. She smiled and led me back to the others. There she shuffled and made me cut the cards, but then began turning them over on to a pile without any concession to the usual elaborate patterns common to most fortune-tellers. She also began the standard empty patter when my friends interrupted:

'No, no! Manchi, tell him first the past so that he knows it's true. Go on woman, tell the past!'

She took my hand but never glanced at the palm, never raised her eyes to my face.

'There are three women about you.'

There was a roar of laughter: 'There are ten thousand! Come on Manchi!'

But she continued in this atrocious mixture of languages which robbed her words of seriousness and conviction. She continued, giving me a perfect description of my Mother, of Princess and of Sena! I was used to and immune from the usual claptrap, I myself had learned the way to make it convincing – but this was not the same. This was uncannily precise, spoken quietly but without a pause, without hesitation. It was impossibly accurate though nobody in the camp ever heard of my Mother, and only Teddy knew about Princess, and few suspected anything about Sena and me. She kept talking without changing her manner, but now just spouting ordinary Gypsy rubbish. She stopped, and I asked whether I would survive the war. She scattered more cards and, for the second time, looked into my eyes:

'Yes, you live long and very happy. But you will be ill, very ill. You think you die, but you live. There is a journey over the water, journey over the sea, there is money, good money. I know no more. I finish.'

'But will I marry the Gold Woman?' – describing Irka she did not use the usual 'fair' but just 'gold' which I had never heard a Gypsy applying to any woman. The others joined in urging her to tell me more. She hesitated a long moment, still looking straight into my eyes.

'You sure you want to know? No good for you to know much!'

And when I nodded she said:

'Gold Woman not for you. You never see the Gold Woman. But you live, and you happy!'

She left the room quickly, leaving behind a hubbub of noise and the banter of my friends.

Toothy was becoming unbearable, taking more and more from the store, as well as demanding cigarettes and vodka which had to be purchased from other SS men. From time to time he ordered me to give food directly to some of his pals and this I hated and feared. In addition to being German, they were stupid, semi-literate beasts who had no idea about 'organisation'. One of them was caught red-handed with a cube of margarine from my store. The sergeant in charge of all the kitchens stormed into the magazine dragging along the small, thin SS man and his greasy packet. The big bully reduced the little man to tears and made him admit that it had been I who had given him the margarine. In the next few minutes I acquired cut lips, wobbly teeth, and a burst ear drum. I was also promised hanging for stealing food and for corrupting the SS guard – and this was a serious matter. It was also the only hope as all 'crimes' implicating the SS had to be submitted to the Gestapo and Eva was soon coming for their coffee.

The same afternoon she gave me back my life, bringing the torn-up report of the kitchen sergeant.

'This is the end of it and you will never hear about it again. Neither that son of a bitch nor even the camp commandant will dare to enquire about Gestapo matters. But of course you will lose your store job and be transferred to Sector D.'

CHAPTER 17

THE OLD NUMBERS

The thwarted kitchen sergeant did not give up and, through the SS Work-Führer, had me placed in the group assigned to deepen and straighten the nearby river. There, waist deep in icy water, the prisoners had no chance of living more than a few weeks. Not satisfied with this he had gone to the trouble of giving the SS man in charge of the group my number with his request for 'special attention'!

I was transferred to Sector D and the next morning, after the roll-call, just as in Auschwitz 1, we marched towards the camp gates. It was again a grim and terrifying moment to be back where I began years ago. Yet it was not quite the same: I was now a marked man but also an experienced old number with many friends.

The usual count of heads at the gates slowed down the marching columns and our group almost stopped in front of the kitchens. There, from an open door emerged, with his own SS supervisor, the Chef of Section D kitchen. They both strolled casually to the capo and the SS man leading our river-column, and chatted a moment. Then the Chef came to me and ostentatiously shook my hand:

'Don't worry, mate! They have *our* instructions now, and if anybody lays a hand on you they know what will happen!'

We arrived at the place of work, but before I could get a spade the capo was by my side:

'You don't need this. If you want to walk about take a tape or one of these measuring rods. But best come with me to the hut, there are some good sandwiches, and the boss would like to meet you.'

So I lazed happily on the banks of the river, as the capo had been told that if I complained, or met with an accident, his legs would be broken and he would die in the hospital. The SS supervisor was simply promised vodka and cigarettes for his co-operation. I was there less than a week whilst my friends were altering my card in the camp main index. I now became an electrician because there was a recent order from SS Headquarters that all electricians must be employed in their own trade. Work with the electricians was not bad and my army training in overhead lines proved most useful. Soon I was leading a group of linesmen as there was a lot of new work in the fast growing camp. We also had troubles with grossly overloaded cables, overheated transformers and contact breakers propped up by broom handles. Still, I enjoyed the challenge of working on the live 420V overhead network. It required nerve and agility to sneak between the four bare conductors whilst wearing clumsy climbing irons. It also needed steady hands and skill, especially in wet weather when the electric leakage along soaked poles meant a good shock from each wire. When stringing new lines, or repairing old ones, we had many unofficial requests (for stronger bulbs, extra lights or sockets) which we accepted with glee and at good prices. Though I could always call on the kitchens or get extra supplies chucked over the wire from the Gypsy camp, I did not need to bother old friends as my present job paid well enough.

There were also other matters such as thousands of insulators sunk in a bog and coils of wire mysteriously developing kinks at every single turn. But the best was the new high tension line built by the German civilian experts from AEG. Using prisoners' labour they beat and kicked their new slaves no less than did the SS guards. We, the professionals, were not maltreated, and the Germans were only too ready to accept our humble offers of doing their own skilled work. I quickly learned the exacting job of splicing the high tension oil-filled cable which, officially, we were not supposed to touch. The whole project was completed in a few months and when the power was switched on ... it blew up. Not a spectacular atomic bang, but enough to rip open the concrete floor and disable the transformer. The old engineer, who told me what a drop of water can do in a 400KV cable, had been absolutely right. It was really killing two birds with one spoonful of water because the Gestapo hanged for sabotage the AEG foreman - the one that had been so skilled in beating prisoners.

One day under a heavy guard, I was ordered with my group to do a job at the town railway station. We had just reached the railway yards when the sirens sounded an air-raid warning. This was an extremely rare occurrence which panicked the SS men and filled us with joy at seeing some American war effort. Our guards left us sitting in front of a concrete pill-box whilst they scampered to a nearby underground shelter. High overhead we saw the silvery flashes of the toy-like Fortresses as they steadily droned on and on. The anti-aircraft guns opened fire from behind the station and round puffs of smoke peppered the clear sky. More heavy guns sounded from the direction of the SS barracks whilst we sat admiring the show. Then, suddenly, with the whistling sound of the falling bomb, the show was brought straight to us. To our left black fountains of smoke erupted along the rails and showered us with flying debris. Chunks of concrete, lumps of wood and a hail of stones fell all around us as we cheered and called for more. But the planes were already past, vanishing into the distance. The artillery stopped, the skies resumed their natural deep blue and out of this blue the last bomb smacked right into the entrance of the shelter. Its flash blinded us, its deafening explosion left us flat on the ground, stupefied, semi-conscious. Ages passed before life reasserted itself with shouts, cries and screams. We were called to dig up the shelter and as the entrance was almost clear, within a few minutes we entered the concrete tomb. It seemed empty except for a red heap of wet manure piled against the back wall on which several silhouettes appeared as if freshly painted and smeared. In the centre of this concrete surface was one silver pocket watch with a length of chain, both twice the natural size but flat as a sheet of paper. We found it hard not to cheer when we heard that this was all that remained of some fifty SS men and German civilians.

Then came the evening when, after the roll-call, we were herded into the barracks and locked up. But through the ill-fitting roof joints we watched strings of lorries driving in and out of the adjoining Gypsy sector. They came empty from the right and when fully loaded went to the left, to the gas chambers. They came and went all night whilst we listened to the cries, wailings and shouted commands, all muted by the continuous growl of the engines. About a dozen Gypsy girls were sent to the women's camp together with the female hospital staff. The male staff was transferred to our Sector D. Of the original twenty thousand Gypsies the rest disappeared as if they had never existed and only the four overworked chimneys belched flames and smoke above the rising mists of dawn.

The next morning Teddy was allotted to the small and select group of engineers and surveyors employed in the Camp Development Office. They were responsible to the SS Engineering Officer with the rank of Hauptsturmführer which was equal to that of the Commandant of the whole Auschwitz Camp. Within a few days Teddy asked me if I would like to join him and, on the direct orders of the Hauptsturmführer, I was transferred to the Development Office. There were about twenty of us and hardly any work. Maps, plans and detailed drawings of the camp were almost ready and showed roads, streets, barracks as well as water supplies, sewer systems and electrical network. All of this was divided into stages, several of which had been completed whilst the further schemes had ground to a stop. On my first day Teddy introduced me to the Hauptsturmführer. A young man in immaculate field-grey rose from behind his desk and met us halfway to shake hands! He was learning Polish but it was still an uphill struggle to communicate adequately, especially as the conversation took a most unexpected turn. The officer began by apologising for the terrible situation in which we all found ourselves. A Finnish engineer, he had joined the German forces to fight for his country against the communist hordes, but was put in charge of building a concentration camp for people who, like himself, struggled for freedom. He gave us the real news of the rout of the German Armies in the east, of the slow but irresistible Allied progress from the west, of the desperate shortages of all materials, and the inevitable end of the Third Reich. But he also pointed out the standing orders which clearly stated that, whatever the situation, no prisoner should be left alive to fall into enemy hands.

Armed with some insignia of our superior jobs we could wander freely within the outer ring of guards. Thus, with a sketch pad and a roll of drawings, we could go almost anywhere in Birkenau, though for the women's camp it was advisable to bring a theodolite or other showy aids. To get into any of the crematoria we required a pass and a guard, but this was no problem as our boss used to sign anything we asked for and would also allot to us the SS guards, telling them in our presence that their task was to protect us and help in the execution of our duties. This solved the problem of delivering food and clothing to Sena in the women's camp. But most of the time I was helping Teddy in his fast growing 'business' which, however fascinating, began to worry me more and more. Without the convenient hiding places and other facilities of the hospital we still ate well but did not cook or prepare special dishes. I also had plenty of cigarettes but Teddy no longer enjoyed the protracted bargaining of all the past wheeling and dealing. With an ingeniously marked and pivoted pencil, he weighed and pocketed any and all of the gold articles that came his way including the 'biters' which was the slang term for the gold teeth stolen from the crematoria. Now, prisoners were no longer hanged for possession of currency or even gold, but the 'biters' still meant the gallows, as the Germans did not wish such a proof of mass murder to seep out of the camp. So, in spite of their high gold content, the teeth were relatively cheap and Teddy accumulated them fast. His main circuit was simple and incredibly profitable. Civilian specialist workers, like the AEG electrical experts, brought and sold to him fresh tomatoes and other fruit for which he paid in dollars ten times the market value. These were carted in instrument boxes to our offices where we loaded them into the empty soup containers which were then returned to the camp kitchens. There, for a fair 'donation' of cigarettes, they were repacked into a clean container, flooded with black ersatz coffee and shipped to the crew of the crematoria.

Strong young Jews were chosen by the SS for this duty. Once there they never left the area of their crematorium, working three eight-hour shifts. They slept, ate and rested in their own dormitories and enjoyed all food, drink and treasure brought 'for resettlement' by the Jews whose bodies they kept loading into the ovens. After three months the SS liquidated the old crew and chose a new one. But, for their short working life, they had everything except fresh produce for which they gladly paid anything, especially in 'biters', which we collected and transported in the most ingenious ways, proof against strict checks by the SS men at the main gates of the 'cremos'.

In the office I made more friends. There was Krystyn, an ex-pupil of my old Batory's College and 'Tiger', a student of architecture, who, with his lady-love in the women's camp, shared my labours in carrying supplies for her and Sena.

One sunny morning Teddy called me aside and without preliminaries came to the point:

'Today I blow if you'll help, and I need at least one more man. Who would you suggest?'

So Teddy was escaping. He was going and leaving me behind. He took for granted that I would help - well, of course, I would. But the fact that he was leaving me behind was a terrible shock. Still, with all my heart I hoped for his success and, for the second man, I suggested Krystyn.

Arriving from different directions the three of us met at the beginning of the mid-day break in a slight depression of the abandoned building site. The shovel gangs never finished the levelling of this area and mounds of earth overgrown with tall weeds and willow bushes screened us from a casual glance. The wilderness was criss-crossed by paths and dirt roads along which lorries and carts had rolled transporting soil and building materials. Here and there stacks of planks and parts of prefabricated barracks showed their bleached timbers above the lush greenery of the waste land. Behind one of these piles, seemingly abandoned, stood a civilian lorry, one of many such vehicles contracted by the SS as extra transport.

'Put the top three plates aside and load the others, please,' called Teddy, disappearing into the bushes. From behind the lorry emerged two prisoners in civilian clothing with bright pink stripes on trousers and jackets. Suddenly it dawned on me: for the past week Teddy had been experimenting with toothpastes of vivid colour. Some of them could be easily brushed out of the fabric though they looked like the official prisoners markings. This was it, and this was why Teddy spent last night sewing new bright patches on to his clothing. In addition to the painted stripes, our jailers cut square holes in the garments which were then machined with patches of red and black fabric - but Teddy's patches were cleverly stitched on top of a complete, uncut suit.

The plates were very heavy, almost too much for four men, but we just managed. They were thick, double boarded, hut wall-units about four feet wide and seven or eight feet long. The top three were standard ones but all the rest were window plates with the actual windows removed. Thus, when piled up on the lorry they would form a substantial cavity in the very middle of the stack. The worst moment came when Krystyn and I had to stand on the nearly completed load and suddenly found ourselves high above all the weeds and bushes. There we were completely exposed. The gunners on the watch towers, the mussulmen of a transport column resting nearby, their capos and foremen must be staring at

Krystyn and myself, the only two prisoners working during the mid-day break! Teddy and the other two were already inside whilst Krystyn and I heaved the last solid plates on top of the pile and wedged securely the whole load. From the bushes emerged the civilian driver and his mate. Without a word, I passed to them two small but extremely heavy packages and watched them unscrew the top of the gas generator (all private vehicles ran on wood), drop in the parcels and cover them with hardwood blocks. This, half a kilo of gold per head, was payment for the escape. This was also the insurance against potential treason by the civilians who would also hang for the 'biters'.

There were terrifying moments of the evening return to camp with one man missing from our group, but the SS guards did not dare to beat us up because of the Hauptsturmführer's protection. It all finished with a few slaps and a lot of cursing. A month later, a coded message reached us from Teddy – free and back in Cracow with his beloved Sophie!

Krystyn and I had our own escape plans, but before we could complete the preparations the Germans decided to evacuate Auschwitz, beginning with the Poles. The situation grew more tense as every day some Poles were recalled from work and loaded into trains departing to other concentration camps in the west. Krystyn, Tiger and I talked and argued daily. With the shrinkage of the camp we were losing friends, the security of our preferential position and the chance of survival. At the same time, with every passing hour, the Russian front approached bringing life or death – death because the Germans had planned the destruction of the camp with all its inmates. This autumn of 1944 the three of us still had the choice. We could try to remain in Auschwitz, counting on the help of our SS boss though he had volunteered for active service on the East Front and could disappear at any moment. Then we would be pushed out on the next transport, possibly to the stone quarries of Linz or Mauthausen ... Alternatively, with the help of other old numbers, we could still choose any 'good' transport and continue our slavery in another camp, hoping for the ultimate end of hostilities. Finally, we decided on the latter alternative and, using all our wiles and connections, chose a small transport going to Breslau-Lisa, a minute 'working' camp. Then, in spite of all the SS checks and controls, we reached the train well supplied by our friends with warm clothing, extra food and even some small treasures for the 'rainy day'.

CHAPTER 18

TRAVEL IN THE THIRD REICH

Most transports from Auschwitz were packed tight into closed railway trucks but with only fifty of us travelling a hundred miles, a passenger coach was used. The windows were boarded up, doors padlocked and the SS guard promised to shoot us all if anybody tried to escape. After long delays the train rolled north-west to Breslau. We disembarked at the junction of Breslau-Lisa and were marched to an enormous SS depot to join three hundred prisoners of the maintenance crew. Our new camp consisted of only one large hut where an inmate with a 'capo' armband received us. First we were given the new prison numbers issued by the Gross-Rosen camp, to which we now belonged. Then we began to learn about our environment. As Auschwitz was unique with its treasures, corruption and 'organisation' so Breslau-Lisa was the only camp where the inmates formed a homogeneous group, helping and protecting its weakest members. The reasons for such altruism were manifold: the small number of prisoners; the same Auschwitz background of all inmates; the object of the camp – the maintenance of the depot and not the annihilation of the incarcerated; and, last but not least, the personality of the capo in charge.

The whole depot was one vast area of fields and barracks containing untold masses of building materials and fitments. Acres of boggy ground were stacked with mountains of timber, piles of prefabricated buildings and row upon row of ceramic wash basins and water closets. Temporary huts were stuffed full of metal fittings, boxes of screws, cases of nails – all materials unobtainable in Germany except for the SS. In this maze we moved in small groups re-stacking uneven heaps, pulling out of the bog items sinking into the ground and generally contributing to the war effort. Semi-literate SS men knew but one deeply ingrained maxim:

'Ordnung musst sein!' (order must reign) and this was satisfied by rearranging prefabricated wooden parts so that dry ones were exposed to the inclement weather whilst the already rotting top ones went out of sight deep into the pile. Also, when marching smartly to the next job, we developed a slight sideways stagger when a heavy crowbar would swing unerringly to tap the bottom of a water closet or the back of a wash basin; the neat rows looked just the same but most of the articles were just so much scrap. We used to show some of the cracks to the NCOs, pointing out how badly they were fired to break with the changes of season! However, we had to stop this practice as they, anxious about their own jobs, ordered the damaged units to be carried to the more inaccessible parts of the depot and this was too much hard work.

This passable existence, without the constant threat of whip and death, was sweetened by the knowledge of the considerable damage which we caused. On the other hand, the hard labour from dawn to dusk, the inadequate food and the bitterly cold weather were almost unbearable. Food was our first priority so the three of us spent the dark autumn evenings on 'art' work. Soon our spreading fame brought us plenty of SS customers and pay. We charged half a pencil, two sheets of paper and four loaves for a portrait done from a photograph. I would begin by wrapping the photograph (invariably a girl) in a square grid of black thread and copying the outline in a similar but larger grid on a sheet of drawing paper. Then Krystyn took over the main shading and finally Tiger, who was the only one with a spark of talent, finished eyes and lips giving the thing some life and semblance to the original.

There was also another source of food, pitifully small and irregular but doubly welcomed as it came unsolicited from the outside world. Along the periphery of the depot ran a country road on which passed peasant carts loaded with sugar beet. Usually a thin horse, led by a farmer, dragged a cart full of rounded yellowish lumps. Covered with mud, and frozen hard, these resembled large turnips. On top of the heap often sat a little child and, if there were no SS in sight, the child would squirm and kick some beet so that it would fall off and roll under the barbed wire fence. Rarely, very rarely, they would also call in Polish a few words of greeting or the news about the advancing Russians. All this in spite of the Gestapo, in spite of one and a half centuries of intense Germanisation of the province which for ages had been indisputably

Polish. The sugar beet tasted bitter-sweet and gave everybody terrible heart-burn. But we learned to slice it thinly and boil it till it disintegrated into a syrupy mess which was not palatable, but was nourishing.

In 1944, our last summer in Auschwitz, the Russian Armies reached Warsaw which rose in arms. But our good Allies halted and waited until the insurgents were murdered and our capital razed to the ground. Now, as the wet autumn became colder, the Russians were again surging forward. Snows wrapped our world in white silence through which came the distant rumble of heavy guns. The steady rhythm of the depot was broken as we frantically loaded SS lorries only to tip out the contents and begin again with other goods. Our SS masters ran hither and thither or froze immobile listening for the approaching doom. We waited for the coming of our second mortal enemy and hoped that in the chaos of a battle we might escape from both.

Then, on a dismal, frosty morning, instead of work we faced evacuation – a march of seventy miles to Gross-Rosen. It was in this hour of need that the unity and spirit of our little camp paid dividends. Extra clothing was distributed fairly, hoarded food divided and we formed quickly into a marching column. An unwritten truce with the guards had been arranged by our capo as an extension of good camp management. There it was our 'willing' co-operation (with only the discreet sabotage), and now we were to give no trouble whilst they refrained from violence.

The wooden soles of our clumsy boots skidded on ice and snow, the thin prison overcoats flapped in the northerly gale, but we trudged on, supporting the weaker ones, whilst the guards marched on the side of the road as blue and cold as we were. It was a grey day of unbearable frost and a vicious wind with blinding snow showers. It was an endless day on forgotten farm tracks of the Silesian plain. At night, after a meal of bread and water, we huddled and shivered in a draughty barn. The next morning we reached a highway flooded with a continuous stream of German refugees. It was almost like Poland of '39 – almost, but not quite. Apart from being winter instead of late summer, the people were uniformly poor, uniformly drab, equally miserable but still disciplined as befitted the master race. The police motorcyclists, the grey cars of the SS and the black limousines of the Gestapo were given the right of way. People too weak to keep up moved off the road and rested in the ditches. The sight of men, women and children, all white and wan, cheered us considerably. They shuffled on, even more slowly than we did, they carried rucksacks and bundles, pushed prams loaded with all their possessions. Most of them had already lost more than they had stolen and looted in our country.

At the first major crossroads the military police ordered us off the road. Catching a glimpse of one black Gestapo uniform in the background our SS masters ceased to argue and took us again into the maze of narrow country tracks which severely tested our strength. Deep snow drifts, tortuous ruts frozen hard like steel rails, hunger and bitter, penetrating cold. The stronger ones (or the more stubborn ones?) helped the weaker. So, staggering, falling, we marched on and on. Another night, another freezing barn, but this time only a very small piece of bread, and water with floating lumps of ice. The third day was the worst, but we continued moving, dragging or even carrying those who had collapsed. To the physical ordeal was added the fear of failing strength and failing spirit. At some crossroads we saw signs of the passage of other columns like our own. Wide trodden tracks smoothed by dragging feet, also more and more striped uniforms in the snow. They lay flattened like empty rags, blue grey rags with blue grey faces. Sometimes just a neat hole in the back of the head, sometimes half the head blown off in the mess of blood and brains, frozen as hard as the mud and the ice. Sometimes one, or two together, but once there was an even row of twenty or thirty – so we kept on till late at night we passed through the gates of Gross-Rosen. We arrived without losing a single man and the SS sergeant in charge of the escort was rewarded by our capo who slipped him three good watches – almost the last of the treasures brought from Auschwitz by the old numbers.

It was still perishingly cold and, sitting in a camp street, we saw little through the flurries of snow – just white waste ground, half-finished buildings, lighted windows full of moving shadows. Soon our crowd was led further to the rickety fence dividing the camp proper from the undeveloped site with its stacks of materials like our old depot. Here were our new quarters: a concrete cellar, or really the deep foundations of a future building. It was a large room, damp and windowless, lit by a storm lantern. There was no door, just an open entrance with a large snowdrift outside and a smaller one inside. But, except near the entrance, there was no wind and no snow. We were given bread and water as the kitchens of the overcrowded camp could not cope with the influx of prisoners evacuated from the east. In three shifts they cooked a thick soup which was distributed continuously, reaching each group of blocks at intervals of twenty-seven hours. Thus we had our main meal almost daily but always some three hours later than the preceding 'dinner'. Nobody went to work and long roll-calls took place only once a day. Heavy frost and unceasing blizzards kept masses of prisoners huddled in their barracks. This terrible weather masked our own forays into the fenced-off storage areas. Padlocked shacks could not resist our skills and yielded their tools. Then, cutting the inner fences, we stole everything of any possible use. Within a couple of days our concrete tomb was transformed into a livable dormitory filled with two-tier bunks, fitted with a proper door and well lit by electric lights hooked up to a new line stretched precariously from the nearest substation. Only then, waiting resignedly for the next issue of food, we could relax in relative comfort which did not last long.

Big, burly men with yellow armbands of capos burst in brandishing thick cudgels. Somebody caught in the arctic draught from the open door shouted abuse and the nearest ruffian smashed him to the floor with his mace. Our own capo sprang into the centre of the room and the newcomers got down to business demanding a ransom of five thousand marks, or, with the help of the SS, they threatened to take all the treasure that 'you have brought from Auschwitz!' Explanations and arguments about Breslau-Lisa did not get us anywhere and their ringleader attacked our own capo, who, dodging the blow, shouted in Polish to take them. Men sprang down from the upper bunks, others surged up from the floor. Not the mass of half-dead mussulmen, but a vicious pack of starved wolves closed over those capos. The press of bodies, like some nightmarish rugby scrum, writhed in the middle of the dormitory in a panting, almost silent, struggle. One or two hollow-sounding blows, one or two whistling sighs. But dozens of hands grabbed each stick, dozens of arms anchored each foot, claw-like nails and fang-like teeth tore and rent the enemy whilst the grotesque shadows jumped and tottered under the swaying lamps. The spasmodic heaving steadied, subsided and, one by one, our men scrambled to their feet and stood back from the heaps of torn rags and bloody meat. Somebody near the door spitting out his own teeth pointed into the night and moaned that one bandit had escaped and our own capo immediately organised a collection to buy our way out of the trouble. In half an hour, when the escapee returned with three SS men, all was ready. It was rather cheap at a watch and a few hundred marks for each soldier. The surviving Gross-Rosen capo got a kick from one of the SS men.

In the beginning of February 1945, only four months after leaving Auschwitz, we were herded towards trains destined for Buchenwald camp in the centre of Germany. Long strings of waiting wagons seemed lost in the labyrinth of railway lines. Endless columns of striped uniforms squatted in the snow blown horizontally by a merciless wind. A loaf of bread for each pair of prisoners and, at last, the command to entrain. A hundred men counted carefully to a wagon which, at its door, had the old army inscription '8 horses or 40 men'. When the door slid shut we all stood packed tightly shoulder to shoulder, unable to move even our clumsy clogs. But as the train started and jolted we were gradually shaken into a looser formation. We halted at many unknown stations, sometimes for minutes, sometimes for hours. In the evening the train stopped in an open field and, under the muzzles of machine-guns, the prisoners were allowed to relieve themselves. Some wagons had already many dead which the SS ordered to be piled up in the fields and left there. The journey continued but the guards locked the doors on a second latch leaving a three-inch gap which allowed glimpses of the outside world and a paralysingly cold draught. We saw no bomb damage but were cheered by the impression of austerity and downright poverty. At night we discovered that forming groups of five allowed two men of the team to squat and doze. But even this problematic rest was interrupted by cramps and falls.

The second day was just like the first though our bread was finished, thirst overshadowed tiredness and tempers began to fray. At odd junctions we waited hours for a gap in the military traffic and felt forgotten in drab marshalling yards. In Poland the poor and the wealthy alike threw to the prisoners bread, fruit, cigarettes. In East Germany we had sugar beet and fag-ends. But here, in Central Germany, civilians passed our train with averted eyes and ears deaf to shouts and moans begging for water, whilst only feet away stood fire buckets under a dripping tap. Waiting at these forgotten stations we swore to remember for ever Germany and the Germans.

On the third day we were allowed to fetch water and relieve ourselves. The field was broken by a ditch with the remnants of an old hedge and suddenly a small group of prisoners nearest to these obstructions, took off like a flock of partridges. They were all squatting in the deep snow and, the next instant, up and away they went. Most of us saw it happen and, like the old hands at this game, we flattened ourselves seconds before the machine-guns opened up over our heads. They just hosed the field and soon dozens of prisoners were flopping on the ground. Only the fastest few reached the ditch and disappeared into the bushes. The guards waded into the prisoners nearest to the place of escape shooting and clubbing more victims. We heard the SS talking and gathered that very few got away and were expected to be killed by the alerted Hitler Youth Organisation.

The next day we rolled into Weimar and marched up the icy, ever-rising road. Behind us the clouds of smoke still hung over the recently bombed town. Before us, against the pale wintry sky, stood out the black watch towers with their lines of electrified fences. The four or five thousand hungry, thirsty and exhausted men hoped for water and food. But the camp authorities, obsessed with the fear of typhus, ordained that nobody entered the camp proper without six weeks quarantine in the 'Little Camp'. Even there they would not admit prisoners without bath and delousing. And the last air-raid had cut off the water supplies to the town and the camp. However, even this emergency had been envisaged and we were herded into a fair-sized field, surrounded by a barbed wire fence. There was a single tent occupied by Russian prisoners of war who slugged anybody trying to enter. In the quickly falling dusk, barrels of steaming soup were brought and deposited between the double gates of our compound. When the outer gates had been locked behind the retreating porters, the inner gates were opened. Only the Russians and our Breslau-Lisa group, anticipating what was to follow, readied the strongest men to fetch and defend our share. It seemed to take hours before all of us received our portions ladled carefully into twenty basins which we had secured. In the meantime, the hunger-maddened crowd fought like a herd of wild animals over the spilled soup. Later, in the blinding spotlights of the watch towers, the sub-machine guns of the SS ensured that all prisoners were given their ration of bread, and the darkness of night shrouded the living and the dying, whilst the snow sparkled in the arctic frost.

In the morning flat-decked carts were loaded with the corpses that the quiet night had harvested. A few of us decided to spend the next night in the tent or die in the attempt. Armed with a few pieces of barbed wire broken off the fence we stormed the Russian citadel at dusk. At the cost of one man we were in and discovered that the damned Russians kept a guard at the entrance but occupied only the very centre of the shelter, so that now dozens of us gained a better chance of life. But the flat cart came twice a day and left piled higher than before. Many of us had severe frostbite, and eyes that grew bigger and sank deeper and deeper. The big and tough died as quickly as the small and weak. The pious and devout collapsed as fast as did the blaspheming rogues.

Many died but I was amongst the lucky ones who survived. I staggered about when exhaustion and cold bade me to stay curled up in the snow; I rubbed my freezing hands till the pain of the returning circulation made me groan. I tried to work out, to analyse why and for what I chose to suffer more instead of quietly going to sleep. But my thoughts broke and jumped, refusing to focus, to stay with any one image or idea. Infinitely distant and uncaring stars of the Great Bear; Princess as remote as the stars; bloody Germans and the all-pervading cold; Krystyn and Tiger asleep on my feet, fools whom I must kick and prod before they froze to death ... Later, aeons later, warm showers almost drowned us and, in tatters of old striped uniforms, we dragged ourselves to the barracks of the quarantine. With smaller than ever rations we spent our days huddled on overcrowded bunks. There were long roll-calls and daily visits of hospital orderlies shouting for the sick to report. They dressed the most severe frostbites and dismissed other complaints, looking only for the high fever of typhus. Then, one day, I saw the familiar face of the senior orderly, and realised that it was Little Peter from Block 21 of Auschwitz. His eyelid came down in a slow wink of recognition.

'Stretcher bearers! Here, this man!' - he yelled, pointing at me - 'Suspected typhus!'

Then I had a glorious fortnight in a clean hospital bed. Peter was in charge of the isolation ward and, though his powers were incomparably less than would have been the case in Auschwitz, he managed to slip me some extra food. The Germans, mortally frightened of typhus, gave the place a wide berth, but I could not stay there too long. Peter, with his knowledge of the local conditions, advised me to get away quickly from this overcrowded camp. He managed to have me discharged at the right time and to the right block which was scheduled for a transport to Natzweiler. He even wangled the transfer of Krystyn so that, only a month after our arrival, we both left Buchenwald.

In the milling crowd Krystyn discovered his own class-mate Joseph and, as experienced travellers, we surged forward together, securing an advantageous place in a corner of the wagon. We knew what to expect and how to organise sleep; we could rest against the walls and shorten the time in reminiscing about the past.

On the fifth day of the journey, near the French and Swiss borders, the train slowed down as if frightened by the persistent wail of air-raid sirens. Only when we came to a complete stop did the heavy beat of distant aircraft come in surging waves, and all around the guns opened up. Then terrific explosions rocked the world and the crowd stampeded inside the locked wagon. In panic they trampled one another, beat the unyielding door, cried and wept. My dislike of crowds and contempt for this mass hysteria stifled my own fear as I pushed harder against Krystyn and Joseph. Squashing them into the corner, I protected all three of us with fists and clogs. Now came the shriek of straining engines, the staccato of machine-guns – fighters at zero level. And suddenly utter silence. Again the approaching growl of aircraft rose into an unbearable roar, and lines of holes appeared in the roof of our wagon. The puny cage began to burn, somebody released the outside bolt and the wagon spewed out its maddened cargo. But Joseph stayed down and I yelled at him to get up. Krystyn's mouth moved but I could not hear. The wounded dragged themselves past the smoking craters in the platform. From the burning train flames shot higher, and I began to hear the roar of the fire and Joseph's cries.

'You can't be hit! We were on top of you!' – but I slid my hand inside his coat and felt hot, sticky blood. We dragged him on to the platform and stripped off his coat. On top of his shattered shoulder rested a flattened lump of a 0.5 slug. The last bullet of the American Mustang had ricocheted from the stone edge of the platform, ripped upwards through the floor of our wagon, through his armpit and had come to rest inside his jacket. I made a pad from a torn shirt, told Krystyn to hold it in place and ran for help, leaving Joseph my warm overcoat, the parting gift from little Peter. I passed the wrecked train, found the station building equally deserted, and stopped, bewildered and lost in this emptiness. A thought of freedom flashed through my mind but, even forgetting Joseph, one did not run in this country of dense and most regimented population of armed murderers in brown, black and green uniforms of HJ, SA, SD and Gestapo. I saw the slopes of the valley dotted with groups of prisoners and SS men still hiding behind bushes and rocks. Nearer was a small Red Cross hut with three nurses who shrank away from me. My plea for help restored superiority of the master race:

'Get out, you swine! This post is for Germans only!' shouted the senior one, brandishing a pair of enormous scissors. On the table were laid out bandages and field dressings but the harpies would not yield one scrap of gauze or cotton wool. Then, from my broken German I switched into Greek and Romany curses, gesticulating violently with my right hand, whilst my left quickly scooped as much material as I could hold. When they called for help I fled with the paltry loot and did my best for Joseph. It took hours for the guards and the prisoners to reassemble. With the rails blown up and the train destroyed, the remnants of the transport were marched to the nearby camp of Shörzingen whilst Joseph with other wounded was taken to some hospital.

Without my overcoat I arrived at the new camp in a pitiful state, and by the next morning had a raging temperature which made me light-headed. At mid-day the German doctor in charge began sorting out the newcomers. Krystyn, familiar with the medical inspections of Auschwitz, tried desperately to make me appear normal and fit. But by then, I was happily ordering people to bring me lemon tea and take me to bed. Vaguely and out of focus I saw the wide face of Rhode, the Auschwitz pupil of Mengele. 'Hello, Doctor! How goes it?'

An enraged SS man pushed forward to deal with me for such an unprecedented familiarity, when Rhode stopped him. I think he talked to me but I remember only finding myself in a hospital hut. There two SS men told the capo in charge that Herr Doctor himself ordered for me the best care and attention.

There were no drugs but I had water and quiet. Time telescoped into vague light, silent darkness and a continuous cough stabbing me right through with hot knives. Then the temperature dropped, the cough subsided, and I became ravenously hungry. The pneumonia was over but there was no chance of a recovery on the meagre rations. During his nightly visits Krystyn told me that Joseph had died and suggested that I leave hospital, as the 'working' prisoners received slightly more food.

The work involved quarrying and firing oil-bearing shale but, under the frequent attacks of American fighters, it had already come to an almost complete stop. The anti-aircraft defences had been destroyed and the mine shafts blocked by bombs and rockets. Now the fighters swooped low, hunting individual SS men and members of the Todt organisation who supervised the site. Most of us did not even bother to lie flat but waved enthusiastically when, with the staccato of guns, the planes pursued the running Germans. There were also our own casualties, but after the millions of deaths in the gas chambers it was a negligible price to pay for carrying back the dead Germans. Because we often brought them dead, as even those with only light wounds seemed to catch splinters of rock in some vital part of their anatomy.

In a few days I realised that I could cope neither with work nor even with the march from the camp to the site. But a transport of mussulmen was leaving for Dachau and I could go or try to dodge. It was a choice between starvation here and the risk of another journey, with either the gas chambers or life in Dachau. Yet Dachau had no large crematoria and was not the worst of the camps – so I decided to go. In the last moment Krystyn joined me though I never knew whether he believed in my superior judgement or my incredible luck.

The journey began on a frosty April morning after we had been stripped of our overcoats, sweaters and footgear which, they said, were needed for our working comrades. We did not get any food and were loaded into the low coal wagons with their open tops closed by a barbed wire mesh which did not stop icy gales but scalped anybody who tried to stand up. In our emaciated state and without outer clothing we just sat and shivered together through freezing nights and days punctuated by air-raids. Repeatedly the train stopped and the SS guards ran into the fields whilst the enormous 0.5 bullets ripped through the wagons, through the cargo. And the cargo cringed in panic fear, burrowed under the corpses, huddled in squirming heaps. There remained only shreds of private dignity in which one could sit quietly wondering whether death would come from the bullets of the Allies or in the knacker's yard at the end of the journey.

We never reached Dachau and when, after five days journey, the train finally stopped at Dachau-Allach, we scrambled out on to the platform. Blackened by coal dust, with hollow cheeks, sunken eyes and lips cracked by cold and thirst - a shambling crowd of skeletons. Many walked slowly, but more just crawled the few hundred yards towards another lot of barracks, another milestone of German *Kultur*. This was not the concentration camp which we knew for long years. It was just an enormous cage, a refuse bin for what remained of the German conquest of Europe. Even the sacrosanct roll-calls became vague and purposeless as nobody knew how many prisoners there were. During daytime the huts were closed and the slaves strolled and sprawled, or died quietly in the warm sun, in the cold rain showers. In the mid-day sun many discarded their jackets and I soon spotted a group with the numbers tattooed on their arms - the Auschwitz brigade. They told me that water would not be turned on before night and, as we were literally dying of thirst, I set out on a search of my own. Soon, behind the washrooms hut I prized open the cover of a manhole and, seeing a clean-looking trickle of water, had a long, life-giving drink. Krystyn, shocked to the marrow, tried to stop me from guzzling the doubtful fluid but, under my ironical glance, gave up and drank his fill. Within an hour we felt like new men whilst the inexperienced, the finicky and the stupid were dying of thirst.

Being without shoes was a great disadvantage and Krystyn soon found some odd, broken clogs whilst I noticed a fine pair of boots on a corpse lying between two huts. Still, in this new place, it seemed prudent to have some back-up for the acquisition of the boots, and I approached the Auschwitz crowd. Their high tattoo numbers indicated only a short camp experience, but even so, I was staggered by their disgust at the idea of robbing a corpse! So, with only Krystyn's backing, I took the boots which fitted me well. I had just finished tying the laces when, from around the corner, emerged a group of five or six men. They too must have been after the boots and, taking in the situation, began to shout and threaten: French curses and truly Gallic gesticulation. Krystyn, in his wooden boats, shuffled to my assistance when I reached for a half brick laid by for emergencies. Their encircling movement stopped, and, after a moment's hesitation they ran away.

When we arrived at Allach the food was appalling. But incredibly it still deteriorated day by day. A loaf of bread, bitter with the horse-chestnut flour, was cut into more and more portions till we received one daily slice. Soup, a mess of boiled nettles, lost the additive of ground bones and became translucent blue-green liquid. In a week even the nettles gave out, and we were left with boiled grass. Then there was no more bread and no more salt. We, the Polish prisoners, looked with envy at the French and the Dutch who were still frequently receiving Red Cross food parcels. But we did not resort to robbery, which remained the prerogative of the Russians.

The SS men were not much in evidence inside the camp until the afternoon when a heavily armed detachment entered to separate the Russians who tried to hide amongst other nationalities. A few bursts of machine pistols put a stop to this game. Soon a column of several hundred Russians trudged south along a dusty road. The same night the squeak of our barrack door was followed by two explosions of hand grenades chucked in amongst the sleeping prisoners. The pandemonium of shouts and moans subsided with automatic fire lashing and splintering the wooden walls. The wounded and the living cowered in the corners, under the bunks, amongst the corpses ...

The following morning, 30 April 1945, we stacked the corpses behind the huts and dragged the wounded to the hospital – another overcrowded building where prisoners lingered before their corpses were transported to the ovens of Dachau. Suddenly, the sleepy crowds were electrified by news whispered quietly, spoken aloud, shouted from barrack to barrack: the guardhouse at the main gate was empty and on the watch towers stood only the camp capos armed with rifles! The whole camp seethed and boiled with gossip, with claims and counter-claims. A group of prisoners pushed tentatively against the still locked gates, a couple of shots rang out, somebody screamed and the crowd dispersed to gather again in another place. Then, on a hill beyond the wire, we saw an open army car and the silhouettes of two soldiers. Rounded helmets, not the square piss-pots of the Germans. An utter silence enveloped the camp and the crowds surged towards the fence. The car stopped, both men standing up, staring at us. The silent, mute crowd pressed against the barbed wire, the wire bulged, groaned and collapsed. The mass of people flowed over the fallen, up the hill to the two bewildered, speechless soldiers of the VII American Army that brought us Freedom and Life.

PART 3

WANDERER AND CITIZEN

CHAPTER 19

DISPLACED PERSONS

The thin people walked, the starved skeletons crawled, and the human tide continued to spill from the camp up the gentle hill. As they crossed the broken wire many glanced back at this magic line which, after years of slavery, was now behind them. Then, like all the others, they turned and gazed silently, as if in a religious trance, towards the high altar - the jeep on the brow of the hill. There, above the silent sea of blue-grey uniforms, incongruously sat the two GIs, their faces reflecting surprise, horror and then compassion. Somebody spoke, breaking the eerie silence and a thousand mouths opened in cheers, in blessings and prayers, in a million unanswered questions. Not believing their own eyes and ears, they tried to touch the jeep, the real, live Americans. But it was a quiet, gentle crowd, at the gates of heaven. The soldiers talked and asked but there was little communication in this babel of Polish, Dutch, French and what I later learned to recognise as the Texan drawl. The driver, seeing an emaciated, swaying body, threw his own tunic over the naked shoulders. The gunner extracted a crumbled packet of Chesterfields and distributed the cigarettes. Then they both dipped into the back of the little vehicle for their emergency rations, sweaters, cigarettes ... They took off their watches, their shirts ... Now they sat helmeted but half naked in a jeep stripped of everything except guns and ammunition. With my school English and the help of some Dutchman I managed to explain about the camp, the hunger, the night flight of the SS. The Americans had to move on but promised help within a few hours.

In a delirious euphoria we watched the lorries full of infantry. We saw the light tanks refuelling and disappearing as fast as they came in pursuit of the fleeing enemy. We saw officers and their men looking in horror at the camp, at us, at the piles of corpses. The armed capos fled from the watch towers but a few were seized and killed by the mob. Later, an American reconnaissance unit brought back some of the SS guards. There were no meaningless formalities of invoking international law: the front troops saw the hell created by these men and without further inquiry proffered loaded pistols which were eagerly grasped by the survivors.

Later, another detachment stopped to take care of us. With the roar of cheers, a tank flattened the main camp gates and rolled on to crush one by one the dark watch-towers. American lorries brought food from the SS stores and our kitchens began cooking tons and tons of thick soup, soup with real potatoes, with fat, with meat even. The people ate, and ate, and were sick, horribly sick ... some died. I also was sick and ate more. The sickness passed and I, the same as Krystyn and many others, began to put on weight, to resemble human beings again. In these first days we were desperately weak. Once, acting as an interpreter for some American, I came to a building with six wooden steps at the entrance but I could not mount them till, blushing furiously, I climbed up on all fours.

In came a medical unit with showers and the most wonderful invention of DDT – the powder that magically cleared us from all vermin, without shaving, without the stings and burns of the old disinfectants. Our prison uniforms were burned whilst we were issued with the new, warm and soft ... black uniforms of the SS armoured divisions. Then, no longer *Schutzhaftlings* (prisoners in protective custody) but DPs (displaced persons), we were transported to the nearby empty barracks of the SS centre in Freiman. It was an enormous 'U' shaped block with offices on the ground floor, luxurious flatlets on the next level and dormitories above. Krystyn and I seized a three-room apartment all for ourselves, but soon took pity on an oldish chap with an Auschwitz 'millionaire' number who seemed incapable of fending for himself. For a few days the soft furniture, comfortable beds and spaciousness of the surroundings fully absorbed our attention. Then we began exploring and getting involved in the community life of the new camp. The escaping Germans had exploded demolition charges in the boiler-house but in no time we had one boiler working and supplying hot water for baths and showers. Damaged kitchens were also repaired and soon the various administrative committees began to function. With my store-keeping experience I was roped in to manage the food distribution which was becoming a problem. We were supplied by the army with bread, potatoes and cereals requisitioned from the Germans and supplemented by irregular issues of tinned meat, cigarettes and other American luxuries. Whilst the calorific value of the rations was more than adequate, the monotony and blandness of the perpetual soup created considerable discontent. In prisons, in camps, we all dreamt of the END, of return to the loved ones and finding all as it had been before September '39. The end had come but it shattered our dreams just as thoroughly as the invader had shattered our towns. The French and the Dutch departed to their own free lands. But our Allies, those who went to war for our freedom, and these who proclaimed the Four Freedoms, they sold in Yalta, to the other invader, our birthright and our Polish lands. So we, the flotsam and jetsam of the war, stayed in the SS uniforms, in the SS barracks ... and grumbled about the soup.

Whilst I bargained with the Americans for more corned beef, Tol, our newly acquired companion, became the mainspring of various activities and enterprises. With the camp management he decided to issue our own postage stamps! As a pre-war publisher and a graphic artist of repute he designed the 'Freiman-Munich-Post' stamp which was soon printed in the famous Bruckmann's works. The stamps, utterly useless and illegal, but all with the Polish National Emblem of the White Eagle, sold like hot cakes. Soon they were replaced by a newer design of 'Dachau' stamps issued in various colours and denominations with a surcharge for the Polish Red Cross. These were bought in thousands by Americans, the Germans and the ex-prisoners. At that time there were no mail services except the USA Army post and many letters carried by it bore our stamps. Some of these letters which did not find the addressees were returned overstamped by post offices of various countries and provided ammunition for vicious 'war' amongst the international philatelic firms.

In the meantime the Polish Red Cross, as well as the camp treasury, acquired much-needed funds, whilst the hard work involved bound together our trio. The long hours in the food store and the effort required by Tol's enterprises absorbed me so completely that I hardly noticed the further deterioration of the camp life. Bored and disillusioned, the mass of incompatible individuals seethed and fermented. The intellectuals would no longer put up with the uncouth labourers, the soft-spoken southerners argued with the hard Silesians, the spivs and criminals exploited the simple peasants. The more enterprising forayed into the surrounding country, terrorising and looting the German population. The main gate closed with a clang and GI sentries patrolled the periphery – we were imprisoned again.

Tol co-opted another man to our team, a poet whom I christened 'Puppy' as he was not only very young but behaved like an unruly whelp. He did not gnaw furniture, but worried and needled everybody with his leftish views and merciless exposure of people's hidden weaknesses which he spotted unerringly. We all understood the reasons for the closure of the gate and other restrictions. But understanding did not mean acceptance, and many not only blamed the Yanks but even transferred to them some of the hatred felt for the Germans. Krystyn swelled and reddened, the poet stamped and spluttered, denouncing the locking of the camp gates as the reintroduction of collective responsibility. But the Americans did not care a hoot for anybody. They did not know, and did not wish to know, anything about Europe or Europeans. Now they culled the camp and repatriated all Ukrainians, totally disregarding their protests and mass suicides. Some of the Poles shrugged their shoulders with the all-embracing 'serves them right', some were sorry for the poor beggars. But all were frightened by the precedent which could send us via Warsaw to Siberia. Then came the 'Polish' liaison officers flaunting the new uniforms with the Eagles no longer bearing their crowns. Though two centuries had passed since Poland ceased to be a monarchy, the national emblem always retained the crown. Now these men displayed the mutilated device and talked to us in atrocious Polish full of Russicisms. With promises of generous land grants they repatriated a number of peasants, but, despite official pressure, the attitude of the majority remained such that these officers did not venture into the camp without an American escort.

Another cause of discontent arose from the camp management which was taken over by the Black Mafia. Some Polish clergy had been imprisoned in Dachau and now several Jesuit 'fathers' came to Freiman. The few who once had been stationed in the States seized power and, protected by the cloth and their American experience, exploited their position to the full.

Amongst grievances and worries the passing days also provided some light relief. Working in the basement of the store we had crowds gathering at the windows, gawking at our books, at the arriving victuals and commenting crudely and sarcastically on our efforts so that at last, we put up some net curtains. But one could not close one's ears to the remarks floating in through the open windows:

'Look! The thieving buggers, like some bloody dukes they hide behind the curtains!'

'You know why? All day long they guzzle macaroni! Nothing but thick macaroni!'

Yes, for very many of us the solid, almost dry noodles or spaghetti remained the epitome of plenty, the ultimate heaven filled to the brim with ambrosia. But, though eating our fill, we did our best for the camp. In a separate block the American Quartermaster had built up a stock of provisions from which only a surplus trickled to us. Amongst many treasures there was a room lined with shelves full of corned beef which we craved and considered the gourmet's delight. This, I decided, must be ours and, strolling past, managed to find a very few tins bulging with putrefaction. These I unobtrusively shifted into a corner of one shelf and pointed their position to one of my mates. Next day I pleaded with the Quartermaster Captain for more meat which he refused, explaining that the rations were entirely satisfactory and well balanced.

'But Cap, you have tons here and it's all going bad!'

He laughed at the possibility of American tins going off, though he admitted that in the thousands of tins of old stock there might be a single bad one, and this was my chance:

'You blindfold me; he' – pointing at my friend – 'can spin me round! If, at first go, I get two dicky cans you issue all of it to the camp!'

Staggering in a fit of laughter he shook my hand accepting the challenge and, a minute later, I handed him two tins bulging ready to burst open. We had double rations of meat for quite a time and, when I got to know him better, I restored his faith in the might of America by telling him how the trick had been worked.

Still, the overall feelings of frustration, disappointment and monstrous injustice grew, and we had to do something more than sit locked up in the nice comfortable prison. Then Tol, who rubbed shoulders with all the high and mighty, came with an unexpected proposition. All four of us could be released from Freiman to join the Polish Committee in Munich. Though we knew nothing of this organisation, nor what we could do there, we accepted with alacrity.

The gate of Freiman barracks with its GI sentry faced empty fields stretching away to the far horizon. From left to right ran a cobblestone road separated from the perimeter fence by a narrow pavement. There, the three of us stood close together, uneasy in the new-found freedom. For years we had waited for this moment, but in our vague dreams freedom was synonymous with Poland, home, the loved ones and the pre-war time. But this time had passed and vanished for ever. The flow of events, the gaping holes in the continuity of our lives, left us confused, lost and frightened of open space, of foreign lands, of our ex-jailers. It was an overwhelming feeling akin to agoraphobia: behind us was the safety of the barracks, the protection of the Americans – before us was Germany and the Germans. The green landscape was not as empty and rural as our first impression of it. The horizon was not so distant, the trees hid the sprawl of suburban houses and down the road a few civilians waited for the bus. They eyed suspiciously our black uniforms and on our approach closed into a small tight group. Till the last few weeks we had been the subhuman creatures from whom the power and wisdom of the Führer had protected them. Now, liberated and fed by the new masters of Germany, we were sometimes given the run of the backyard, like unchained dogs. So, in the old bone-shaker of a bus they kept away, leaving us, the untouchables, separate and alone.

In his ungrammatical German, Puppy asked for tickets to the town and the conductor shrugged his shoulders:

'Ich verstehe nicht! Spricht du Deutsch?' – so he did not understand and, using the rude pronoun of the second person singular, asked if Puppy could speak German! In the sudden silence some passenger giggled, others turned around with sneering smiles and, forgetting all doubts and misgivings, I knew that their time had also passed, even if they tried to bring it back. I looked straight into the conductor's eyes and said quietly but distinctly in my freshly acquired best American:

'Three to the town centre, you son of a bitch!'

'Yes, sir!' he acknowledged, handing over three tickets.

Munich was a beautiful town bisected by the green waters of the Isar river. Some bridges were down, but except for in the vicinity of the railway yards there was little war damage. We crossed to the right bank where, facing Pinzenauer Street, stood an opulent villa which overlooked the river. For years the house had been occupied by the Gestapo and now it was requisitioned for the Polish Committee. In the basement there was a spacious canteen for the staff and guests, whilst the first two floors housed the offices. The storey above and the attics nestling into a mansard roof were used as dormitories for clerks and typists. Tol was already installed in a room of his own whilst we acquired a cubby-hole with a narrow three-tier bunk.

The Polish Committee was born as an anomaly of the period, but soon became an important necessity. It established itself and grew, barely tolerated by the occupying powers who had no interest in, or time to deal with, the masses of foreigners. Shortly, the Committee was recognised as an unofficial Consulate and, trusted by both sides, formed a bridge between the Americans and the Poles. We regulated food supplies to the Displaced Persons' Camps of the district, protected the interests of our 'citizens' but curbed their unreasonable demands and tried to weed out spivs, thieves and bandits. Our activities extended even to successful co-operation with CIC (American Counter Intelligence Corps). We maintained liaison with General Anders' Second Corps in Italy and condescended to receive the Liaison Officers from Warsaw. The registers of the Committee contained the names of tens of thousands of Poles in Bavaria. All this work was handled by untrained staff. Most of them were honest and hard-working, but there were a few chancers. In this motley crew common sense and a little administrative experience went a long way and soon I became the Secretary of the Committee. At this time Tol left the Committee and began working for the London based Polish Red Cross which recruited a number of employees in Germany. Pushing and intriguing, Tol had himself and his two older friends appointed as the Munich Legation. These were most coveted posts as they paid a substantial salary, offered endless perks and entitled one to a uniform with officer status recognised by the Americans.

The Munich Legation soon co-opted more men as auxiliaries but not accredited members. Two of the early helpers were Krystyn and Puppy who organised the Missing Persons Bureau. Most of the Poles in Germany were looking for wives and families lost somewhere between Narvik and Monte Cassino, Arnhem and Katyn. In most of Europe there was still no mail service and, anyway, we did not know where to address our letters. Of course, long before these two began their endless typing of lists, I had already written dozens of personal letters. Copies were addressed to our home, to Princess, to the hospitals where my parents used to work and also to the Polish Medical Association and the University. Their dispatch presented more problems, but they went into the Army Mail through friendly Americans, they were given to acquaintances who chose to return home, they were entrusted to various semi-official travellers and smugglers pushing their way to the east. And the letters, cast widely, sought out my Princess, my parents and the news of Sena. In the last months of the war, starved, ill and weak, I had no time and no will for thought. Now, however hard and long was the daily work, there was too much time for remembering the regal grace of Princess and ... the beauty and love of Sena.

I was sorting out the morning mail, the whole load brought by messengers from the outlying camps and from the American Administration. There, in the bag of letters from the SS barracks of Freiman, my eyes lit on an envelope outstanding even in this collection by its dog-ears, creases and encrustation of dirt. The smudged address in the round script of my mother bore both my names – the camp one and the real one! I slit open the soiled envelope and smoothed the crumpled letter from which, without conscious reading, leapt at me the news of the deaths of my father and Irka. I told my secretary to deal with the mail and, folding the letter into my pocket, left the office. The overgrown garden, the boulevard, the open banks of the river. Sitting under a willow I read and re-read the letter. My father had died of TB and hunger a week after the Russian 'Liberation' of Poland. During the Warsaw Rising Irka and her sister had been taken prisoners and murdered by the German Army. There was still more to read: Mother had been left totally alone but she had met Sena. Irka had been in love for a year and had married just before the Rising. Thank God that she had a taste of happiness but ... but ... she wanted to be honest and tell me about it but my own mother had stopped her! The Gypsy Camp and Sena – I had written to Irka about her, but there, they had interpreted my free cryptic as a reference to some adventure in France. Nothing could have been more ironic and now, there was not only the feeling of loss, but also one of betrayal. I had survived the war and from a German slave had become another sub-human of a Displaced Person. But there was no Poland, no home, no family. Only vague, and now soiled, memories left: pictures of the past or merely of another dream? And at my feet the ice-cold, bottomless, green water of the Isar – the true, the real Nirvana ... But this would be an admission of defeat, of a German victory, and to them I had not surrendered and would not surrender.

There were other ways, other ventures: I remembered the young Jew arrested by the Americans. I saw his little black note-book accounting for the forty whole German families which he had killed in retribution for his own people. I served unofficially as an interpreter and when I finished they simply deported him. I believed that he was right but doubted the strength of my own will if it came to cutting the throats of small children ... Then there was Mother, and I had to take care of her. But I was so tired, so alone. As the evening dew dripped from the willows I realised that I had sat there a whole day. Back at the office I told the others that my father and Princess were dead and that it was a subject closed for ever.

The next day began inauspiciously with various 'reminders' about a Miss Lola whom for weeks the Committee President had been recommending for the position of my secretary. But in spite of the post-war chaos I had obtained information concerning her and her father. Now more Polish than the White Eagle, both had been Volks-Deutsch (adopted German Nationals) who had worked for the Germans – he in commerce, she in bed. In spite of the mounting pressure from various quarters, I was resolved not to have such people near me, though I promised to interview her. She arrived dead on time, truly beautiful and dressed in a white blouse and navy-blue skirt. But however proper the clothing itself, on her it was anything but demure. The skirt rode higher and higher up her thighs as we talked, and as my questions revealed that she had never worked in any office, the buttons of her blouse began to pop open. At the third one I said simply: 'Get out.' But instead she almost slipped out of the flimsy silk and I roared:

'Get this whore out of here!'

I must add that, whatever other people said, it is not true that I kicked her down the stairs.

It was a bad day as, after arbitrating in a stupid dispute where the 'honour of Poland' was at stake, I had to see self-appointed members of some kangaroo court who wanted to dishonour and preferably hang an old Auschwitz acquaintance 'Capo Johnny' whom I now managed to save from a lot of troubles.

Germany began to settle down under the new régime. The re-established local authorities issued identity cards and ration books, UNRRA came to help and stayed, shops opened though they offered only the rations. The deeply ingrained German obedience to any orders stabilised the community whilst the lives of the DPs remained in turmoil. They were fed and housed, and the panic caused by the forcible repatriation of Ukrainians and Yugoslavs had abated, but it left the atmosphere of uncertainty and dread. The mass suicides were not forgotten and our yesterday's saviours were no longer trusted. Black market prices of handguns soared as they were sought equally by those terrified of Russia and those who believed that the world owed them an easy life after the havoc of the war.

The camps with their communal existence did nothing to settle the nomadic masses. For centuries Europe had accepted Christian ethics, though these were considerably modified by the war experiences. But now, as the one common enemy disappeared, so vanished all moral rules and restraints. Individuals, as well as large groups, competed for food, recognition and a better life. The Polish people were divided into innumerable factions. To the pre-war political parties was added the London Government in Exile. Nearer to us were the proud and disdainful heroes of the Armed Forces – those who won the war. The ex-prisoners of war argued about the battles of '39 but were unanimous in their contempt for the rabble of the DPs. The latter split into the pariahs of the labour camps and the aristocracy of the political prisoners, as now all bearers of the green triangles (professional criminals) claimed to have been wrongly labelled 'politicals'. The survivors carried forth their banners of 'martyrdom' and sowed the seeds of future legends. They wanted glory – I wanted to bear witness for the tortured, gassed, burnt; for all the unknown, unnamed, already forgotten dead. So I coaxed Puppy and argued with Krystyn and Tol, till we sat down and wrote a book about Auschwitz. We swore to write only the truth, and agreed that nothing would be printed until endorsed by all of us.

The Missing Persons Bureau began to reap its harvest. In the reciprocal lists arriving from other parts of Germany, from Switzerland and Sweden, here and there odd names matched, a man, a woman, a child was found. Some wept with joy, some walked away with bitter tears. Krystyn's parents were back in Warsaw, Puppy discovered his girl in Sweden, Tol's wife had been killed by the Germans after the Warsaw Rising.

Politics were creeping into the Committee and because of my uncompromising views I left the office to become Tol's assistant and driver at the Polish Red Cross. From London the goods for the Polish DPs went into main depots and we had to fetch our share from Frankfurt. The bulk transport was provided by a paramilitary organisation so famous for the rampant banditry of its lower ranks that I was put in charge to minimise the expected theft. For three days I slept only a few minutes at a time, but arrived back with the whole cargo unbroached, though after my motley crew had stolen an American Army motorcycle, I had to resort to the Military Police. To distribute amongst our DPs the bales of clothing, cigarettes, even combs and needles, we had to acquire locally the necessary vehicles. With a few cartons of cigarettes and a little blackmail, chauffeurs of the Legation were 'buying' German ex-army trucks and cars which, after a respray, were registered as Red Cross property. Naturally, the head of the Legation, a distinguished barrister, did not authorise such transactions but he disported himself in a Mercedes, whilst Tol acquired an enormous Horch saloon. So the chauffeurs were promoted from auxiliaries to the Accredited Personnel. The next vacancy was filled by a Polish lady with a good knowledge of English, whilst Krystyn, Puppy and I remained in the background slogging twelve hours a day. Then we began to have doubts about Tol. A member of an odd religious sect, often 'holier than thou', and always ready with his 'come to Jesus' call, he lavished on us endless but rarely fulfilled promises. His Christianity was for export whilst he looked after himself, the Horch and his two, newly 'organised' Leicas.

Our world remained in turmoil. DP camps were continuously reorganised and moved from place to place. After the forcible repatriation of the Ukrainians, the victors kicked out the Yugoslavs whom Tito demanded, got and promptly shot. The US army relinquished to UNRRA all responsibility for the DPs whilst the new German authorities were given more and more power. In these stormy, ever-changing surroundings there was for me one fixed bearing: England and my friends there. Actual, real people whose names, addresses and whole way of life remained unaltered. To them I wrote, as even addressing an envelope to the pre-war destination seemed to provide a strong anchor to windward. I also wrote to Mother that I did not wish to return to Russian-occupied Poland but would do so if she wanted me.

The uncertain future and doubtful present were taking a heavy toll of us all. Puppy got 'stoned' at every opportunity and grew viciously sarcastic about the West. Krystyn talked only of home between bouts of silent gloom. I worked, till there was no time to think about the future. We lived well on German rations with Red Cross extras and our main meals in the Committee Canteen. However, after years of Auschwitz experience I frequently brought home a carton of cigarettes, or a case of sardine tins from Freiman, from American friends, or just because it 'fell off a lorry'. Yet after scraping a margarine paper we always fried it to get out all the goodness. As associates of UNRRA we obtained a modern flat. On the floor below was lodged our English-speaking lady with her two young protegées. She had a firm grip on these 'adopted' girls who were well taken care of and strictly supervised. They were an ill-assorted pair of a small, well-rounded blonde and a thin, tall brunette. The round one made eyes and flirted with anybody coming within her orbit, whilst the bean-stalk was extremely shy and demure. Both were not much to look at and even less to talk to but, with the scarcity of girls, I was not surprised at the ardent attention paid to these young ladies by my two friends. What did surprise everyone was the pairing-off of the parties. The short, grinning Puppy trotted at the side of the tall, reserved Antoinette, whilst the giggling, almost spherical Helen rolled fast around the big, grim Krystyn. But I had no right to laugh at my fellow sinners as, a week later, I too was well and truly caught by a vivacious, auburn beauty. In my travels for the Red Cross I met her by chance and in rather startling circumstances. In her bedroom, with the skirt of the trim khaki uniform hitched up to her waist, she was taping a small automatic to the inside of her thigh! I never found out much about her as her blood-curdling stories of the Home Army and her escape from Poland changed frequently. Our affair soared like a rocket, blossomed and faded. I realised that there was nothing between us except our own fears and loneliness, which unfortunately remained unshared and unabated. Fortunately, she found a handsome lieutenant and disappeared from my life fast and for ever.

Autumn 1945 was followed by a winter of deep snow and hard frost.

The drivers of the Legation were so often 'ill' that I drove a lot more than I wanted, usually a three-ton Skoda. This was the strange 'end-of-the-war' period when neither human life nor the official vehicles counted for much. The Yanks had more equipment than sense and drove hell for leather, laughing their heads off when they smashed a heavy five-tonner. I was always in a hurry and would not be outdone by their four-wheel drive. So, when faced by a snow-drift, I just reversed for half a mile, wound her up to the full speed and ripped through. Sometimes I came out back to front, but by good luck stayed on the mountain roads and reached my destination. It was not all a happy-go-lucky existence. There were moments of exhaustion and despair, like the time when broken snow-chains forced me to stop in the deserted highlands and scratch and claw with half-frozen, bleeding fingers at the unyielding steel wedged between the twin wheels. Such incidents were few and compensated by the satisfaction of the delivery of goods to a remote camp or, even more dramatic, the rescue of a few chilled and semi-conscious Americans from their stranded vehicles.

During this same winter, after endless sessions of re-writing and correcting, our book was completed. There was no printing without an official permit, and no permit for anything unessential. Luckily we found an American with a weak head and a taste for vodka. He was in charge of Sewers and Sanitation but, after a bottle or two, he signed and stamped a permit. Cigarettes opened the gates of Bruckmann, the famous printers of Munich. My crude camp-German clinched the deal at pre-war prices and soon the ten-thousand edition was out! As we expected, it had a mixed reception: praises from the Polish Western Press, but, for debunking the 'heroes', vicious threats from many ex-prisoners. Still the book was good enough to be later reprinted in Poland.

One Saturday, I decided that, in spite of sporadic sweeping, the flat looked like a pig-sty and ordered spring-cleaning. Krystyn grumbled, Puppy threatened revenge, but we got down on our knees, scrubbed the floors white, washed the doors and windows, and dusted the lamps. In the evening we collapsed, exhausted. The whole place shone and there was again a view through the windows. The bell rang and, as the other two professed to be paralysed and dying, I went to open the door. There, accompanied by one of the Committee clerks, stood my Mother.

CHAPTER 20

GOD HELPS THOSE ...

My meeting with Mother was a great emotional experience, but seeing her after the six years separation was a real shock. I had said my goodbyes to a mature lady, small but healthy and well-dressed, shaken by the war but still sure of herself, a doctor of repute. Now I held in my arms a shrunken old woman, weeping uncontrollably. She was dressed in the worn-out coat of my grandmother, scuffed shoes and a piece of blanket for a head-scarf. Her only luggage was a small, almost empty sack. Then we were inside the flat with the chaos of a thousand questions, with Krystyn and Puppy milling around smiling and happy as if they had found their own families; and Mother, like a small child, holding my hand and refusing to let go for a second. Puppy offered a cigarette and Mother's eyes opened wide at the luxury of a full packet of Camels and each of us lighting a whole, separate cigarette. Krystyn, who was the only cook amongst us, dashed to prepare a special feast whilst we tried to bring some order into our chatter. And as we filed into the dining-kitchen, she broke our three hearts with a casual remark:

'It's terribly dirty here, but I'll get at it tomorrow!'

I took a few days off work whilst Mother, still unable to credit our prosperity, was settling in. She had received most of my letters and had decided to visit me in Munich as she could not comprehend my reluctance to return to Poland. The Polish authorities had offered her a professorship with all the governmental perks and, as a further inducement, had tried to arrange her visit to the West. But at the time no occupying power would grant a visa for Germany so, using her contacts in international medical circles, she travelled as a doctor with the Swiss repatriation train which quietly dropped her in Munich. She intended to stay a month or two before returning to Poland. Above all she wanted to be with me but did not try to influence my judgement.

We talked endlessly to catch up on the lost years, though only once and very briefly, she told me about Stalek's death and about Irka. She could not bear any reminders of the former, whilst the latter was my problem which I would not discuss with anybody. Mother was also hesitant to tell me about Sena, who, though starved and ill, had survived Auschwitz. In Warsaw she had recovered well but could not forget her overwhelming feeling of bitterness towards me for abandoning her in the camp. Logically she knew that I was no more responsible for the separation than she was. But the feeling remained and she refused the offer of travelling to Munich with Mother. And that was another dream lost before it had really begun.

We also discussed the present and the future. Mother thought that Poland was free, whilst I believed that our country had been taken over by Moscow. And after five years of concentration camps, I did not intend to try Siberia and thought of settling in the West – though of course not in Germany.

The first postponement of Mother's departure occurred on purely sentimental grounds as now I was all that she had. The second time was different as in the past few months she had begun to perceive that occupied Germany had more freedom than 'free' Poland. She saw that her original opinion arose from the contrast between past and present: during the German occupation of Poland thousands had vanished, now in the Russian freedom only individuals disappeared without a trace. So she came to share my views and we began to consider our future, preferably in England though there was no official way out of Germany. However, it was whispered that Italy was easy to reach and might offer other opportunities. It was a difficult decision and a gamble to leave the flat and the steady work, for the unknown of Italy, for a doubtful chance of further progress West. But in spite of the sweet talk from Tol, and the warnings of the barrister heading the Legation, against the pleadings of Krystyn and Puppy, in the early summer of 1946 Mother and I boarded a lorry which was returning from Munich to the Polish Second Corps in Italy.

It was an illegal enterprise but small Polish groups were frequently smuggled in this way. South went officers from POW camps, relatives of men serving in Italy, VIPs liberated in Germany and, unavoidably, a sprinkling of adventurers. Now there was an even dozen of us crowded into a lorry. Mother in brown slacks and I, in an unbearably hot battle dress, sat between two couples. One of these was a pair of old forlorn people, he in a worn-out dark suit, she in a nondescript dress as grey as her head. On my side was a young woman leaning and rubbing against me whenever she was not bickering with her husband. Opposite, in his sombre black robes, was a very young but quiet priest in charge of a girl and three boys 'from an orphanage'. The four teenagers, rough in dress and speech, gave a first impression of suburban hooligans. However, when the boys became too noisy one word from the girl had them standing to attention. The last person of the party was a beautiful, ageless woman whose raven hair and black, high-heeled shoes contrasted with the tight sheath dress of flame-coloured fabric.

The noisy engine, the flapping of the canvas hood and the rolling clouds of dust prevented conversation. Before the Austrian frontier the driver, assuring us that it was only a formality, lowered the tarpaulin at the back. Soon we stopped again and, silent in the dark, stuffy interior, we heard the broken English of our escort, the nasal American drawl of the frontier guard and then, most unexpectedly, they were both chatting in Polish. A few minutes later we sped into Austria. That night and the next day we spent in an overcrowded mountain chalet. We had plenty of bread and black coffee, and in the evening we were told that after a short drive to the Brenner Pass a guide would take us on foot across the frontier.

'Don't worry, and leave all the luggage in the lorry – it will be waiting for you on the other side. I send a group every second day and there is nothing to it!' finished the Liaison Officer in charge of the chalet. But, as an experienced campaigner, I quickly repacked our meagre possessions: two sweaters, four cartons of cigarettes and some food went into my rucksack with which I was not going to part.

After a short drive the lorry stopped, the back gate was lowered and we jumped down on to the road. The engine growled and the vehicle moved off. Above, a black sky with a million silver stars before us, a valley full of misty darkness with brilliantly-lit customs barriers and guard-houses. The dim mountains towering around us were bathed in blue moonlight and the golden glow of frontier floodlights reflected on our faces. To escape discovery we dived into the roadside ditch as uneasiness and apprehension turned into fear. Whispers in the dark, somebody crawling forward, somebody turning back. It was the girl who called from the front that there was no guide there. Now in panic we all gathered close: all twelve of us – but no guide. Noise in the distance and the blinding lights of another vehicle flattened us into the relative safety of the ditch.

'We can't stand here!'
'They will find us!'
'Let's hide ...'
'No, further into the bushes!'

And somebody running away. Then the quiet voice of the girl:
'Boys! We are going round the mountains!' And almost immediately the clump of a few pairs of heavy boots. I was close to Mother and whispered that we should follow the boys. The younger pair already ran to catch up. The old couple wept, and Mother encouraged them to follow, promising to help if the going got rough. The priest must have gone with the young ones, and the flame-coloured dress followed us staggering on the high heels. There was some sort of path leading away from the road and at the moment it seemed good enough. We left behind the lights of the frontier as, stumbling and falling, we marched into the unknown. I asked Mother to keep close behind me, and led slowly, warning her of bushes and boulders hidden in the shadows as the path began its endless climb, up and up for ever. Soon even curses stopped as people ran out of breath. It was a real blessing that in the spring, Mother and I had spent several long weekends walking and climbing in the Bavarian Alps – it had been a perfect training for this adventure.

Dawn mists covered the mountains and exhausted, shivering people huddled against a grey rock face. Mother and I, in sensible clothing and sweaters, were almost comfortable. The first rays of the sun revealed the ravages of the night. The dusty and torn red dress barely covered long, bluish legs and the dark eyes sank deep into the face on which tears etched lines into the artifice of paint and powder. The young couple were too weary to quarrel, and the old pair, though looking extremely tired, seemed still capable of more effort. The priest lay sprawling as if crucified on a small piece of flat ground. Even the youngsters, now silent and subdued, appeared completely spent. Unobtrusively, almost surreptitiously, they dug out some bread from their packs. I turned to the girl:

'I have some corned beef here, but we all are in this together and we share whatever we have.'

She stared at me, her grey eyes angry, mouth pursed, her small jaw jutting out ready for a battle. But suddenly she relaxed and, with a casual 'OK,' turned to the boys saying, 'Equal shares for all!' We were extremely thirsty but there was no water and the stale, half-dried bread with the greasy meat was hard to chew and swallow. Then the girl with the priest came to me asking what we should do next. We were miles from the Brenner, high up in a wide valley, but the path had long since disappeared and we were left in a mountain wilderness with a maze of criss-crossing sheep tracks. I had already thought about the situation and answered readily:

'The frontier runs east-west and if we march south' – I pointed up the long, steep slope on our right – 'we should, in theory, arrive in Italy.' They both stared at the rising pasture behind which rocky ledges and craggy faces reached straight up into the sky blocking all view and hemming us in.

'You mean – climb up there?'

Apparently none of them had ever been in the mountains; now they were completely overawed by the scale and majesty of the scene, and the proposal of attempting the sky-high peaks seemed to them wild, frightening and impossible. I explained carefully that reaching the first ridge would be easy though time-consuming, the real risk and danger lay further ahead if we pushed blindly without a path or map. Still, half an hour later, we all were moving on, slowly, painfully ever higher. The old man panted and moaned, clutching his left side, but walked on helped by his weary wife. The young couple almost sprinted a few hundred yards to sprawl exhausted before the next effort. The girl also set too fast a pace and, zig-zagging slowly but steadily, Mother and I caught up with them. It was then that I heard one of the boys complain about the weight of his pack, addressing the girl as 'Sergeant'. Unexpectedly, it was the black and red woman who, though grim and miserable, seemed to manage best. Earlier on she had broken one of her high heels, and limped like a camel till we restored her balance by tearing off the other spike.

The high sun was unbearably hot when we all settled for another rest.

The group was scattered wide with everyone seeking a flatter or softer cranny when suddenly we were confronted by an Austrian border guard. With the springy step of a born mountaineer, he descended silently into the midst of our exhausted, sweating band. His rifle at the ready he inspected us one by one and smiled, not unkindly:

'Holy Mother of God! You are the most miserable, the most amateur band of smugglers that I ever saw!'

Now that the pregnant silence was broken, two men of our group jumped up. In fluent German they tried to explain the situation and plead with the guard who remained adamant. He had to obey American orders and we would have to spend a couple of months in clink, in Germany. During this voluble exchange I took Mother's hand and slowly, quietly, edged towards a cover of rocks and boulders. I had no responsibility for the group and knew that the guard under American control would not dare to shoot unarmed DPs - we had a good chance. The argument was still going strong when we slid behind the rocks and then, to my right, I heard a sharp, metallic click. There, behind a low boulder, flat on the ground, lay the girl with a dark blue MP 40 in her hands - it was the click of the thirty-two round magazine that I had heard. By her side knelt one of the boys ready with two more magazines - no wonder they had complained of the weight of the packs!

'Hey! What do you think you are doing? The war's over and you can't just shoot people out of your way!'

She turned her head scowling at me:

'Germans are not people!' - and her hand jerked the loading lever. This was ridiculous and we all could get into a hell of a mess. Now I could no longer opt out, I had to do something and I barked in my old army manner:

'Sergeant, put the gun down! You will not shoot without my order - I will deal with this!' and, not even looking at her, I marched back to the still arguing group. I squatted amongst them and ordered a carton of cigarettes from each, and all but the priest and the young ones unearthed the goods from their bags and packs. With an armful of cigarettes I approached the guard and in my atrocious German explained:

'Enough foolishness! You take the cigs and go,' and, without giving him time to think, added, 'but first you'll tell me where is the frontier and how to get over to Italy. Now talk fast!'

And he did. The frontier was on the nearest ridge but the descent on the other side was tricky. We had to traverse a mile or two west and cross a dangerous scree to miss the unscalable cliffs. He saluted smartly and departed with his small rucksack bulging with the booty, whilst I wiped the sweat off my face.

Our little crowd of incompatible individuals suddenly became welded into a single homogeneous group which I led onward. Now they kept together, sweated together and helped one another, whilst the girl and her boys, no longer cheeky, addressed me as 'Sir'. In the early evening, with bleeding feet and totally exhausted but deliriously happy, we all bathed in a mountain stream at the bottom of an Italian valley. An hour later, an army lorry gave us a lift to the nearest Polish garrison. There we found out that the crossing of the Brenner was unofficially arranged with the Americans so that each group marched straight through, parallel to the main road and only yards off it, whilst the GIs looked away. It was just half a mile stroll across a soft meadow! Somehow it had to be our guide who missed us by a few minutes during which we panicked and disappeared into the mountains. For the past twenty-four hours, whilst we struggled over the peaks of the Alps, endless patrols scoured the countryside in search of the lost flock. We were offered transport to the nearest DP camp, but only the two old people were glad to accept. The heelless lady, with miraculously restored flame dress, disappeared in a gaggle of officers, whilst the rest of us still cogitated the future. The young ones wanted to explore Italy, but, with no money and no contacts, I was apprehensive about Mother who too was set on sightseeing. So, when the priest suggested that we join his 'orphans', we accepted the offer and, in no time, I began to appreciate his black garb. Even the lorries that rushed past short-skirted girls, would squeal to a halt at his casual gesture, and all military camps and garrisons, whether Polish or American, hurried at his word to lay out a meal for the whole party.

We spent a day exploring Venice and Mother loved and admired every stone and brick – as I had done six years previously. Now, my old enthusiasm vanished, leaving the oppressive heat, the stink of the canals and the anxiety of finding the next meal, of providing for the morrow.

We saw Padua and Verona, passed Ravenna and Bologna, slept in tents or barracks and lived on green grapes interspersed with an odd army meal. Then we were 'processed' and 'verified' by the counter-intelligence people in Modena - the name and experience so similar to my original 'welcome to France' in Modane. The interrogation began with innumerable questions about religion, Mother's maiden name and all the inevitable 'bull'. When I was questioned about Auschwitz some intelligence genius expressed the opinion that I was 'putting on a good show - old boy' but that I had never been near the camp. I lost patience and told him in unprintable language what I thought of him. I must have raised my voice somewhat because people from adjoining rooms crowded around us and suddenly the boss of my interlocutor was slapping me on the back! Ages had passed since we both had served as orderlies in Auschwitz hospital, but we had also met later in equally dramatic circumstances. He had been liberated by the Americans in a camp where a severe epidemic of typhus raged unchecked. There, to obtain quickly the necessary help and drugs, he assumed the title and prerogative of a fully qualified medical practitioner and took charge of the situation, saving many lives. But then with the misery of the camps and the uninviting future of DPs, he kept the professional status and continued in private practice as an MD! In the early days of the Polish Committee I had helped to extricate him from criminal charges and troubles. Now, I was doubly pleased to see him without his medical halo, but happy and well.

It was a reunion celebrated with my friend's lavish hospitality and deference to my Mother. But as the three of us talked I began to feel the enormous gap that the experience of the camps had created between us - the old numbers and all outsiders. Even jokes which amused us seemed like macabre humour to Mother, but we all laughed heartily about 'our orphans'. Apparently they, a small group of the Polish Home Army, had fought in the Warsaw Rising but managed to escape the Germans and even the Russians. Seeking freedom outside Poland and still led by their girl sergeant, they experienced hunger, suspicion and mistrust. Then, with one brilliant stroke of stealing priestly robes they became the poor orphans to be pitied and helped along! But at last, happy amongst the Polish soldiers, they found a new home in the Army.

Soon I was briefed on our situation. With the end of hostilities the Polish Forces could not enlist more men, and newcomers were to be accommodated in the DP camps. In practice, a few 'special cases' were still recruited by the use of back-dated forms which had been 'delayed in the administrative procedure'. The Second Corps expected a recall from Italy to England for demobilisation and it was rumoured that its 'dependants' would also be taken there. With my service in Poland and France, as well as the long imprisonment, I was offered the privilege accorded to 'special cases', and it was a tempting opportunity. On the one hand, the uniform, the long overdue commission, not to mention food, pay and cigarettes. On the other side a dubious existence as a Displaced Person pushed from camp to camp. But the war was finished, the armies were to be disbanded and the ex-soldiers would probably become equally unwanted foreigners ... No, I would rather remain an independent individual and hope to fight my own way back to human dignity. And so, with a rucksack replenished with food and cigarettes, the two of us moved on down south.

In Ancona, almost halfway through Italy, we saw the Polish Army Hospital which Mother decided to investigate. Within a quarter of an hour we were seated comfortably in the senior staff canteen whilst more and more doctors fussed about her. Many of the younger ones were her former pupils but there were also older men, the pre-war colleagues and friends of my father from the first world war. I knew very few of them but enjoyed her happiness and popularity. We slept in most comfortable beds, appreciating the mosquito nets which were a necessity in this marshy land. In the next few days we decided our immediate future. Mother was 'joining up' and, though she was employed in an auxiliary capacity, her own entry to England was assured. I would go further south towards Bari, where in Barletta, was a civilian camp for the 'dependants' of the Polish Second Corps. It was only another three hundred miles, half the distance that we had already covered from Munich. But though there were no frontiers to cross and no Alps to climb, the journey was made harder by the poor, war-weary country and the scarcity of troops. My complete lack of Italian and ignorance of the local customs did not help either. But when really exhausted I received help from a most unexpected source. Hunger had forced me into the hills above some God-forsaken town where I was stuffing myself with ripening grapes. Suddenly from a higher terrace somebody shouted in Polish:

'You will get better diarrhoea there than in Auschwitz! Come over and I'll show you fields of really ripe, black ones!'

And when we met face to face he glanced at the number tattooed on my arm and then he could not do enough for me – 'the old numbers must stick together'. On top of all the 'info' where to get army food and how to obtain lifts, he forced on me the most generous loan which, incredibly, I was able to repay in London a year later.

Barletta camp, the usual huddle of tents and huts, was like all the others: greasy and unpalatable food, bored crowds of lost and disillusioned people from all walks of life. In late summer Southern Italy was unbearably hot and the water of the nearby sea was too warm to be refreshing. In day-time the panting people sought relief in scanty shade, at night they talked desultorily and waited till midnight when the corrugated iron roofs ceased to radiate heat into the barracks and clouds of mosquitoes forced everyone indoors. As hardly anybody was prepared to work, I had no trouble in obtaining a clerical job in the camp administration. It paid little but there was a premium of cigarettes. We started work very early but by eight o'clock everybody sweated so that the drill shorts and flimsy skirts were wet through and stuck firmly to the wooden chairs. At noon and in the evening we trailed from the office to the sea in our heavy boots as the sand was too hot to walk on with bare feet. I used to swim long distances but even with this exercise I found the humid nights most uncomfortable. In the overcrowded camp I still had only a narrow stretcher to sleep on, but the real misery was caused by the mosquitoes which buzzed and bit till in desperation one pulled a blanket over one's head to sweat and gasp in the stifling cocoon. To make it worse my old nightmares returned to plague me again. Soon after the liberation I had been afflicted by these awful recurring dreams which had almost disappeared with the hectic pace of work in Munich. Now every night back came the same frightful visions. The dream became a hell of terror with demons coming nearer and nearer till I woke up bathed in cold sweat and shaking all over. I had to get up, to walk, to be sure that the reality was here and not there. Ultimately, it took some ten years to get rid of the beasts.

Then came the long-awaited news: a special commission was in Italy to adjudicate who could go to England. So, the prospective emigrants from Barletta were picked up by army lorries and delivered to the transit camp, yet another conglomeration of dilapidated huts. The milling people, each one bent on his own progress, looked already harassed and harried in their anxious wait for the interview with 'THE COMMISSION'. Nobody had the slightest inkling what questions might be asked, what criteria would be applied, and everybody was frightened and hesitant of taking the first place in the queue. To me it seemed simple enough. I had fought the Nazis, I was a Pole, one of the Allies who had won the war and my own country was now occupied by Russia. Young and strong, I wanted to settle in England and had already received two letters from my English friends offering me their hospitality. As to the interview itself, I had dealt often enough with awkward brass hats to volunteer confidently as the first candidate of the day.

The interior of the hut was scrubbed and arranged to resemble a board room. But no amount of polish could hide the shabbiness of the place. Behind the table sat the dignitaries: one or two uniforms with enough brass to sink a battleship, and three or four dark, immaculate business suits. They were obviously high grade civil servants and an MP or two. But there, and to us, they were an intimidating epitome of the wealth and power of the Empire. They were extremely polite, asking questions of what and how, making allowances for my slow English. They glanced at my letters from England and conferred a few seconds. Then the one in the centre of the group shook his head:

'We are bound by the regulations which say that only the dependants of Polish soldiers can be admitted into the U K. We sympathise with you and have no doubt that you would be an asset to our country. Unfortunately, in the circumstances, we cannot authorise your application, however sorry we feel about it.'

I stood speechless whilst the sentence of continued exile was slowly sinking in. They still seemed to argue among themselves but I no longer listened, determined only on not showing my disappointment, on not letting a single tear roll down my face, and swallowing hard before I could utter just the two words of 'Thank you'. I was at the door when one of them called me back. He walked to the window, outside which seethed the crowd of civilians interspersed with the uniforms of Polish soldiers.

'Mr Siedlecki,' - his pronunciation of my name was almost perfect - 'You Poles are all closely related. I have no doubt whatsoever that, if you walked out there and looked carefully, you would find a relative. What we need is a name, army number and unit. And come back as soon as you have found your uncle.'

The thin, small corporal was not even astonished at my request:

'It's all right with me, mate. Just write down my number and give it to them!'

I was extremely grateful to him and regretted that I could only offer him one of my last packets of Camels. I also felt slightly guilty at the sneaking thought that I would have preferred it if he had been a commando or a tank man instead of a functionary in the field laundry. But when I came back into the hut of the Commission they all looked really pleased and, congratulating me on finding a lost relative, entered my name for the first transport.

CHAPTER 21

THE FRIENDS IN NEED

The train carried a mass of people whose individuality had been leached out by the turbulent waves of war. The Germans had uprooted them from remote Polish villages; Allied transports and camps bewildered them no less than foreign languages and customs. Now a train bore them still further to the hoped-for reunion with their dear ones. There were also some Ukrainians and a sprinkling of other nationalities represented by young women – those who played their cards right and only surrendered their virtue for a marriage certificate. All had heard of England and many knew that it was 'overseas' – a frightening knowledge to those inland people for whom the biggest body of water was the village pond.

Our transport with its sealed carriages meandered slowly through Europe to deliver us to a Channel boat that tossed and danced on the leaden-hued sea. A chilling autumnal gale drained the last vestige of energy and spirit from the people. A slow disembarkation, an ordinary train where English travellers tried to be friendly to the bewildered immigrants in shorts, in thin rayon dresses, but the language barrier remained unbreached. A bus ride and another camp, this time in lush greenery half hidden in rain and mist. Nissen huts, brick-built washrooms and lavatories, the small woebegone reception committee. A dismal beginning after the scorching sun of southern Italy.

The next day the camp 'Administration' changed my last few dollars into pounds and directed me to the nearest public phone. An hour later I found one at the crossroads and remembered the real meaning of 'you can't miss it'. The operator at the local exchange was most helpful, listening patiently to the mixture of my school English and American slang. Soon I was talking to my friend's sister Ann who, in his absence, asked me to come and stay as soon as possible. It was only a couple of hours by the local buses and I sat glued to the window trying to spot the names of passing villages. But the signs were either hidden in the overgrown hedges or screened by hoardings and advertisements. Then, I burst out laughing: I, who had twice crossed occupied Europe, was worried about getting lost in this little island of my own choosing. But the journeys were not to be compared – there we had thrown into the balance our own lives and were prepared to kill or be killed; here and now I wanted to be unobtrusive, to be absorbed into the crowd, to become fully and truly one of them.

I passed Castle Hill, the little shopping centre and the stone pillars at the entrance to a large, wild garden. Away from the road stood the old house, unchanged and unchangeable, just as I remembered it from before the war, just as it had stood for centuries. There was a warm welcome though I was no longer an honoured European visitor, but an unfortunate lame dog of a foreigner to be helped over the high English stiles. After the inevitable tea, served in cups of the thinnest china, I heard the news. Bob, my best Polish friend of school and war adventures, was dead. After our parting in 1940 at Paris he had joined the RAF and had been killed over France in the last year of the war. But, on the first floor, his bedroom remained just as he had left it two years previously. His clothing hung in the wardrobe, freshly laundered linen lay on the shelves, on the dressing table were hair brushes, shaving kit and a small tray still full of cuff-links and tie-pins. Even now the room brought tears to the eyes of Ann, but to me it remained an empty, dead place. Bob lived or died in his friends' memories but never in this spotless shrine. Still, I did respect feelings and beliefs of other people and was really touched when, after a silent but no less obvious struggle, Ann offered me a loan of Bob's oldest suit. Then we went downstairs to meet Anthony. He, a school friend of Bob and myself, had passed through Russia, Siberia and the Middle East to serve with the RAF. Through Bob he had met our English friends and was now almost adopted by our hostess. We shook hands and gossiped but it was not a happy reunion. The greetings and talk were so cold and casual that later Ann took me aside to explain what a terrible time dear Tony had had in Siberia, and I refrained from the obvious rejoinder that I myself had not come back from a picnic.

My visit was too rapid a transition from years of communal life in overcrowded conditions to this conventional, tranquil house. Before dinner dainty glasses were half filled with pale sherry from a crystal decanter. There was often a delicious Yorkshire pudding and home-grown vegetables which for me, as for all Poles, were marred by a 'goo-ey' white sauce. The deep, soft carpets and masses of brittle antiques did not go together with the well-fed white bull-terrier which was always chastised and reproved for dirty paws and boisterous behaviour. He took an immediate fancy to me and the fifty pounds of hard dog full of claws and teeth frequently thudded into my lap at the most inopportune moments. Everybody was so kind, so friendly, but somehow I never did feel at home there. It seemed impossible that Ann resented the affection her dog showered on me. And Tony certainly could not be afraid of me as a potential competitor for the favours of Ann. It was also difficult to fit into the settled custom and routine of the English middle class. I had just begun to adapt myself to the situation when it was time to go: my other friends, the Fords, insisted that I come and make my home with them.

As the train stopped at the station I realised that Ann had not given me the Fords' address, remarking casually, 'Oh, everybody knows them - you won't have any trouble finding them.' But Ilkley was not that small, and in reply to my enquiries I received only odd glances. Seven years had passed since I spent a few days there and I could not recollect the name or even the look, of any street. However, my old sense of direction, or some subconsciously remembered details, led me slowly but surely to The Pines. Three noisy spaniels raced down the long drive to meet me and through the open French windows came Jane to welcome me. She looked more mature than my mental picture of her. John, back from POW camp, seemed thinner and smaller. Mr and Mrs Ford were absolutely unchanged. He was extremely quiet with the politeness and reticence of the English gentleman. In contrast, always in a hurry, Mrs Ford moved and spoke at such a rate that I never caught more than one or two words of any sentence. In time I learned to understand a bit more and was overjoyed to find out that many people could not follow her either. The family and the house were as English as roast beef and the Tower, but somehow, after the first few days, I felt better there, and incomparably more at home, than at Ann's place.

We talked a lot in spite of my language difficulties. From the beginning I could understand best Mr Ford, as he scorned slang and spoke only the King's English of impeccable grammar and distinct pronunciation. To help me further, he remembered to use words of Latin or Greek origin like 'sufficient' instead of 'enough'. I also got on well with Jane who, uncannily detecting any doubts in my mind, was always ready to repeat her remarks in another form and more slowly. I was surprised how quickly and completely they had got over the war. It had been a catastrophe, but for them it had passed, was dismissed and best forgotten. I never even heard of John's adventures in the desert except that, severely wounded, he had been taken prisoner in one of the tank battles. Similarly, they did not want to hear any details of my past, but were eager to help in shaping my new life. Taking for granted that I would stay on as a member of the family, they encouraged my plans to complete, or even start from the beginning, my engineering studies. And I, deeply touched by this magnanimous offer, accepted with gratitude though I realised that I should never be able to repay their generosity.

I went back to the camp to arrange my final discharge and, though I had been only a fortnight in England, this third journey seemed so simple and effortless that I wondered at my recent timidity and groundless fears. The authorities were only too happy to be rid of even one of their charges, and quickly issued me with clothing coupons, a food ration book and a battle dress, khaki of course, but thick and comfortably warm. Back in Ilkley Mrs Ford, who was an active officer of the British Red Cross, offered to supplement my meagre wardrobe from their stores. I had great doubts about accepting public charity but took it gladly when told that the clothing was intended solely for Displaced Persons. She then drove me to York where I acquired a pair of grey flannels, a sweater and a couple of shirts which made me feel like a millionaire.

Of the subsequent frantic search for further education I remember most the quickly alternating hopes and disappointments. All colleges and universities were already filled with demobbed ex-servicemen. The remnants of the Polish Government-in-Exile were giving scholarships and grants but their funds were running out. In her little MG Jane took me to Bradford College where everybody was extremely kind but equally firm – there was not a single place left on any course. Next day Jane asked me if I remembered Marjorie and, seeing my blank expression, she elaborated further:

'It doesn't matter, the point is she remembers you! You played cricket with her and her cubs in '39! She liked you no end and wants to help.'

It took me a good minute to think out and articulate a suitable reply to the effect that it was very kind of her indeed, and I was really proud of the 'indeed'! Then Jane explained that her friend's father was the head of a big company which used to donate to Bradford College a considerable amount of equipment.

'We pick up Marjorie tomorrow morning,' she continued, 'and she will introduce you to her father. It will be perfectly all right!'

But it did not seem to me as simple as that, even if Marjorie and her father wanted to, and could help. In Poland nepotism and any similar practice involving protégés was frowned upon and I knew that Stalek would not have it in any circumstance. Here, in England, still lost in the language, ignorant of customs and the way of life, I decided to tackle Mr Ford on this matter. He concentrated on the practical side of the problem: if I wanted to study it was only sensible to use proffered help. However, I persisted, trying hard to explain my doubts in stilted school English desperately short of abstract words. His answer was now more to the point and brought out aspects which I had never before considered. These concerned the will, the ability and the interest the possession of which, he thought, I had amply demonstrated in the recent past.

'If I had to train one engineer for my factory and had the choice of an unknown teenager or you whom I trust and respect, my decision would be obvious. The same applies in the wider case of giving preference to a person with previous studies and experience, somebody known and proved.'

I saw his point but was not entirely convinced. None of them knew much about me, and my survival proved more luck and adaptability than aptitude for engineering. On the other hand, it seemed that without their support I would not even have a chance to study. So the next morning I met Marjorie and was introduced to her father. After a talk about my pre-war studies and more recent adventures he made a couple of telephone calls and told me that I could have a place in the College. Next day, in the College, I was assured of an admission as soon as they received a notification about the grant which had been promised by the Polish Authorities subject to an interview.

I borrowed enough money for a return ticket to London where I presented myself at the appropriate offices. There I ran into the brick wall of slow and uninterested clerks of the Polish Government-in-Exile. During a long morning and a hungry afternoon I filled in many forms and succeeded in obtaining an appointment for the next day. It was one of those few hot autumn days and, leaving the stuffy offices, I took off my, or rather Bob's, jacket and rolled up my shirt sleeves. Walking slowly through the rush-hour crowds I considered the relative merits of a park bench and a railway station when I heard distinctly a remark in Polish about 'such an old number'. Behind me were two girls, one in an ATS uniform, the other in a neat, short-sleeved blouse, an Auschwitz number tattooed on her forearm. This was an indisputable sign of brotherhood often stronger than any blood ties and immediately we were all talking together. They had both been in Auschwitz and were now studying in London. It did not occur to any of us to ask whether we originated from north or south Poland – 'from Auschwitz' was the one and only meaningful identification. On hearing my predicament they decided immediately:

'Come with us and have something to eat, we have enough!'

We wolfed a large loaf with a thin scraping of margarine and I was introduced to their kind old landlady ('we give her our ration of tea and she always has a surplus of bread'). Then they planned the night – I could kip down in an armchair whilst they shared the 'Put-u-up' settee in their large attic room.

'But you must leave before nine as she is awfully Victorian! She goes to sleep early and you come back about eleven. We will let you in, only take your shoes off not to make any noise!' – and everything worked perfectly.

I left them early the next day and during the interview was promised the grant of £20 a month on production of a certificate that I was a student of Bradford Tech, and no amount of explanation or pleading could change it or get out of them a written statement to this effect. Back in Bradford the administration explained even more slowly and patiently to the dumb foreigner that in no circumstances could they admit me into the College before receiving the confirmation of the grant! Boiling with fury and frustration I appealed to a high-up College executive who shall remain nameless in this tale. He listened to my recital and, after a moment's thought, called his secretary and dictated a letter 'to whom it may concern' that Mr Siedlecki has been accepted as a student ... She brought it back in a few minutes and, after reading it carefully, he turned to me:

'Well, that is about what you need? But of course, you realise that I cannot possibly give it to you as it is not true, and anyway it's an administrative affair of the College Secretary. It also needs the College stamp and a signature.'

He carefully picked out of a wire rack two stamps and laid them between the typed letter and the open ink-pad. He hesitated and added:

'The big one goes at the top and the facsimile of my signature goes at the bottom ... But excuse me for a moment - I must see what my secretary is doing. When I come back we can discuss your choice of subjects.'

He left the room, quietly closing the door. I pressed the stamps firmly on the typed sheet, folded it into its envelope and hurriedly put it into my pocket. It seemed ages before he came back, suggesting that we have another chat soon, and shook hands wishing me success. I received the grant by return post and began my studies.

CHAPTER 22

BACK TO SCHOOL

I entered the College with mixed feelings. The apprehension of coping with the new surroundings and the language overshadowed my satisfaction of beginning a new life. The grimy streets of Bradford, the soot-blackened façade and the maze of College corridors further dampened my enthusiasm. The large classroom was full of students congregating in separate groups of ex-servicemen eyeing disdainfully a motley collection of young boys straight from school. All were talking at the same time so that the hubbub of voices rose in waves and I couldn't catch a single word of the broad Yorkshire. At the entrance of the lecturer the noise subsided to erupt again in a gale of laughter at his short speech – a joke presumably, though, as before, I did not understand anything! But then he plunged into his subject and, miraculously, I began to hear and understand. The logical, consecutive statements concerned with one narrow field of knowledge came across plainly and clearly. Still, I was glad of my decision to start the first year course instead of the second to which I was entitled by my pre-war studies. In time to come I began to understand some of the local dialect, but the gap of age and background between me and other students was so wide that I did not make any friends and remained solitary and alone.

It was hard to accept the school-like College, so different from the free-and-easy continental universities. Conversely, the technical subjects I followed and assimilated quickly, but found unexpected trouble with simple arithmetic as I had learned the multiplication tables to 9 whilst any two figure numbers we dealt with 'on paper'. Of course, at the time I did not even suspect that the systems of 12, 14, 16 and 20 parts per unit still existed in the modern world. I also took the additional 'basic English' taught by a Mr Kay who treated the whole class as young and retarded delinquents. Nevertheless I soon saw that he was a born teacher with a staggering knowledge of his subject. At the beginning I must have been the worst case in the class and he seemed to give me more than a fair share of his time. In a few months my essays and précis improved enormously but my spoken English remained so poor that I still had to concentrate fully at all times to keep up with the lecturers. Exhausted by these efforts I returned home to Ilkley to be plunged into the family conversation and cross-talk where I could follow, at the best, one person at a time. Every night I went to bed with spots before my eyes and crazily tumbling words like aunts and ounces, cogs and clogs ... It was mostly Jane's understanding and friendship which carried me through this period.

The next setback came when the Head of my department explained that the Tech was not a university and to obtain a degree I had to become an external student of London University and take their exams in addition to those of the College. I went to London University where, after the long interview, I was promised admission, subject to passing the 'Special English for Foreigners'. This, I soon found out, was regarded as impassable, and indeed, taking it a month later, I failed dismally. My second attempt in spring 1947 was equally disastrous and the language barrier, instead of decreasing, loomed higher and higher. In desperation I approached Mr Kay about private tuition. Hesitatingly he asked if I could afford half-a-crown per hour. I accepted happily and only a whole year later learned that, at that time, he had refused students offering one and two guineas an hour.

College lectures, homework and especially English filled my days, but on Sundays I always managed long walks on the ever-changing moors. The emerald green of bracken darkened into deep russet. The mists thickened into fogs, and hoary frost announced the coming of Christmas. Academic term ended and at last I had time for a long letter to Mother, who had settled in Edinburgh on a small stipend from the Polish Government in London. Around me the festivities rolled on: lights sparkled on a Christmas tree, the table sagged under the abundance of magnificent food, and wine-filled crystal shone like rubies. The family joked and chatted, including me in their circle, but in spite of their friendliness, this Season of Good Will brought me too many memories of Irka and Stalek, of Bob and Joseph ... all those who loved life and had been robbed of it. And suddenly, caught unprepared amongst the joyous crowd, I felt more alien than ever. Was I just sorry for myself? Or was it the language barrier which exaggerated the disparity between Polish emotionalism and English reserve?

My English progressed so imperceptibly that only some new difficulties signalled the improvement. Initially, any question directed at me registered subconsciously in a short-term memory store to be replayed slowly and silently, translated into Polish and understood. Only then an answer was thought out in Polish, translated back into English and spoken if all the intermediate steps went without a hitch. Now, at least the simplest exchanges like a 'Good morning' or 'Thank you' occurred automatically and without the two translations required earlier. This process however ran into a difficulty with numbers. I could count, or recite a multiplication table, in Polish or English, but when concentrating on something else, the two languages tended to get mixed up and I was stuck unable to multiply, or even add, the Polish five to an English three! The only way of reaching the answer was a conscious effort to keep the calculations in one language only.

Another measure of my progress was the ability to chat with fellow students. One of these exchanges resulted in an odd episode at the College. The engineering drawings were supervised by junior assistants but, quite often, a senior lecturer came to check the progress. As I usually finished well before the allotted time, he used to lean over my board asking about my war experiences. On this occasion some students drifted across steering the talk to the beginning of the war and, remembering the Ukrainian banditry and Russian tanks, I made my point in crude American Army slang. It was at this moment that I noticed the puce colour of the silent lecturer who suddenly turned and walked away followed by a gale of laughter. Only then I learned that they all knew the strong communist sympathies of the gentleman. Though the joke was aimed at the lecturer, I did not like being used in that way and told them so. The giggles ceased and I went to see the 'red' gentleman in his study. In my determination to explain what had happened I must have appeared rather belligerent as he quickly retreated behind his desk. I apologised sincerely, but stressed that it was due to his position and seniority, whilst on neutral ground, I would be happy to shoot on sight any communist. The episode ended in a handshake and an amicable parting but, throughout my course, I felt that, in his subject, I received marks higher than my work warranted.

The deep, slowly melting snows of the exceptional '46-47 winter swelled the grey waters of the Wharfe. New growth of bracken and wiry heathers covered the moors, and the hesitant spring gave way to the sunshine of summer. The College year came to its end in a flurry of exams and, at home, my adopted family was preparing for their holidays. For me the time had come to stand on my own feet and, finding digs in Stanningley, I secured a summer apprenticeship at English Electric in Thornbury.

My everyday life altered as dramatically as did my employment. I exchanged the palatial house and its beautiful park for an attic room in a long, grey terrace. Chips with microscopic chops and black pudding took the place of pheasants and salmon. I missed the long walks on Ilkley Moor but was satisfied with equally aimless wandering through sprawling hamlets which were already being absorbed into the ever-growing city. Occasional whist drives took the place of the frequent cocktail and bridge parties of my former hosts. But, after my war experiences, the material changes affected me very little indeed. Even the emotional change of the family life for that of a lodger was tempered by the simple and friendly attitude of the working folk which contrasted with the formal and undemonstrative behaviour of the upper middle class. But I began to appreciate even more than before how much I owed to the people who had taken in a stray foreigner, given him friendship and showed him the English culture and way of life.

My grant of £20 per month covered bus fares, books and other College necessities, but, after paying for digs with breakfast and 'high tea' included, there was little left. The luxury of cigarettes was cheap, but to accumulate a financial reserve I dispensed with lunches, and as a result often felt hungry.

My second College year required more work but passed quickly and with less strain. The autumn brought me the first success of a pass in the London English exam. But this achievement was marred by my doubts about the means by which I had obtained it. The exam comprised two main parts: a précis and an essay on one of the given subjects. I had chosen 'My first impressions of England' and made it into a glorious panegyric of England and the English. Presumably my language was better this time but I wondered whether the contents of the essay influenced the marking. Anyway, the language barrier was conquered, and now appeared of no significance. I became a student of London University, though it was a year late, as in spring I had to take 'Part One' of Bradford Diploma and only the 'Intermediate' of the London Degree. Still, dropping the study of the English language left me more time which I invested in night classes in mathematics which was my weakest subject.

There was no chitter-chatter and no waste of time. The students of mixed age and sex represented all strata of society though there was a disproportionally large number of foreigners. They were easy to recognise by rather shabby, frequently ex-army, attire and the most intense concentration caused by their limited knowledge of English. There I met Marija, a Latvian girl who had been taken to Germany for forced labour and had arrived here under the European Voluntary Workers scheme. Nobody beat her any more, and at night she was free to study chemistry, but there was little difference between the labour on a Bavarian farm and the heavy manual work in a Bradford woollen mill which retained three-quarters of her wages for inadequate food and accommodation in their own hostel. Soon after our first meeting Marija left the hostel to move into digs with two English girls. One big room contained the most unlikely trio: the small and subdued ash-blond Marija, demure Margaret with six foot bean-pole frame, and buxom Sheila of flame-red hair. The Latvian went all out for a degree in chemistry. Margaret had left the comfortable farm of her parents and, regardless of her shape, was set on becoming a dancer. Sheila, an adventuress, was working as a waitress to save for a treasure hunt in the Caribbean! But in spite of a doubtful past and an uncertain future, she had a firm, practical grasp of life and took Marija and me under her wing. Having decided that we both were badly underfed, she instructed us to come after the night classes to 'her' café and sit in the back corner where she 'slung hash' with gusto and speed. It was a totally dishonest swindle but in the circumstances we did not resist too strenuously. Twice a week we would find our way to the dingy and smelly 'caff' where Sheila plopped in front of us two plates piled high with red-hot greasy chips under which were invariably two large lumps of fish. After consuming both mounds we always paid with a ten-shilling note and received ten shillings change in silver and copper. Dear Sheila!

– she certainly eased our lives though after a year of this diet I could not bear fish and chips for a long time.

Once, as I walked Marija home, she asked me in and we found a note from Margaret: 'Mum and Dad are taking me to dinner - home late - M.' Sheila was still in her 'caff' and so the two of us settled down to some troublesome differential equations. In an hour both girls arrived together and I was just leaving when a ring of the bell was followed by importunate knocking downstairs. The landlady always retired early and Sheila dashed to the front door. We heard voices, heavy steps, and suddenly the room was full of people: two large, hard-faced women and Sheila followed by a huge man blocking the door. Almost in a whisper Sheila announced them as CID. One of the women asked our names and I realised that I was standing behind my armchair with a carving knife in my hand. The visitors politely but firmly asked me to leave as they wished to interview the girls. Usually pale but now chalk-white, Margaret turned towards me:

'Don't go! Don't leave us!'

She was on the verge of hysteria and one of the women reached reassuringly for her hand, which was a mistake as the girl jumped back ready to scream. The woman also backed away, trying to retrieve the situation by quiet persuasion - nothing to fear, just a few questions, the gentleman can stay if you all wish it, and the girls nodded silently.

'Well now ...' began the woman, but I interrupted:

'First let's see your credentials!'

They all flashed some hard-covered booklets but I was not satisfied:

'Put them on the table!' - and I stepped from behind my armchair, no longer concealing the knife. I told Sheila to watch them whilst I perused the documents. By the time I was satisfied, and had laid the knife on the table with the handle towards them, they all seemed a little smaller and less intimidating.

The man was taking notes while the girls hesitated and stammered barely audible replies. In a few minutes it was obvious that they tried to find out whether all three girls had alibis for the late evening and I volunteered a quick summary: Marija had been with me, Sheila had spent all her time at the café, whilst Margaret had been with her parents. Then I asked for an explanation of the whole proceedings. They exchanged a few whispered words before telling us the story. The girls' landlady, severely injured, had been found at the bottom of the cellar steps and her nephew had informed the police that her valuable collection of postage stamps was missing. He also maintained that the crime was committed by the three girls. The CID people thanked us politely, apologised for the intrusion and departed. The incident was closed some weeks later when one of the original visitors returned to tell the girls that the nephew had been arrested and charged with attempted murder and theft. The landlady recovered, but Margaret's parents insisted on her changing the lodgings. Sheila found another boyfriend to replace the Caribbean dream, and Marija moved to Frizinghall.

In late spring she approached me in her usual brusque manner about a loan of ten pounds for a trip to London – the first step in her efforts to reach Canada. I brought the money a few days later and we had an almighty row when she insisted on giving me, as security, her mother's wedding ring, the only memento of her home and her murdered parents. In the end I took the ring as nothing could resist Marija's iron will. A few months later she had repaid every penny of the loan and only then proudly slipped the ring on her finger.

In the meantime I passed the London 'Intermediate', the College 'Part One', and found a summer apprenticeship at Jowett Cars in Idle.

My English improved so that I could not only communicate but also began making friends amongst workmen and staff. Some introduced me to their families and to the dirt-track racing, others showed me round the factory, explaining various aspects of design and manufacture. For the first time I saw engineering in a broader sense than pure technology and, more important, I began to perceive the hard nature and the big heart of Yorkshire.

To save bus fares I acquired a push-bike. Consumer goods were still in short supply and anyway I could not afford a new machine so I bought an old tourer which, when rebuilt, served me well. After two years of hard work I cut short my summer apprenticeship and used the last week of the holidays for a bit of cycling. I renewed my acquaintance with the Yorkshire dales and ventured further to visit Mr and Mrs Sinclair, my Manchester hosts of 1939. There I was deeply touched as they welcomed me as a long lost son. They were poor, hard-working people, but I had quite a task fending off their persistent offers of a substantial loan for an indefinite period.

My third College year began in the study of my Departmental Head.

He congratulated me on my success in the London as well as the College exams but pointed out that it would be almost impossible to manage in one year the College Finals and the London 'Part One'. With his support I requested the Polish Authorities to extend my grant for another year or to allow me to take only 'Part One' instead of the College Finals. Their immediate reply was an emphatic NO to my request: the grant was for a College Diploma and this I was told to get. All this trouble arose from my initial ignorance of the English educational system and also from the equal and persistent ignorance and pig-headedness of the Polish Authorities.

My mother moved from Edinburgh to Leeds and I tried to spend weekends there as she was extremely lonely. This was not as often as I wished as the last year of the studies took heavy toll of my time and energy. The steady flow of lectures was interrupted by visits from representatives of firms looking for budding executives, but my humble self never attracted attention in this modern slave market. So, swotting for the finals, I began sending out my own applications for work. I borrowed a typewriter and, because of my old and deep interest, directed a stream of letters to all famous motorcycle manufacturers from AJS and Ariel to Triumph and Velocette. I was surprised that all the addressees answered, though all replies were equally polite and negative. The next batch began with AC and Alvis and finished with Vauxhall and Wolseley, but was equally unsuccessful. I tried national giants and small local firms – all to no avail as war production had ceased and conversion to consumer goods took time. Also the labour market was swamped by demobbed servicemen whilst for the unpopular manual jobs EVWs – people like Marija – were in ample supply and happy to slave just for a chance to escape from Germany. Disheartened by the situation I did not feel equal to the finals which, to my great surprise I managed to pass, and a day later received an offer of work: car-washing in a local garage! But, the same night, Shirley rang up. We had met at Fords and I remembered her well as the only English person with a good command of Polish. On the phone she told me that her friend, a local industrialist, had complained of personnel shortage and she had already arranged an interview for me.

CHAPTER 23

APPRENTICE

After the College Finals I quit Stanningley digs and secured a small attic above my Mother's lodgings. So I travelled from Leeds to Ilkley for my interview.

From behind his large desk the Chief Engineer of 'Spooner Dryer' hissed at me one word which I did not catch, but before I could enquire he shouted:

'Gears, man! Gears! Cog wheels – you understand?' – his hands splayed wide and came together meshing finger to finger. And gears I did know – theory from College, and from Jowett the machining, fitting, tolerances ...

'Kinematically they are all cylindrical, conical or hyperboloidal pairs rolling together with line contact but without slip ...' I could have gone on for hours but he stopped me and switched to vibration. But again I was soon stopped and an impossible, heretical thought flashed through my mind that the swarthy man behind the desk had long forgotten, or never knew well, the Theory of Machines. He offered me Drawing Office work at five pounds ten shillings a week. It seemed a pitiful remuneration but it was a tenth more than my old grant and, as beggars can't be choosers, I accepted. He then took me to the Chief Draughtsman, a young man with a sense of humour but a bit of a martinet. Mr Loveday told me that I could start the following Monday but would have to produce a Labour Exchange certificate, still necessary under the war time regulations.

In Stanningley Labour Exchange, I had a head-on collision with ignorance and prejudice personified by a slob of a clerk who would not even listen to me:

'All Poles go to the mines or mills and I'll see that you go there, and fast! You had no business in Bradford Tech!' – and, however hard I tried, I could not get through to him. I felt the blood rushing to my cheeks, my ears ... Some of my fury must have reached him as he suddenly turned and ran from the room. A girl came in and asked if I wanted anything else but would not talk about my work permit.

I walked all the way back to Leeds to cool down, but inside I was still boiling and ready to explode: Germany, Italy, slog through the College, the language barrier ... I could not even think sensibly. At home I quietly told Mother that I could have the job but had run into difficulties at the Labour Exchange. She was overjoyed and remarked that I should phone Dora who was somebody in the Ministry of Labour. I just couldn't talk about it any more and, at my blank stare, she explained that she had met Dora at the Anglo-Polish Society where the lady was doing an enormous amount of work for the Poles. In the end Mother talked to Dora who advised that I should go again to the same office where they would sort out everything.

The next day I cycled to Stanningley repeating to myself that I must not, and would not, hit the man first. On arrival I gave my name and was whisked straight to the boss of the outfit.

'Now then Mr S-S-Sh... You must forgive me, it is very difficult to pronounce! Anyway, I really must apologise as there was some misunderstanding yesterday, but everything is all right now and, of course, you can start your work at Spooner's immediately.'

And so in summer 1949 I began to earn my living in England.

It was the first time I used a draughting machine, and this was a vast improvement over the old mahogany tee-square and wobbly drawing board. The drawings were in pencil and appeared simple and rough, but there was an enormous number of them and the speed of the draughtsmen around me was staggering. The Chief Engineer left very soon after he had employed me and, in those early days, I had little contact with Mr Loveday. The next in command was the Senior Draughtsman, Mr Lobley, a young, serious gentleman with an umbrella. He was most friendly and really helped me in my first steps as a draughtsman. Others of the staff appeared then as indistinguishable as a crowd of film extras, but in reality there were only four or five of them and I soon began to know them all. The early days were frightening as I felt unequal to the job. There were millions of simple but all-important rules of standard practice that I did not know. And, whilst trying to remember it all, I noticed the reluctance of the other draughtsmen to give information or help. It seemed odd as in all my previous experience – the Army, prisons and apprenticeships – I had encountered co-operation and friendship. Here, if not open hostility, it certainly was a negative attitude to any beginner. This was further exemplified by the rough treatment of an office boy who was always told, 'I had to learn the hard way and now you sweat it out!' But there was an exception to this rule: on the board nearest to mine worked Alan who, though impatient with my queries, was ready to repeat the misunderstood or forgotten information and help with other difficulties.

On the home front everything went smoothly. Mother had happily settled down in Leeds. We had an excellent relationship with our landlord and his wife, an old, retired couple who often invited us for a game of bridge. With the low rent and my earnings we began steady saving as Mother found the English rations more than adequate and fed us both on a tiny budget. Just as we were congratulating ourselves on our good management, our luck ran out in rather peculiar circumstances. I was at home when her monthly stipend arrived and, noticing that she signed two identical receipts, I pointed out that she had just acknowledged receipt of forty pounds instead of the actual twenty. So we marked the second receipt in red as a duplicate, and the next month she got her usual twenty pounds with a single receipt form and a letter stating that the funds had run out and no more would be paid in future! A weekend began with a scrutiny of our accounts and a careful consideration of potential savings. By Sunday I declared that we could manage on my wages. It was a relief to us both as Mother, after her two wars, could not face more professional work and struggle.

About this time Marija visited us to say goodbye as her dream had come true and she was emigrating to Canada. Her overseas friends paid the passage, but even so she was almost destitute, and gladly accepted my old pair of army boots as a 'going away' present. We wished her all the luck in the world and parted, not expecting to meet again.

To stretch our meagre resources I gave up buses and cycled to work. It was pleasant in summer and acceptable on crisp autumn mornings, but the fifteen miles homeward journey in the darkness of winter was grim. In the office the details of 'standard practice' became obvious and natural. My output increased proportionally and I no longer felt useless. Of course, I had my share of disasters, like the urgent drawing of a chimney cowl completed in the late hours of overtime. The Senior Draughtsman checked the details and, leaving the office, we mailed the drawing. I knew well what this chimney cover was and how to design it but, unfamiliar with its English name, and hearing the sloppily pronounced sound, tackled my companion:

'Jim, you mean that what I have just drawn is called exactly like the four-legged thing that gives milk?'

'What do you mean?'

'Well, I heard you talking of this cow so I put the title C.O.W., and you did not say anything when checking it.'

Short of burgling the Post Office we could not do anything and my 'COW' had gone to the customer.

Another time, when drawing an 'Arrangement of Piping' I was asked to check that all the required components were actually in store. I picked up the stock list, but was stopped:

'They are always running short, especially of nipples, the ones with internal threads, so ring up and confirm!'

Stores were at our works in Leeds but, in the General Office, one of the girls kept a close check on stock. She was a well-built Yorkshire lass always in tight sweaters but, as I was shy of my slow and heavily accented English, I had never spoken to her and now hesitated before using the phone.

'It's all right, just pick up the phone, the internal one, and ask for Joyce.'

The office became entirely silent and I was grateful to them as, with so much noise around, I found conversation awkward, and by telephone, just impossible. I got Joyce and made it short and to the point:

'Joyce, have you got two one-inch female nipples?' - and she answered without taking any time to check the books:

'Yes, I have a pair, but you had better come and measure them yourself!' I turned round complaining:

'She wants me to go and measure them - I can't go just now!'

A gale of laughter swept the office and it took me a long time to learn the less technical meaning of the word.

With drastically reduced domestic budget, even the cheapest cinema became a rare treat, and instead I accompanied Mother to the Anglo-Polish Society, though I never liked the dreary, inhospitable rooms with a few English ladies dispensing milky tea. They appeared to be of a 'do-gooder' type and either could not understand our English or corrected the pronunciation of every word, making conversation impossible. As a result there was a sharp and permanent division between the 'staff' and the 'customers', the former bustling with kettles and tea whilst the latter congregated in whispering, conspiratorial groups. Since Mother used to help with refreshments the two of us were generally left alone with a foot in each camp but belonging to neither. I met the all-powerful Dora who had helped me with the work permit and, on hearing her laying down the law, I ceased to wonder about the abject apology which I had received at the Labour Exchange. I heard that, during the war, the Society had given a whole-hearted welcome to the fighting men of Poland. Now, post-war austerity and receding memories had changed the situation and reduced the English ranks of the Society. There did remain, however, a hard core of ladies genuinely concerned about Poland and the Poles, whilst others stayed from sheer inertia or just to show off a new dress. Both these groups were equally striking in appearance making recognition easy and unmistakable, though there were unclassifiable exceptions like the woman doing most of the washing up with Mother. Her sombre dress and the calm, taciturn behaviour disqualified her from membership of either group. The smooth English complexion and the already greying hair made her melt and disappear in the crowd. Resting between the batches of dirty cups, she crossed her legs, and suddenly there was the most perfect pair of ankles I had ever seen. It was so unexpected amongst the rather solid and short bases of Yorkshire girls that I slowly raised my eyes for a first real look at her: the hair certainly was going grey, but the face was young with blue-grey eyes and a strong, definite jaw. The complexion was light, delicate and devoid of thick war paint which most of the ladies affected. She was a school-teacher with an incredible number of 'E's in her name which began with Eileen. Also, most emphatically, Eileen was not English but Irish, and, as I still strove to improve my language, she offered to help.

In the office I met the owner and founder of the firm. In passing, Mr Spooner noticed an intricate drawing on my board and began chatting about his inventions. Soon I was working on his sketches and calculating details of the new machines. My lack of practical experience was offset by a relatively wide theoretical background, and my speed now equalled that of other draughtsmen. Continuous overtime, whilst welcomed financially, made me tired and allowed little leisure. To make things worse, a bad cold left me with a hacking cough for which my GP kept prescribing quantities of obnoxious syrup. During the weekends I continued visiting Eileen who helped especially with my conversation, which the engineering jargon and office slang did not improve. She was deeply interested in Polish affairs, but we also talked about the Ireland of her childhood and I was surprised by her uncompromising Catholicism, which subject we learned to avoid. There were striking differences in our interests as her first love was music and I still hankered after motorcycling and gliding, though both were out of reach. In spite of these apparent incompatibilities I began to fall in love with this bewitching colleen.

Winter came and, for the first time, I saw the impenetrable yellow fog which stopped all traffic and made life most difficult. There was no more cycling, and at night even the buses stopped, so that on some occasions a group of us had to walk back from Ilkley all the way to Leeds. At Christmas I was given a ten shillings rise in wages, but in view of the work I was doing, my apprentice status and pay seemed quite unfair.

In the warmer days of spring Eileen and I after 'talking' started 'walking' together. With my finances there was little choice of activity and we tried cycling, which was not a success as she certainly was not an outdoor girl. And still, in spite of our different cultures and backgrounds, her attraction grew and I began thinking seriously of a future together. But neither of us was young enough for the spontaneity of first love, and the progress of deepening friendship was hampered by our infrequent meetings and, on my side, the language. I could communicate all right, but the whole gamut of Polish endearments seemed untranslatable. From books and films I knew dears, darlings and honeys, but unaccustomed English words seemed even more stilted than the Irish 'alanna' and 'acushla'. But whatever the difficulties, I made up my mind and had to get on with it, especially as I felt sure of her acceptance. I don't remember the place or the words I used, but only her staggering answer: an emphatic NO. It was beautifully worded, sweetened with many thanks for the honour and justified by her age: 'far too old for you'. There was no more to say and I walked home. The night was cold and empty. I had made a mistake but nobody died of a broken heart. Yet from the past came the memories of Princess who married my friend, of Sena who remained in Warsaw ... Then I re-lived my failed English exams, the Stanningley Labour Exchange, the offensive jibes of the drawing office ...

On the Sunday morning I talked with Mother and proposed going to America. We had friends in São Paulo but I was set on the States and Mother was happy to follow me anywhere. As the first requirement was the health clearance I visited my doctor to ask for an X-ray but, before I could speak, he handed me another prescription for the cough mixture. Finally he directed me to the General Infirmary in Leeds for an X-ray. A fortnight later I called for the results and was invited to see the matron. She was a large and placid but authoritative woman who, after a short chat, told me that I had advanced TB and must cease work immediately. I made sure that there was no mix-up and asked about the treatment. The answer was as shattering as her first information: hospitals were full and I had to wait my turn - a few months, a year ... I went home to dull days and sleepless nights.

A week later occurred the third disaster of the series. Eileen did not want me, the illness which had killed my father and his two brothers had struck me. Now, as I had not paid some optional contributions during my college years, I was not entitled to Unemployment or Sickness Benefit, and Mother and I were left high and dry.

CHAPTER 24

PEOPLE WITHOUT FUTURE

Mother received some social benefit arranged by Dora, but it was Shirley who ferreted out information that, as a Polish Officer, I could be treated at the Iscoyd Park Polish Hospital. So there I found myself in February '51 in Shropshire.

Small, wiry Mrs Banszel was the sister in charge of B1, the officers' ward to which I was directed. Though quietly spoken she was always obeyed instantly. She seemed rather aloof but slowly I realised her deep compassion and saw the care she lavished on young and old alike. Second in command was Maryla of the roving eye and the shape to go with it. Everybody from porters to doctors spoke Polish, and the odd English word that I used evoked raised eyebrows of blank incomprehension. The whitewashed prefab housed some dozen beds, each straddled by a narrow table and buttressed with a small cabinet. In the middle of the polished black floor was a line of larger tables interrupted by two cast-iron stoves. The ward was light and spacious but very spartan and perishingly cold. The sister told me to get into bed and relax before the examination. She also introduced me to one of the patients. The old, silver-haired man painfully got out of his bed to shake my hand.

'Delighted to meet you, I am Major Kowal of the Fourth Lancers.'

Even with his permanent stoop he was a head taller than I and looked like an old gnarled oak ready to fall in the first winter gale. His old-fashioned courtesy contrasted with the faded pyjamas and the shapeless slippers. He took me round all the beds pronouncing distinctly name after name preceded by military rank and followed by the branch of the Service and the unit.

Like everybody else I had been issued with threadbare pyjamas and the Ministry of Pensions suit. This was a simple, unlined jacket and trousers of a nondescript blue, and the whole set, though softer, warmer and better cut, nevertheless resembled the uniform of the German concentration camps. The box with my own suit went into the storeroom whilst I shrank into the cold, clammy bed, feeling like a new boy on his first day at school. After an unpalatable, lukewarm dinner the Major shuffled slowly to my bed. Now, dressed in the blue uniform and a 'private' scarf wound around his thin neck, he proposed a game of chess which I accepted and promptly lost in the first ten minutes. We exchanged the colours and I lost in twenty minutes. He looked disappointed but commented that I must have once played seriously, and I smiled remembering the Montelupi prison. On the first night confused thoughts and muddled dreams did not give me much rest. The illness – terminal illness? The returning beasts of my nightmares. The ultimate defeat ... but no surrender!

Next morning X-rays were to be followed by a series of tomograms and the explanation of 'slicing you in layers' did not sound greatly reassuring. But, seeing the coupling of the moving X-ray tube with its traversing film holder, I grasped the ingenious principle of making roentgenograms of a single layer of tissue at any depth. Some days later came the examination by the ward doctor of whom everybody said that he was an absolute wizard. The Wizard was small, plump and beginning to go bald. He was also very kind and breathed most reassuring confidence. It was not the blustering bonhomie of 'we will have you right in two ticks', but the quiet assurance of great knowledge and experience. He enquired about my work and background and it transpired that he knew both my parents. After a long and thorough examination he showed me the films of roentgenograms and tomograms and, pointing out the shadows affecting both lungs, explained the proposed treatment of streptomycin injections with oral doses of para-amino-salicylic-acid, 'PAS' for short. Then I asked for the long term prognosis. He hesitated, looked straight into my eyes and spoke quietly. He stressed that no accurate prediction could be made in freshly diagnosed but old cases like mine. However, he thought that in two or three years time I might leave the hospital and, with a bit of luck, might even work again. Some of my relief must have shown as he quickly began to hedge, adding that he meant light work only, and it was too early to speculate. Then I enquired what I could do to help the healing process. Now he was quick and clear.

The patient could do as much as the doctor. The will to live backed by sensible behaviour was as important as the drugs. Stay in bed, read and talk, but do nothing, absolutely nothing, wash and go to the loo by all means, but otherwise stay in bed and don't get up for a game of chess or cards. And eat, eat, eat, put on weight, drink cod-liver oil. Smoking? – well, it never helped anybody, and should be abandoned or restricted, but he would rather see me smoking five a day, than fretting and worrying!

So it was not as bad as I had imagined but one had to consider, to think ... That night I slept like a baby till the lights flared up and the cleaners were again washing the spotless floor. I was the first in the cold washroom and took my time shaving and showering. The Ministry of Health had taken over the complete hospital from the Polish Army who inherited it from the Americans - hence the showers, rather a rarity in England at that time. Back in the ward, I carefully made up my bed before climbing into the doubtful warmth of the thin blankets. Most of us used to make our own beds as a little help which showed our appreciation of the hard-working staff. The cleaners emptied the ashes and lit both stoves which began to radiate the welcome heat. Before breakfast the day sister strolled through the ward placing on each bed-table a little glass tumbler half full of colourless liquid - the morning PAS. Into the dreamily unreal ward a squeaking trolley was wheeled and then, shovelling the grey mess of porridge on to individual plates, the sister woke up the still sleeping patients with a gentle shake, with a cheerful word.

For me it was the first direct challenge to do something for myself and, though not feeling hungry, I tucked into the porridge. It was glutinous, barely warm and slopping dismally in the cold milk poured over it. Choking on every mouthful, I destroyed it slowly, leaving a clean plate. A half-fluid egg with blackened edges and two thick slices of bacon almost defeated me as the bitter metallic taste of PAS rose up and clashed in my mouth with the congealing fat, but I pushed it all back, stuffing another piece of bread down my throat. Across the table I saw the incredulous face of Sister Banszel who, in the preceding days, had tried unsuccessfully to coax me into eating. Smiling she poured a beaker of coffee: 'Mr. Janusz ...' she began and was stopped dead by my enormous and uncontrollable belch, which I was half expecting to see as a dragon's flame scorching her to cinders. I blushed crimson, but amidst the reverberating echoes of this eructation we could not pretend that it had not happened, and suddenly we both burst out laughing.

After breakfast was always a quiet time when most patients lay silent, half asleep, half dreaming. Others read or wrote letters till about ten o'clock when came hot milk and a raw egg per head, a delicacy which I had never touched before. Still, recollecting the doctor's injunction, I stirred it into the milk and drank the resulting fluid – it was no worse than the porridge and could be swallowed faster. More energetic patients pulled on the blue suits over thick sweaters and drifted leisurely here and there to gossip. Refusing to budge from my bed I was soon visited by the older inhabitants and, over the passing weeks, learned the histories of my colleagues. I was too ill and miserable to be sorry for them but I was struck by the number of people who had once been 'cured' and left the hospital to return again a few months later. Some were even a few times on the 'outside' but now they considered the hospital as their true and only home. Individual stories covered Poland, Siberia and the Middle East. They stretched from the First World War to the Polish Campaign of 1939 and from the Battle of Britain, to Monte Cassino and Arnhem. But one aspect was common to all the stories: the people in them lived entirely in the past with unshakable belief in the Return-to-Poland, the Poland of 1939. They neither recognised nor admitted the existence of the Polish Communist Government and considered the present state of affairs as a temporary cease-fire. Against this background stood individual people. There was an old colonel, a silent giant of a man of whom it was said that once at Christmas he spoke for all of thirty seconds. Now, every week whilst collecting penny donations he would straighten his creaking back and say:

'In the name of the National Treasury I thank thee Sir!' – and I never heard him utter another word. At the other end of the scale was a most garrulous, small and wasted second lieutenant, never still, never in bed, but always yarning about heroic cavalry charges and the famous riders he had known. He had a habit of illustrating his tales in vivid, though rather grotesque mime. His knees bending rhythmically at the trot of an imaginary horse would speed up as he leaned forward lying on the horse's neck, the right hand groping for a lance would seize a pen or a fork to stab forward viciously and indiscriminately. Finally he would jerk up, jumping into the midst of the enemy and, invariably, kick his feet forward, causing the hospital slippers to sail one after the other right across the ward. The real trouble was that he was deadly serious, and one had to stifle smiles and bite one's lips to avoid mortally wounding him. Once, when deep in the equestrian Olympiad, he clinched the long story with an unanswerable verification of his intimate knowledge of the hero:

'I knew him well, he lived in the High Street and died of diarrhoea!' - and I almost choked trying to mask my guffaw with a fit of coughing. Much later I learned that his whole army career consisted of nine months in 1920 and three weeks in 1939. The rest of his life the little man was an insignificant bank clerk. There were a few professional army men, but others were reserve officers caught by the war and thrust into this isolated and incredible community.

My birthday I always considered a private affair concerning only the nearest family and, on 16 March, I got up as usual, though I could not help comparing this day with happier anniversaries. Then, having won the daily battle with my breakfast, I saw the sister enter the ward with two porters carrying sheaves of glowing daffodils. It was still a dreary winter with no visitors or flowers in our little universe, but now, out of the blue, the sterile ward bloomed with masses of flowers - like rising suns dispelling gloom, bringing light and hope. A card with best wishes from Shirley. Sister shaking my hand. The talkative lieutenant bubbling with a long, never-finished speech, the silently nodding bulk of the colonel, the smiling faces and the roar of *'Sto lat, Sto lat ...'* (For he's a jolly good fellow).

In spring, the ever-open double door of the hut looked at the gently sloping meadow stretching forth to the forest of rhododendrons. Once, the immaculate lawns and fabulous shrubberies had contrasted with the tracery of birches and the bulk of elms and oaks. Now, in the heart of the ruined park, the grey concrete huts decayed slowly whilst the thin, blue-clad figures of the foreigners shuffled along the overgrown paths.

I was no longer the stranger in the ward and the hospital routine became the natural way of life. I grew accustomed to the rusty squeal of trolleys delivering oxygen cylinders to the single rooms from which a sister or a doctor would emerge at night silent and defeated. A name was crossed out of a register and never mentioned again as those still living went about their business. Rain or shine, I kept to my bed and ate and ate. The PAS was a nuisance with its side-effects of frequent visits to the loo and its metallic taste, more vile than ever. But the food no longer stuck in my gullet, the eggy milk was no more a punishment. I became friendly with a Squadron Leader of my own age – the only patient sharing with me the will to return to normal life. We competed fiercely in gaining weight and drinking tumblers of cod liver oil. In the first three months I put on three stones to the great satisfaction of the smiling Wizard, who, after a consultation with the Chief Surgeon, announced that the time had come for the more radical treatment of phrenicotomy. It was a surgical disruption of the nerve, causing one-sided paralysis of the diaphragm which then compressed the diseased lung and promoted its healing. But, unreasonably, I was not enthusiastic about this proposal. On arrival at the hospital I would have welcomed any operation. Now, used to the secure life of the ward, I was frightened of change, of the unknown. I did not consider stories of patients left with paralysed arms by disruption of the wrong nerve, but the general idea of being cut up remained repulsive. Moreover, my war experience taught me to abhor pain which I would not willingly accept. However, after a talk with our Wizard, common sense prevailed and the next morning I found myself on the operating table.

There was a boxy screen over my head, presumably so that I could not cough into the operating field. Somebody buckled more straps, and, afraid of pain, I argued fiercely, ignoring a nice girl who tried to hush me. My neck and chest went cold and I demanded Novocain instead of the freezing chlorethyl. The voice of the Wizard assured me that everything was all right, and I believed him. There was a pressure on my arm, somebody asked whether I felt anything and, on my affirmative, continued:

'Now you will feel a slap on your tummy and that's that!'

A loud smack reverberated painlessly and it seemed ridiculously stupid to have such a performance just for that! I was warm and deliciously sleepy when Sister Banszel insisted that I eat my breakfast as twenty-four hours had passed since the operation. There was no pain but some shortness of breath.

A pneumothorax followed soon, though the doctor had difficulty in piercing my abdominal muscles – 'only once had I a heavyweight boxer like you.' But, with the X-rays showing an unusually high lift of the diaphragm, the pressurisation was abandoned and I happily pursued the old routine. Now, allowed and encouraged to get up for meals, I continued my gluttony at the central table. The Squadron Leader was sent home whilst I found another friend. It began with our Sister asking me to call at one of the single rooms to cheer up an old patient who once had been in the concentration camps. The shrunken figure seemed lost in the expanse of blankets and, in the corner of the room, I noticed the ominous lumps of the oxygen cylinders. As he turned to look at me, the sunken eyes lit up and the bloodless lips parted in a smile:

'Mr Salski! It's marvellous! Welcome, Welcome!'

My old name – yes – Auschwitz. Though changed out of recognition he really was Adam, one of the engineers in the Camp Development Office. There were explanations of my names and of Teddy's escape, floods of old memories. He enjoyed our chats so much that I visited him daily. For nine months I came watching his ebbing strength and listening to the hiss of oxygen till the main valve was finally turned off.

As time fled by I was making good progress and learning more about TB. The dark shadows among the white rib bones of the roentgenograms were the cavities in the lungs, the impaired hearing of many patients was a secondary result of the disease, as was the increased sexual drive. Sputum tests showed whether the patient was infectious and blood precipitation indicated overall health. But more important than those snippets of technical information were the insidious mental changes. As contact with the outside world grew more tenuous and the memories of it faded, so one's interests were transferred to the cloistered life of Iscoyd Park. Even my correspondence with Mother shrank as, left destitute and alone, she had obtained a clerical job at Leeds University. From there she applied for the post of a pathologist and was already working in one of London's hospitals. In the permanent security of my bed I could not visualise her in that new environment – was she again the assured and commanding pre-war doctor, or still the post-war apprehensive and lost woman? Time and distance seemed to fray the bond between us when the discarded past returned in letters from Eileen. Her impersonal sympathy and my casual replies slowly changed from the politeness of strangers into the concern of friends. Thus a new link to normal life was forged.

When I ceased to be infectious they transferred me to the next ward

B2. The huts were identical and the inhabitants very similar at first glance. Closer scrutiny showed those of B2 to be more mobile and lively. But their faces still appeared too thin and emaciated or bloated and too full, whilst their movements failed to strike a balance between jerky nervous energy and the sluggishness of people obsessed with care for their own health. Mentally there was (as in B1) the same disregard of the present, and preoccupation with the past – people with no future escaping into their own make-believe world. But I could not make myself hope again for the lost Poland, and the future beckoned to me only from the mists and moors of Yorkshire.

Christmas passed quietly and, in the early spring, Eileen came to visit me. No longer chained to my bed, I met her at the gates of Iscoyd Park, and the rare English sun poured warmth over us. Talking, we walked slowly along the narrow lanes of the wide world. Holding hands we looked at one another, at the fresh greenery, at the new life. Kissing, we knew that in front of us stretched the life-long happiness of being together.

The time came that I could leave hospital but was strongly advised to stay another few months to recover fully and to prepare myself for normal life. I still slept nine hours a day and rested after lunch, but spent mornings and afternoons in the occupational therapy workshops. In preference to the tedious course in watch-making I chose woodwork and soon began production of mahogany boxes with designs inlaid in multi-coloured veneers. Then came table-lamps, an occasional table, and an elm-wood cabinet for an enormous communication receiver which I had been given by an old school friend. As I sawed, planed and polished, the date of my discharge was drawing closer, but my anticipation of the event was tempered by a growing fear of the active life beyond the gates of Iscoyd. A dread of bustling, indifferent crowds, doubts whether I could ever measure up to the pressure of work and life without a waiting bed, without a Sister and five meals a day served infallibly and on time ...

I wrote to my old bosses and received, by return post, the offer of a job with a full draughtsman's salary. Another letter to the old couple in Leeds brought an equally quick invitation to stay with them until I had found a place in Ilkley. But, however encouraging, these promises did little to abate my anxiety. After a year and a half of cosseted, passive existence, even the train journey to Leeds loomed as a terrifying enterprise.

If it were not for my own pride and Eileen's help I might have stayed longer in Iscoyd. But my Colleen came to fetch me and together we left hospital at the end of May 1952.

CHAPTER 25

REINCARNATION

The first days in the drawing office dragged interminably. After the long stay in hospital, ordinary, everyday events required a conscious effort. Instead of a quiet rest after washing and shaving I gulped down my breakfast and walked to work, and even this stroll was quite an excursion by Iscoyd standards. Design and actual drawing was not hard labour - for an hour or two. But I had been used only to a couple of hours a day of slow and easy woodwork. Here, there was no mid-day rest in bed and it seemed that the afternoon would never end. But the overwhelming exhaustion of the early days did not last and in a few weeks I had readjusted to normal working life. It was spring with plenty of sunshine and showers, the warm spring with the promise of summer, and of a rosy future.

I applied for British citizenship as soon as the statutory five years of residence in this country had elapsed and I was rather apprehensive of the forthcoming interview. But I could not have wished for a fairer or more sympathetic interviewer than the CID Inspector who saw me in Leeds. Soon afterwards I received my naturalisation papers, swore the oath of allegiance and so became British with the long-coveted rights and responsibilities of a citizen. For some reason, probably connected with King Arthur or Magna Carta, no duplicate of such papers may be issued, but also, no authority is empowered to take them from the owner.

Every weekend I spent with Eileen, often tramping across the moors, walking amongst heather and the green, lacy bracken. It was marvellous being together and, in spite of all the problems of health and finances, we decided to marry in August. With Eileen's deep faith it had to be a church ceremony and, suddenly, from the most unexpected quarter emerged the first difficulty. An officious local padre demanded my baptismal certificate as well as confirmation that I was still single, which had to be signed by the priest of my old parish. The padre appeared totally oblivious of the war, of the complete destruction of Warsaw, of anything but his own ideas of propriety, and neither my explanations nor pleas were going to move him. Finally my patience ran out:

'In that case Reverend Father, we will live in sin which, no doubt, will add spice to our relationship!' – and, with truly Christian meekness, he issued the required permission.

But to make the church ceremony valid in law, we also needed the local registrar, who happened to be a lady as prejudiced against foreigners as the priest. After voicing numerous objections, she asked for my Naturalisation Certificate and announced that she must keep it for verification. Still in awe of officials I left it with her, but back in the office I phoned Eileen for advice. The Irish temper flared into a most unladylike comment about the registrar, and she cut me short to dash straight to the Police Headquarters. An hour later Eileen rang me up to say that the inspector who had originally interviewed me confirmed that the registrar had no right to keep the certificate, and promised to recover it. Soon a knock on the office door announced the arrival of a policeman followed by the registrar and a tall plain-clothes man. The uniformed one asked for me and, as I came forward in the deathly silence of the flabbergasted draughtsmen, the woman handed me my Naturalisation Certificate, apologising sheepishly for the mistake. The plain-clothes man shook hands with me and with an outrageous wink and 'after you madam' headed for the door.

A more mundane, but equally important, aspect of the proposed marriage was the problem of securing a place in which to live. Engineering jobs were still scarce and I already had a steady one in Ilkley whilst Eileen was prepared to move and, as a teacher, could find a post almost anywhere. So, we decided to live in Ilkley, though this 'Gateway to the Dales' was desperately short of accommodation. After trudging miles in a hopeless search I found the solution on my own doorstep. My landlady had a floored attic space reached by ladder-like steps. She did not consider this a habitable place but, swayed by my persuasions, agreed to let it at a nominal charge of a few shillings. She even threw in a basket chair with a broken seat, a card table and a large chest of drawers standing on three legs and a lump of rock. The works electrician gave me an old cooking ring, and Eileen's best friend donated another essential, a magnificent double bed which we used for the next fifteen years. The last item of period furniture we built ourselves: two stacks of tea-chests spanned by a broom handle and screened with a cretonne curtain made a capacious wardrobe veneered with obsolete blueprints.

I had neither inclination nor friends for a stag party and in the darkness of the night came doubt and fear. Looking dispassionately at the two of us it was difficult to find a more incompatible pair. A girl from the Golden Vale of Ireland, sheltered and educated in convents, leading a well-ordered English life, was to marry a Polish adventurer of liberal schooling and outlook. We had nothing in common except sweet words and smiles. Our language, tradition and experience could not be more diverse. And tomorrow 'till death us do part' – no, we cannot possibly ... but it was too late ... what will be, will be.

The wooden hut of the little church, a priest in heavily embroidered vestments, prayers whispered monotonously, Eileen's sisters, my mother and a few friends, all in their Sunday best, but all suddenly strange and unfamiliar. Then, on the arm of her brother, Eileen in a plain costume of blue, shimmering with traces of reds and greens. Her eyes no longer grey but blue and a hint of a smile as fleeting as the iridescent tints of the fabric. The sparkling eyes and the hesitant smile dispelled my doubts and fears. Then, seeing only her face in the dancing lights of the candles, I repeated with total conviction:

'To have and to hold ...'

We arrived from Leeds in a taxi carrying all Eileen's possessions of two suitcases and a tea-chest of books. We were married, we were together, and within an hour we received our first visitor, Mr Ford, who brought us a sheaf of dark red roses. I had only a few days off work and they flashed by in quiet, unbelievable happiness. Thirteen years ago I had left my home and childhood. Thirteen years I had fought for Poland, my ideals, for life itself. Poland was no more, ideals had collapsed one by one, and life was completely changed. But I had survived and the future with Eileen was the shining rainbow of hope beyond lost dreams.

Even by the austere standards of post-war England we were comically poor. A suit, a couple of dresses, a few books and my old army dixie were the extent of our personal possessions. Eileen obtained a teaching post in a nearby village and travelling added considerably to her school hours, whilst I rarely finished overtime before nine o'clock. Food was still rationed and with our limited cooking skills we thrived on tea, potatoes and corned beef, saving a considerable portion of our earnings. In the winter of 1952 my firm transferred its works to Ilkley. The new property included the 'Mill Manager's House' in which I was offered a flat. After our attic, the two rooms with kitchen and Victorian bathroom appeared truly palatial. It took time and hard work to make the new place into a home. Several layers of paint obliterated the black and crimson decor of the twenties, whilst cord carpet and cheap lino covered the floors and we were delighted to welcome into our new apartment Mr Spooner who brought us a wedding present. He was a great patron of the arts and gave us an Ethel Gabain lithograph which used to hang over his own desk. Though not as valuable as his Turners and Constables, it had caught my eye and inspired my admiration.

Long days filled with work passed quickly. Evenings, as well as Sundays and holidays, flashed by, and the months grew into years. For both of us the marriage was a rebirth, a beginning of another life in a new incarnation. It was not a brilliant flash, a miracle. It was the beginning of new tasks and responsibilities, the start of another struggle for a place in the community, for recognition, for better work and a better home. But no longer did one struggle alone. Each had the backing and support of the other, though it required also patience and endless adjustment of the necessary give and take of close companionship. Slowly the intoxication of being 'in love' generated the deepest friendship, unquestioned and unquestionable loyalty and ever-growing love.

From the drawing office I moved to Research and Development and in time obtained several patents. We exchanged our motorcycle for a car and acquired our first house. After the death of Mr Spooner in 1965, the firm changed dramatically and I left for greener pastures where I soon fulfilled my life-long ambition of becoming the Chief Engineer. Eileen and I travelled extensively from Ireland to Greece and from Holland to Tunisia. We bought land and built our dream house with a wing for Mother. I obtained the fellowship of a major engineering institution, and after a few more changes of employment, again accepted a position at Spooner's from which I retired in 1981.

I have not forgotten the forests and mountains of Poland. I have not forgotten Warsaw with the grey waters of the Vistula. I am proud of the thousand years of Polish heritage and our unceasing fight for freedom. But forty years of life in England, years of work and achievement have overlaid the earlier times. My friends and, above all, my wife have helped me to grow new roots which have sunk deep into the soil of Yorkshire. In spite of my foreign origin and atrocious accent, I was accepted by the workmen, the engineers, the neighbours, the open-hearted people who are now my people just as England is now my country.

Map of Poland 1939

285

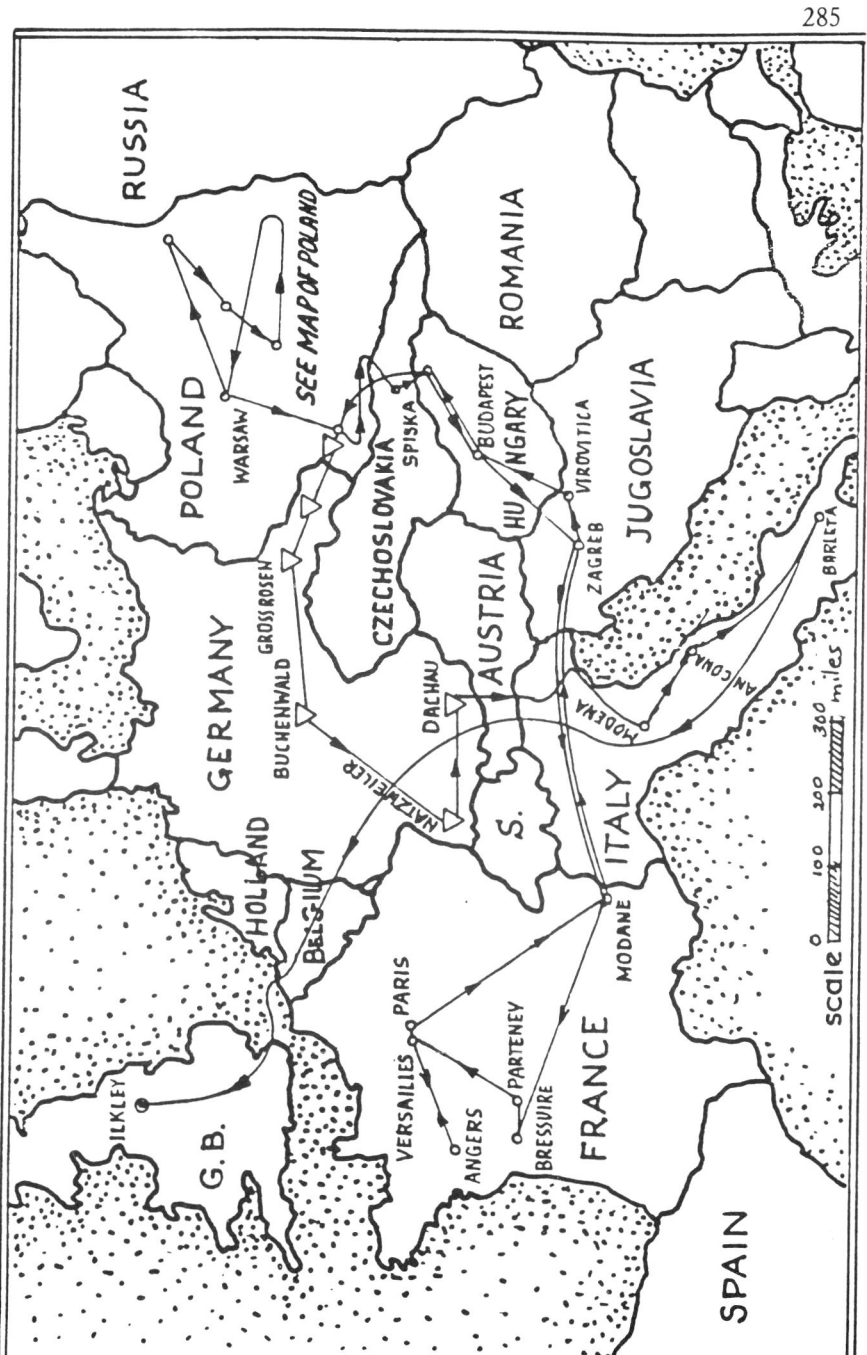

Map of Europe 1939